Winning Their Place

Winning Their Place

ARIZONA WOMEN IN POLITICS · 1883–1950

BY HEIDI J. OSSELAER

With a Foreword by Governor Janet Napolitano

The University of Arizona Press   Tucson

The University of Arizona Press
© 2009 The Arizona Board of Regents
All rights reserved

www.uapress.arizona.edu

Library of Congress Cataloging-in-Publication Data
Osselaer, Heidi J., 1958–
  Winning their place : Arizona women in politics, 1883–1950 /
  Heidi J. Osselaer ; foreword by Janet Napolitano.
     p. cm.
  Includes bibliographical references and index.
ISBN 978-0-8165-0239-4 (alk. paper)
  1. Women in politics—Arizona. 2. Women legislators—
  Arizona. I. Title.
HQ1236.5.U5O77 2009
324.082′09791—dc22   2008050722

Manufactured in the United States of America on acid-free,
archival-quality paper and processed chlorine free.

16 15 14 13 12 11   7 6 5 4 3 2

Contents

Illustrations and Tables

Illustrations

Tables

Foreword

I am a woman and a politician, first elected to office in 1998 as Arizona's attorney general. Shortly after my announcement in that race, a reporter asked a question I will never forget: "So, do you plan on running as a woman attorney general?"

I feel confident my opponent was never asked whether he would "run as a man."

Yes, as women in office we've made progress; and yes, there is still work to do.

On one hand, that race for attorney general indicated how high women had advanced in politics in Arizona. When I was inaugurated the following January, I was among a group of women who held all five of the state's top elected offices—the first time such a sweep had happened in American history.

When I was elected governor in 2002, I became the first woman in the history of our nation to succeed another woman as a state's governor.

But on the other hand, the fact that reporters, voters, and observers still ask questions about women in politics—and the fact that, nearly 90 years after women nationwide won the right to vote, women are underrepresented in Congress, state legislatures, and governors' offices—shows that challenges remain.

I am governor today in large part because of the pioneering spirit of Arizona's first women politicians. And although the accomplishments of today's women leaders in Arizona have made headlines both statewide and nationally, historians have paid less attention to the women leaders so important to Arizona's early history. Whereas many noted the milestone when I was elected Arizona's attorney general in 1998, few knew that Elsie Toles had pioneered women's ability to seek statewide office in Arizona when she was elected superintendent of public instruction in 1920.

Heidi Osselaer describes these women's experiences, their stumbles, and their triumphs to help us understand why a small southwestern state like Arizona emerged as a leader in cultivating women who take on political office. Office holding is exhilarating yet challenging. In light of the women's movement in this country, some people thought women would advance quickly in the arena of national politics, but change has come slower than many expected. As women such as Nancy Pelosi and Hillary Rodham Clinton gain greater attention, perhaps the experience of Arizona's early female leaders will offer insights into the obstacles that remain.

As you read Osselaer's stories of Sharlot Hall, Isabella Greenway, and others, think not only of following in their footsteps. Think, too, of honoring them by surpassing even their great achievements.

—Janet Napolitano
  Governor of Arizona

Acknowledgments

This book started as a research paper for a graduate seminar taught by Mary Rothschild at Arizona State University. Mary had done some research on women in Arizona politics and knew the topic had potential, but she expressed concern because it was so difficult to find primary documents. Aside from Congresswoman Isabella Greenway, Arizona's female politicians rarely kept their papers. State Senator Frances Munds asked her daughter to destroy her papers on the suffrage movement after her death, and Sally Munds Williams dutifully carried out her mother's instructions in the 1970s. I was able to cobble together a collective biography of Arizona's early female politicians from incomplete letter collections, obituary files, legislative files, census materials, newspaper articles, and other documents scattered in various archives. Although only bits and pieces are known about most individual female politicians, certain patterns emerge when they are viewed as a group, and it is easy to see what type of woman gravitated to electoral politics. As Barbara Nielsen, the grandniece of state legislator Claire Phelps, told me, these early female politicians were not the type who stayed home and baked cookies.

Phil VanderMeer supervised the original research for my dissertation and made sure I looked under every rock (and pebble) along the way. He also encouraged me to keep going even when I thought I could not pull all the bits of material together in a way that made sense. Mary Rothschild and Gayle Gullett were always helpful with their suggestions and words of encouragement. Special thanks to Poncie McDearmon and Patricia Biggs for bringing this project to the attention of Governor Janet Napolitano, and thanks to the governor for taking the time from her busy schedule to support the study of Arizona's early female politicians. Kristie Miller provided sage advice. I am especially indebted to my husband, Tom, for putting up with this project for the last fourteen years and for reading chapters with a nonhistorian's eye. Tom and our children, Ryan and Shannon, were always enthusiastic supporters.

It would be impossible to name all the wonderful archivists who helped me gather documents over the years, but several stand out. Christine Marin at the Chicano Research Collection at Arizona State University was a valuable resource, and Deanna Beaver uncovered wonderful material on Nellie Trent Bush at the Parker Area Historical Society. This book is dedicated to the archivists at the Arizona State Library, Archives and Public Records, Arizona History and Archives Division. Wendi Goen was relentless in her pursuit of photographs, and without her assistance and that of Melanie Sturgeon, Nancy Sawyer, Donald Langlois, and all the other wonderful staff members at state archives, I never could have completed the project. Historians just write history, archivists keep it. I wish them all the best in their new home, the Polly Rosenbaum State Archives and History Building.

Introduction

On January 4, 1999, five women were sworn in as the top executive officers in Arizona, a first in United States history. The national media dubbed them the "Fab Five" and celebrated them as examples of the progress women were making in politics. U.S. Supreme Court Justice Sandra Day O'Connor, who already had made history as the first woman on the nation's highest court, administered the oath of office to Governor Jane Hull, Secretary of State Betsey Bayless, Attorney General Janet Napolitano, Superintendent of Public Instruction Lisa Graham-Keegan, and Treasurer Carol Springer. Most of these women, including Justice O'Connor, had started their political careers in the Arizona State Legislature, so it was appropriate that Edwynne "Polly" Rosenbaum, the longest-serving member of the legislature, was a guest of honor at the ceremony. In addition to dominating state executive office, women held 37 percent of the seats in the Arizona legislature that year, well above the 20 percent national average, and a woman, Brenda Burns, was chosen by her peers to preside over the state senate. Some observers assumed that the success of Arizona women during the election of 1998 was the result of the modern woman's movement, but others noted that the state had a long history of female political participation. The *New York Times* suggested that Arizona's "newness, open political system and a certain gender-blind libertarian bent among the populace" might have contributed to the unusual number of female elected officials. Indeed, decades before anyone had heard the phrase "women's liberation," Arizona voters were electing women to office in abnormally large numbers.[1]

The first demand for female political equality in Arizona was made in 1883. Women finally won the right to vote and run for public office in 1912, when 68 percent of male voters supported a suffrage ballot initiative—the largest popular vote for a state suffrage amendment in the country. From 1914 to 1950, when women nationally occupied on average only 1 to 2 percent of all state legislative seats, Arizona women averaged between 5

and 6 percent. By the 1960s and the dawn of the modern woman's movement, women had made some progress nationwide; they held 4.5 percent
of all state legislative seats and 6 percent of all state executive offices. In
Arizona they averaged 10 percent of state legislative seats and 22 percent
of statewide offices. Their work was well chronicled in newspapers by
their contemporaries, but as historian Marshall Trimble commented in
2006, "No matter the paths they chose, pioneer women have something in
common besides their gender: They got little credit for their accomplishments." This book is an attempt to document the historical contributions
of Arizona women to early state electoral politics and to establish the
reasons they succeeded as candidates at a time when most people felt
women were unsuited for public office.[2]

Perhaps the reason women's political roles in Arizona history are
often ignored is that popular culture—particularly western movies and
novels—has given us an image of a place that was distinctly masculine.
Most people, when they think about Arizona history, conjure up visions
of the gunfight at the OK Corral or the U.S. Cavalry tracking Geronimo.
It seems incongruous that such a turbulent and dangerous environment
could also be a backdrop for female politicians. To understand women's
roles, we must first get past the myth that early Arizona was a wild and
lawless place. Recent research on the territorial criminal justice system
proves conclusively that Arizona was no more violent than most other
parts of the country. Gambling, drinking, and prostitution were rampant
in early mining towns, but outright lawlessness was not endemic. Anglo
businessmen and political leaders were eager to establish justice systems
that would provide for order in the territory and to promote businesses to
boost the economy, so they worked with female reformers to ensure that
community services were available to attract new settlers.[3]

To fight alcohol abuse and vice, Arizona women joined the Woman's
Christian Temperance Union (WCTU) in large numbers. The first local
branch of the WCTU was started in Prescott in 1883, and other branches
quickly followed in most major towns. Members were dedicated to lobbying
their elected officials to pass laws to curb alcohol consumption, but early on
Josephine Brawley Hughes, president of the Arizona WCTU, recognized
that without the vote, women were powerless to influence politicians. In
1890 she founded the first territorial woman suffrage association. As its president, she lobbied the territorial legislature for woman suffrage but had little

success. In the early 1900s a new generation of more ambitious women, led by Frances Willard Munds and Pauline O'Neill, turned the movement in a new direction. They resembled other suffragists in the West, whom Rebecca Mead has characterized as "innovative [and] energetic" and who "operated relatively independently of the increasingly conservative eastern leadership" of the National American Woman Suffrage Association (NAWSA). Tired of following the national suffrage leaders' orders to appeal to the legislature, Munds and O'Neill formed an alliance with labor unions and third parties that forced Republicans and Democrats to support a suffrage amendment to the new state constitution. In 1912, eight years before the Nineteenth Amendment to the U.S. Constitution gave all women the right to vote, Arizona joined Wyoming, Utah, Colorado, Idaho, Washington, California, Kansas, and Oregon as a suffrage state.[4]

By 1914, all western states and territories with the exception of New Mexico had extended the franchise to women, but it was not until 1917 that New York became the first state east of the Mississippi River to pass a suffrage bill. The national suffrage movement was founded and head-quartered in 1848 in New York, so why did the East lag behind the West? Rebecca Mead, who has documented the western suffrage movement, argues that there was no single reason the West led the nation with suffrage. Rather, a variety of local conditions influenced the decision process. Western territorial and state legislatures were smaller and easier to influence than large eastern legislatures, and as western territories aspired to become states, constitutional convention delegates were forced to debate voting rights publicly in forums where suffragists made their voices heard. Settlers in the West were more open to new ideas and experimentation than their eastern counterparts, and they often flirted with third party movements such as Populism and Progressivism that supported woman suffrage. Women's leaders used this to their advantage, throwing their support behind popular third parties and forcing Democrats and Republicans to take their demands seriously. Some businessmen and politicians saw suffrage as a way to boost publicity for their state, which they hoped would encourage new settlers. Finally, most western states had progressive constitutions containing provisions for direct democracy in the form of the initiative and the referendum. With these political tools, sympathetic voters could bypass legislatures filled with entrenched politicians who had little incentive to add women to the electorate.[5]

If the general public in the West was more receptive to giving women the vote, it was because many voters assumed that Anglo women, not women of color, would enter the electorate to help shape the political agenda. Race played an important role in impeding suffrage in many states. In the 1890s in the South, white state officials began to amend state constitutions to severely limit the vote of African Americans. During the Jim Crow era, white northern suffragists, eager to dispel southern fears that extending the franchise to women would increase the political power of African Americans, discriminated against black women, often preventing their membership in suffrage clubs or segregating them in suffrage parades. African American women's leaders were critical of the racist stance of the national suffrage organizations, but a majority of white women's leaders remained committed to gaining the right to vote even at the expense of the rights of black women.[6]

In the West, African Americans were few and did not pose the threat to Anglo dominance that Mexican American voters did. In Arizona, African Americans made up 3.5 percent or less of the total population before 1950, but the Mexican American population composed somewhere between 20 and 25 percent. Arizona's Anglo territorial leaders worked to neutralize the votes of those they deemed "uneducated," mostly working-class Mexican Americans who spoke little English, and in 1909 passed a literacy requirement that kept many from voting until 1972. Federal law denied citizenship to American Indians until 1924, but Arizona state law barred American Indians from voting until 1948 and denied those living on reservations the right to hold public office until 1973. Prior to statehood, whites assumed control of the economic, political, and social organizations in the territory, a control that included authorizing the segregation of public schools. They created communities "run by Anglos for Anglos." Minority populations organized in political clubs and mutual assistance leagues but remained largely segregated from Arizona's political culture until after World War II and the civil rights movement. Rebecca Mead notes that "woman suffrage was easier to accept in the West in part because it could not alter the balance of racial power in the region, where white racial hegemony was firmly established by the turn of the century." This was certainly the case in Arizona.[7]

Although many women in the United States participated in campaigns to win the right to vote, few were interested in seeking public office once suffrage was won. The goal of the national woman suffrage movement was to create female voters who would clean up politics, not to create female politicians. When they demanded the vote, women did so as an extension of their domestic role as "social housekeepers," hoping to elevate government with their moral influence. They petitioned and lobbied legislatures to advocate temperance and on a variety of other issues of concern to women and children, but few were knowledgeable about tax codes, tariffs, banking policies, or the myriad economic issues routinely tackled by legislators, congressmen, and governors. Most felt uncomfortable seeking public office, where deals were brokered in smoke-filled hotel rooms and candidates traveled extensively to speak with voters. After women won the vote, polling booths moved from the local saloon to the neighborhood school or church to accommodate female voters, but women's groups and political parties did little to encourage potential female politicians.[8]

Despite all the challenges, some suffragists felt compelled to run for office. These women had developed speaking and organizational skills during the suffrage battles and put them to use in their own political campaigns. Political commentators speculated that female politicians would champion laws that benefited women and children, end corruption in politics, and challenge men for control of government. A public expectation existed that these women would alter the political landscape as they won seats in Congress or became governors. But women were newcomers to politics in the 1920s, and novices rarely win high office. It takes years to develop the name recognition and financial backing to run for state or federal office, and the handful of women who won those positions usually did so because they were the widows or daughters of prominent male politicians. Women's lack of success at the national level led many historians to conclude that they could not overcome the many barriers to office holding. The political parties were too hostile to female candidacies, and women felt out of place competing with men. The assumption was that women, who had been barred from electoral politics for so long, were more comfortable in the separate female political culture of women's voluntary clubs, where they could influence government indirectly by lobbying legislatures. As a result, recent historical research has focused primarily on women's organizations and their influence on politics. The problem with this approach is that it ignores the majority of early female politicians who worked their way up the political ladder, starting in county offices or state legislatures and paying their dues on local political party committees. Their stories remain largely untold. In this book I refocus the examination of women in electoral politics to the local and state level, where female candidates did enjoy successes after winning the right to vote.[9]

Historians note that in the western states where women won the vote early, women often had more success running for office than in the rest of the nation. Yet only a modest amount of research has been directed at uncovering the reasons for this difference. Some theorize that the experience of growing up in the West might have socialized women to participate in politics to a greater extent than women in other regions. As Rita Mae Kelly observes, "local custom and tradition in the Southwest gave women the expectation that public participation—at least in their special spheres of influence—was not only acceptable but also desirable." Paula Petrik's study of women in Helena, Montana, reveals that the generation of women born in the West to frontier mothers was more independent, more likely to work outside the home, and more likely to assume positions of leadership in the community than eastern women.[10]

Even in the West, however, the success of female candidates was uneven. Elizabeth Cox identified the states in which few women were elected, such as California, Wyoming, Idaho, and Montana, and the states that consistently elected above-average numbers of women, such as Washington, Colorado, Oregon, and Arizona. Until more studies appear on office holding in other states, we really will not know why opportunities for women varied so dramatically from state to state. In the meantime, it is apparent that women in Arizona had an advantage because they played such important roles in the economic development of the state.[11]

Arizona remained a frontier well into the twentieth century, and its economy was among the poorest in the nation, so women's work was important to helping families make ends meet. Labor was scarce, and so many men were employed in physically demanding industries such as mining, farming, and ranching that there were shortages of workers to run businesses, teach school, and perform clerical services. Women, regardless of marital status, often took these jobs. Additionally, Arizona ranked high among states for widows. In other states single women, who traditionally held jobs only temporarily before marriage, dominated the female work force, but in Arizona working married women and widows outnumbered single women. Their contributions to the economy, according to Donna

Guy, led to opportunities for Arizona women "unimagined in earlier frontier societies."[12]

Far western states like Arizona attracted a disproportionate number of professional women who were lawyers, doctors, teachers, and business-women. They paid taxes and were sued in court, yet they could not serve on juries and faced discriminatory laws in the workplace. They were not paid as well as men, had fewer job opportunities, and were treated as second-class citizens. In 1920 the Arizona Federation of Business and Professional Women's Clubs (BPW) was organized and became an advocate for female advancement and equality in the workplace. The Arizona BPW found strong support among the state's large female, Anglo professional class and acted like a political party for women, encouraging them to run for office and admonishing members to support female candidates with their votes and campaign contributions.

The Arizona BPW filled a void for Anglo women in Arizona politics. In most states after suffrage, women's leaders were invited to serve on party committees or to run for office if Democrats or Republicans believed they could deliver female voters. The political parties in Arizona did not absorb the most talented women; they ignored them. The Democratic party, with two-thirds of the registered voters, dominated state politics until the 1950s. Without party competition, there was no need to win over female voters by running women candidates. Women's leaders were outraged by the Democrats' indifference to women and became convinced that the majority of male politicians, regardless of political stripe, could not be trusted to represent women or their interests. This conviction stimulated many women to run for office themselves.

The women elected to office before 1950 in Arizona represented the different religions found in the state—Protestant, Jewish, Catholic, and Mormon—but not the different races. Office holding is a reflection of who holds power in society, and Anglo men dominated Arizona's public offices until very recently. With the exception of a handful of Mexican American male politicians, Arizona's minority populations, male and female, were largely excluded from public office before World War II because they lacked the economic clout, educational opportunities, and sufficient numbers to overcome the pervasive discrimination they faced. Yet Arizona voters seemed comfortable offering well-educated, professional Anglo women a small degree of power—far less than Anglo men, but far more than African Americans, Mexican Americans, and American Indians—by electing them to public office.

Like their counterparts in other states, Arizona's early female politicians promised to represent the interests of women and limited themselves primarily to positions in county office and the state legislature. But a successful politician cannot appeal to only half the electorate, and female office holders quickly recognized that they were responsible for representing male interests as well as female. During the 1930s they expanded their political agenda and tackled the economic problems facing the state, emphasizing their qualifications both as mothers and as businesswomen. In the state legislature they sponsored bills to aid widows, overhauled the tax code, funded construction projects, and chaired important committees. Isabella Greenway became such a powerful force in the Democratic party through her political talents and personal connections that she became Arizona's sole representative to the U.S. House of Representatives in 1933. By 1950 women had established themselves as professional politicians and started to run for offices such as sheriff, superior court judge, and even governor. The higher the political stakes, however, the more resistance they met from male politicians and voters. Arizona's early female politicians did not overcome all biases against their gender before 1950, but they did test many traditional notions about a woman's proper role. In the process, they paved the way for future generations of women to make accelerated gains in state politics—including the five women who took the oath of office from Justice Sandra Day O'Connor and assumed control of state government in 1999.

Winning Their Place

CHAPTER 1

The Battle Begins

The Early Woman Suffrage Movement, 1883 to 1903

Women's political participation in Arizona began in 1883 when Murat Masterson, a Mormon attorney from Prescott, introduced a bill in the territorial legislature to allow women to vote in all elections. The bill was defeated, seven votes to three, with "a great many ladies present listening to the debate." Masterson and his fellow supporters believed that giving the vote to women would help end corruption in politics, but their opponents argued that it "would degrade women from their proper sphere in the home circle." Similar arguments had plagued the suffrage movement in the United States ever since Elizabeth Cady Stanton made the first public demand for the vote in 1848. In the nineteenth century women were supposed to remain in the domestic sphere, taking care of their family and home, shielded from the public sphere of business and politics. They had been excluded from politics for so long that, as historian William Gienapp noted, most Americans believed "they simply had no more business at a polling place than they did drinking, gambling, and smoking with the boys back at the clubhouse."[1]

When Masterson introduced the first suffrage bill into the territorial legislature, few Anglo or Mexican American women lived in Arizona. As a northern frontier post first under Spain and then, after 1821, under an independent Mexico, Arizona saw the establishment of a handful of missions, presidios, and settlements, but these were often threatened by indigenous tribes, so few families ventured into the territory. The United States and Mexico signed the Treaty of Guadalupe Hidalgo at the termination of the Mexican-American War in 1848, which forced Mexico to cede to the United States all the land north of the Rio Grande and the Gila River and south of Oregon — encompassing most of present-day Arizona. An additional 30,000 square miles of territory, including the settlements known today as Tubac

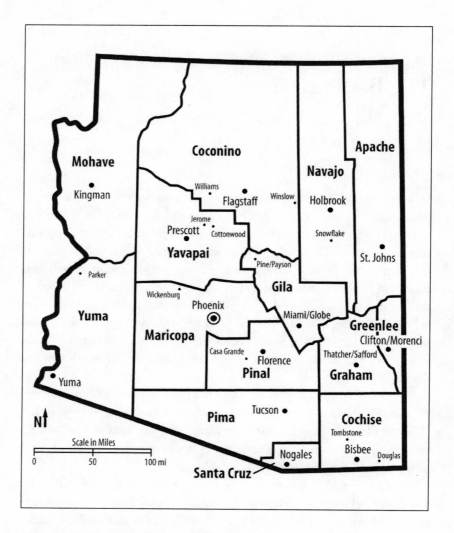

Arizona counties, county seats, and cities, 1910–1982.

and Tucson, were added with the Gadsden Purchase in 1854. Arizona was part of the New Mexico territory until 1863, when Congress passed and President Abraham Lincoln signed the Arizona Organic Act, creating the last territory in the continental United States. Although members of Congress were eager to gain the fertile soil, mineral wealth, and strategic harbors of California, they considered Arizona an arid wasteland that stood between the East and West coasts. As writer Robert Alan Goldberg described it, "the Arizona territory was land scraped raw, with rock and bare, baked ground exposed. . . . The country offered no comfort or amenity. Hostile to change, the desert pressed existence to its margin. . . . The sun, sky, and land humbled and overwhelmed the individual. Distances isolated physically and psychologically—an isolation felt even more profoundly because travel was slow and often uncertain."[2]

Anglo and Mexican American families continued to avoid the region until after 1872, when the U.S. Army had moved most of the Indian population to reservations. Important mineral strikes in Wickenburg, Tombstone, Jerome, Florence, and Globe in the 1870s attracted fortune seekers—primarily male—to the territory. In 1870, only 25 percent of the non-Indian population was female, but by the 1880s, with the completion of land reclamation projects and the railroads, more wives had joined their husbands in the Arizona territory. By 1890 the percentage of women had increased to 35 as Mormon families from Utah and settlers from Texas, Oklahoma, and Mexico came to farm, graze livestock, or work in Arizona's mines.[3]

Arizona's early economy was dominated by mining, farming, and ranching, industries all notorious for boom-and-bust cycles. Some years were prosperous, but most were not, so wives and daughters worked to supplement families' incomes. In the East in the 1890s and early 1900s, married middle-class white women rarely worked outside the home and often had servants to help with arduous chores. Labor was scarce in Arizona, so few women, regardless of their social standing, could afford domestic help. When women arrived in Arizona in the 1880s, they often found themselves without running water, electricity, or indoor plumbing, conditions that persisted in rural areas well into the 1940s. Married women, in addition to their household chores, almost always worked to make ends meet by taking in boarders or laundry, teaching school, or assisting at their husbands' stores or newspapers. In 1900, married women in Arizona constituted almost 43 percent of the female labor force, in comparison with a national average of just over 15 percent.[4]

Widows also played an important role in frontier Arizona. Dangerous work in copper mines left many men injured or dead, and numerous families came to Arizona seeking cures for lung ailments such as tuberculosis, mistakenly believing that the dry desert climate could alleviate their condition. In towns where precious ore was discovered and growth was rapid, overcrowded and unhealthy living conditions often prevailed, creating a lack of potable water and poor sanitation and leading to diseases such as typhoid. Arizona led the West in the number of widows, many of whom were young women left to raise small children alone. A 1900 census showed that one-third of all Mexican American households in Tucson were headed by women, and 10.5 percent of the total female population of Arizona was widowed. Early territorial and state laws concerned with widows were liberal, perhaps because territorial leaders understood how many women were heads of households and how difficult it was for a woman at this time to support a family by herself. The Arizona territory was governed by community property laws, a legacy of Spanish control, which gave ownership of all property acquired in marriage equally to a husband and wife and allowed married women and widows to control their own property, a right denied to many women outside the West. In 1887 the territorial legislature passed a bill giving a widow with children an additional one-third of her husband's separate estate. In 1914 the state legislature passed the first old-age pension and widowed mothers bill in the United States, a law that primarily benefited Anglo women. Citizenship requirements were attached to aid to widows, a disadvantage to Mexican American women, who often had difficulty providing documentation of their spouse's citizenship. Even with government aid, most widows found it necessary to work outside the home, because state funding was rarely sufficient to support a family. Many men who survived illness or disability were so weakened that they were unable to work, forcing wives and children to become primary wage earners for the family.[5]

Discrimination against women in employment and education and as U.S. citizens was first publicly identified in July 1848, just three months before Arizona became a part of the United States, when Elizabeth Cady Stanton and a small group of supporters launched the national women's rights movement in Seneca Falls, New York. In the East, women were active in moral reform societies that focused on eradicating slavery and alcoholism, and through their work they learned that they had little power to challenge injustice when laws and customs kept them in positions inferior to men. Susan B. Anthony soon joined Stanton and others to lead a national movement demanding equality for women in property laws, education, divorce, and, most controversial of all, political participation. In the nineteenth century most middle-class white women tended to the domestic sphere, overseeing the education and religious instruction of their children and the cooking and cleaning for their families. A proper woman was not supposed to work outside the home or show interest in the "corrupt" sphere of government or business; instead, she was expected to rely on her husband or male relatives to represent and support her. Women could not vote and had limited access to education. Those who had the financial means to attend a secondary school could become teachers, but they usually earned only half what their male counterparts earned. Married women could not control their property or wages, and they lost custody of their children in the case of divorce. Women's rights advocates who demanded access to higher education, control of their own finances, and the vote were ridiculed as "hyenas in petticoats" who threatened the natural social structure. Political cartoonists often portrayed early suffragists as cigar-smoking, masculine women setting off to work while their husbands slaved at home, cleaning and tending to the children.[6]

It was slow progress convincing women that they could become, in Elizabeth Cady Stanton's words, "a self-supporting, dignified, independent, equal partner with man in the state, the church, the home." Most middle-class eastern white women did not have to work outside the home and could rely on a husband or other male family member for financial support and to represent their interests in government. Arguments by Stanton and Anthony that woman's status was analogous to the slave's fell mostly on deaf ears until the 1870s, when social problems appeared that challenged women to demand a greater role in politics. After the Civil War, rapid industrialization dislocated many workers in the economy, and alcohol consumption increased dramatically. Wives experienced abuse, abandonment, and bankruptcy because of the irresponsible actions of their alcoholic husbands. Progressive thinkers began to argue that good

Christian women should play a larger role in rectifying the evils of the world outside their own homes, eliminating vices such as prostitution, gambling, and especially alcoholism.[7]

In the 1870s women of all social ranks were attracted to Frances Willard's organization, the Woman's Christian Temperance Union (WCTU), a national evangelical Protestant organization limited to female members. Willard believed that women were society's housekeepers and could protect their homes from abusive, dissolute husbands only by passing laws that either sharply curtailed or banned alcohol consumption. Her agenda, encompassed in the WCTU's "Do Everything Policy," went far beyond temperance, encouraging women to enter the public sphere to aid and rescue those less fortunate, including prostitutes, the destitute, and drug abusers. WCTU women also endorsed educational reforms such as providing kindergarten curricula in schools and night schools for working women, as well as labor laws, prison reform, and legislation to end corrupt political practices. To accomplish all this, Willard argued that women needed the vote.[8]

Temperance work took women out of the domestic sphere to volunteer in their communities and helped them recognize that without the vote they could not legally protect themselves. Despite female protests and petitions, many male lawmakers were reluctant to close down red light districts, pass temperance bills, or end the corrupt political practices that benefited them as office holders. The WCTU grew to become the largest voluntary organization in the country by the end of the nineteenth century, with 150,000 female members. Because of its efforts, the public began to view suffragists less as radicals bent on destroying the family and more as reformers dedicated to improving society. The suffrage movement grew rapidly as WCTU women joined the cause in the 1880s and 1890s, but these evangelical Protestant women also made the largest suffrage organization, the National American Woman Suffrage Association (NAWSA), more conservative, emphasizing the need for the vote as a method of reforming society rather than as a measure of women's equality with men.

The temperance movement took root swiftly in the West, where saloons, brothels, and gambling halls offended Anglo Christian women. The suffrage movement quickly followed, popular among women who not only wanted to eliminate drinking but also felt they deserved recognition for the role they played in settling the western frontier. In 1869 the Wyoming territorial legislature surprised the world when it passed legislation allowing women to vote, serve on juries, and run for office and requiring equal pay for male and female teachers. Local politicians believed women had earned these rights and would reform some of the wildness out of Wyoming, thereby attracting more families to settle there. Although the national suffrage movement played no direct role in passing the Wyoming suffrage law, Esther Morris, a local women's leader who had helped convince the Wyoming legislature to grant women the vote, had been inspired by the lectures and writings of suffragists Susan B. Anthony and Elizabeth Cady Stanton.[9]

Just after the success of suffrage in Wyoming, Utah's territorial legislature granted women the right to vote. Members of the Church of Jesus Christ of Latter-day Saints dominated the Utah territory, and by giving women access to the ballot box, they extended the franchise to a significant part of the territorial population that would support Mormon policies such as temperance and plural marriage. Joseph Smith, the original LDS leader, encouraged a form of plural marriage that he called Celestial marriage, commonly called polygamy outside the church. The practice of plural marriage in Utah created a firestorm of controversy outside the Mormon community, and many LDS church leaders believed that by giving women the right to vote they could eliminate the negative popular image that their women were drudges and slaves. In fact Mormon women were active in their church organizations and communities, often working as midwives, doctors, or journalists outside the home. However, they were also expected to support church policies, including plural marriage. Mormon support for suffrage was problematic for the national suffrage movement. Susan B. Anthony personally found plural marriage repugnant but endeavored to form an amicable relationship with the Mormon church because it shared the goals of temperance and suffrage. This was a dangerous strategy, for it linked the scandalous practice of plural marriage to woman suffrage. In 1882 Congress passed the Edmunds Act, which disfranchised men and women who practiced plural marriage, and in 1887 it passed the Edmunds-Tucker Act, which barred all women from voting in Utah. Not until after the church denounced plural marriage and statehood was achieved did women finally regain the right to vote in Utah, in 1896.[10]

Latter-day Saint church leaders in Salt Lake City encouraged members to migrate to neighboring territories, including Arizona, where they built communities along the Little Colorado River in eastern Arizona and in the Salt River valley of central Arizona in the 1870s and 1880s. These Mormon settlers were often harassed by Gentiles (non-Mormons) for their "un-American" beliefs, especially the practice of plural marriage. Mormons such as Murat Masterson, who introduced the first suffrage bill in Arizona, believed that women should have the vote because they would support issues such as temperance, but most non-Mormons believed it would simply increase support for plural marriage and the number of voters who would take political direction from church officials in Salt Lake City. As in Utah, the Mormon population was problematic for the woman suffrage movement in Arizona. In Tucson, Josephine Brawley Hughes, president of Arizona's WCTU and the first president of the territorial suffrage association, led a virulent campaign against the Mormon religion through her husband's newspaper in the 1880s. It was difficult for Mormon and Gentile suffrage and temperance supporters to work together until after 1890, when the Mormon church formally renounced plural marriage. Even then, hard feelings persisted for many years.[11]

Early woman suffrage supporters in Arizona, regardless of their religion, were primarily interested in using the vote to limit alcohol consumption in the territory. As historian and suffrage supporter James H. McClintock noted in 1916, "the woman suffrage idea in Arizona rather had its inception in the prohibition movement with the understanding that women would knock out the Demon Rum were she given the ballot." Drinking, gambling, and prostitution were openly visible in the male-dominated mining towns, but as families arrived in the 1880s and 1890s, wives and mothers reacted by joining the growing temperance movement. The first Arizona WCTU chapter was formed in 1884 at Fort Whipple near Prescott by the wife of an army officer. The following year Frances Willard, president of the national WCTU, toured the territory with Josephine Hughes. Together the two women recruited members and organized additional chapters in major towns.[12]

Josephine Hughes's husband, Louis, was a Civil War veteran who had studied law and played a prominent role in labor reform in Pennsylvania. He moved to Tucson in 1871 for his health, was admitted to practice law, and started his political career as a city councilman. In 1872 Josephine

Josephine Brawley Hughes of Tucson was the first president of the Arizona territorial suffrage association.

joined Louis in Tucson, making the exhausting and dangerous trip from San Francisco to Arizona alone with their infant daughter. She traveled first by ship to San Diego, where she caught a stagecoach that brought her across the 500 miles of desert in four days. At the time, thieves threatened travelers, so her stage never stopped except to change horses, and Josephine held a loaded rifle at her side the entire trip. At one point her daughter was jarred loose from her arms on the rugged road, but fortunately she was unhurt when she landed in soft sand. Josephine was one of the first Anglo women in Tucson, and she and Louis soon became leaders in the community.[13]

Josephine Hughes established the first coeducational school in Tucson shortly after her arrival in the territory. She also spent much of her career working with her husband at his newspaper, the *Arizona Star*, managing its finances and influencing its editorial policy for twenty-five years, especially when he was appointed territorial governor in 1893. She was a leader in the Methodist church in Tucson and strongly believed in using her position in the church, as the wife of a prominent politician, and as the editor of an important newspaper to denounce alcohol consumption. Josephine Hughes has been described as the territory's "most persistent and scathing critic of immorality, corrupt government and the social evils of the saloons."[14]

In western towns, the saloon was the center of town life, a place to meet and conduct business, cast votes in an election, and learn the latest news. But saloons also were notorious centers of civic misconduct—gambling, prostitution, and drunken brawls. In 1885, violence in the gambling dens of Bisbee was so problematic that the Phelps Dodge mining company instituted a policy of firing employees caught playing games of chance. In Phoenix, more than half of all arrests in 1891 were for drunkenness. A report by the secretary of the interior in 1895 noted that three-quarters of the inmates at the Yuma Territorial Prison were serving terms related to drunken behavior, and half the residents of Phoenix's insane asylum were alcoholics. In addition to the high cost of intemperance, political corruption was blamed on the saloons because candidates were known to buy drinks for male voters, to win their support. Therefore, the saloon represented two problems for middle-class, reform-minded women like Josephine Hughes: it was the source of crime and corruption in their communities and it was a bastion of male power they could not penetrate.[15]

By the time Josephine Hughes assumed the presidency of the territorial WCTU in 1890, the organization had enjoyed several moderate victories under the guidance of Mrs. R. W. Pearson of Phoenix. The WCTU pressured the legislature to ban the sale of liquor on election day, raise the age of consent for girls to sixteen to thwart underage prostitution, and close businesses, especially saloons, on Sunday. Hughes claimed that the success of the WCTU's anti-liquor legislation was "the work of Christian Women and is only another evidence that woman is one, if not the most important, factor in crushing out evil and encouraging and leading reformatory movement. . . . The seeds of temperance, now planted and watered with the earnest tears of good women, will germinate and grow into the mighty forests of truth which will cover the entire territory." Over the next five years, however, the legislature resisted further WCTU petitions, including bills to eliminate gambling and require the strict observation of the Sabbath. Without access to political power, women such as Hughes had a difficult task eradicating the influence of the saloons. Few territorial legislators were willing to listen to women's complaints if they lacked the ability to vote men out of office. Like her mentor, WCTU president Frances Willard, Hughes knew that "women could not wage effective battles for reform without political recourse."[16]

Josephine Hughes resigned as president of the Arizona WCTU in 1891 to become the head of Arizona's fledgling suffrage movement, because she believed that when the vote was secure for women, "then the victory for home and temperance will soon follow." She requested assistance from the National American Woman Suffrage Association, headed by her friend Susan B. Anthony, to form an Arizona association, and in 1891 Laura M. Johns, a NAWSA field organizer from Kansas, arrived to help. Together they established suffrage clubs in every county, collecting petitions and corresponding with important politicians. With the vote, Hughes argued, women would reform society, close saloons, card games, and brothels, and build a "state, anchored in the soundest principles which tell for 'God and home and land,'" the motto of the Woman's Christian Temperance Union.[17]

With the arrival of numerous settlers in the 1880s, Arizona's population more than doubled, and some residents thought the territory was ready for admission to the union. Members of Congress, who determined whether a territory was qualified for admission, disagreed. They refused to pass enabling legislation to allow Arizona to draft a state constitution, believing that the territory's Anglo population remained too small and the desert too arid and hostile to attract additional settlers. Arizona's political leaders proceeded to hold a constitutional convention in 1891, in defiance of Congress. Josephine Hughes and Laura Johns saw this as the perfect opportunity to convince territorial leaders that women should be included in the new state government. The president of the convention, Colonel William Herring, was a suffrage supporter and close friend of Hughes's. At the time, his daughter, Sarah, was studying law under his direction in Tombstone; in 1893 she would become the first woman admitted to practice law in the Arizona territory. After her marriage to Thomas Sorin, Sarah continued to practice law and in 1913 became the first woman to argue a case unassisted before the U.S. Supreme Court. Josephine Hughes and Laura Johns hoped that such a good friend of women as Colonel Herring would convince others to back a suffrage plank.[18]

At Herring's invitation, Hughes and Johns addressed the constitutional convention, where Johns told delegates, "Our object is not office holding so much as a desire to correct the evils of government." But when suffrage was put to a vote, it was soundly defeated, sixteen to five. Territorial leaders condemned the notion of women voting as "a revolutionary and untried question." Although Herring argued that women would "offset the ignorant Mexican vote," others worried that it would increase the Mormon vote. In the end it did not matter, because Congress refused to hear Arizona's petition for statehood. It would be almost two decades before women would have the opportunity to place suffrage in a state constitution again.[19]

In 1896 Josephine Hughes traveled to her home state and spoke in Philadelphia at the annual convention of the National American Woman Suffrage Association. Susan B. Anthony pledged her support for "suffrage onslaughts" in Arizona and Oklahoma, because those territories seemed ready to give women the vote. Despite strong support from NAWSA, the WCTU, and the local Mormon population, the Arizona legislature would not budge. In every legislative session of the 1890s, Josephine Hughes introduced a suffrage bill, but it was always defeated or stalled in committee. The territorial governors of this period, Nathan O. Murphy and Josephine's husband, Louis Hughes, were both suffrage supporters, but neither they nor Josephine could convince the legislature to seriously entertain a suffrage bill.[20]

Hughes and her Tucson followers had made little progress by 1899, when NAWSA organizer Carrie Chapman Catt arrived in the territory with her assistant, Mary Hay. Under Susan B. Anthony's leadership, the national movement had focused on the continual education of voters and politicians to the merits of suffrage, and during their lifetimes the writings of Elizabeth Cady Stanton and the speeches of Anthony converted many men and women to support voting rights for women. As Catt assumed leadership of NAWSA, a new emphasis was placed on organization and financial support, allowing NAWSA to reach beyond a small cadre of elite supporters to attract the working class as well. Instead of simply holding meetings in churches and parlors, Catt organized parades, outdoor speeches, and rallies to attract the average worker and broaden the base for suffrage support. The suffrage movement was no longer content simply to educate the public about the benefits of women's full political participation but also became adept at mobilizing mass campaigns.[21]

Catt's strategy was especially important in Arizona, with its large working class. The local economy was fueled by copper mining, and most miners were skilled laborers who worked for large corporations. By moving the campaign into the streets of mining communities, she could reach more voters, and to accomplish this goal, she turned to new leaders. She found that Pauline O'Neill and Frances Willard Munds were exactly the women she needed for the job. Both women were much younger than Josephine Hughes, belonged to the first generation of Anglo women born and raised in the West, had close ties to the labor movement, and brought new ideas and innovations to the campaign. Josephine Hughes's suffrage work, more closely tied to her friend Susan B. Anthony's educational style, was hampered by her animosity toward the Mormon community and corruption charges aimed at her husband while he served as governor, so she stepped aside as president of the territorial association. Catt, Hay, O'Neill, and Munds took over and organized suffrage clubs in twelve of the fourteen counties in the territory. They continued to work closely with the local WCTU clubs but also expanded their movement to reach out to laborers, many of whom were gravitating toward a new political movement, Populism.[22]

During the early 1890s the Populist movement gained momentum in the farming regions of the Midwest and South when agricultural prices plummeted. Populism grew out of the Farmers' Alliance, which fought the monopolies of large corporations, especially the predatory pricing policies of the railroads and large mercantile companies. The movement sought economic measures that would help farmers become more profitable, including public ownership of railroads, cheap credit, and other inflationary measures such as the coinage of silver that would bring farmers out of debt. The United States government used both gold and silver to back its currency until 1873, when Congress went solely to the gold standard. Bankers and businessmen felt this policy was more secure for financial markets. The Comstock lode in Nevada produced tremendous amounts of silver at this time, and Populists wanted to remonetize silver in order to increase the amount of currency in circulation, thereby creating inflation. While the economic program of Populism attracted some voters, many others were attracted to its egalitarian ideals. Populists called for the direct election of senators, the secret ballot, the initiative and referendum, and woman suffrage, all radical new ideas that would give the average citizen increased power to combat the perceived corrupt practices of large corporations. Many voters left the Democratic and Republican parties and joined the People's party, the Populist political party, which ran its first presidential candidate in 1892. The movement spread westward because it appealed to miners who believed the free coinage of silver would stimulate mining production and create higher wages.[23]

In 1893 a depression hit the United States that drove the price of commodities down. As the price of copper and other minerals dropped, Arizona mines closed and workers were laid off, devastating the local economy. Ranchers experienced a two-year drought, resulting in the loss of between 60 and 80 percent of their stock, and farmers were angered by the inequitable pricing policies of the railroads, which ate up their profits. Mining corporations and the railroads viewed Populist measures as radical and dangerous responses to the depression, but these reforms appealed to miners, farmers, and ranchers hit hard by the economic downturn and facing financial ruin.[24]

Adding to the dissatisfaction of Arizona residents was the fact that most of them believed mining companies and railroads held undue influence over their government. Railroads had vast investments in laying the track that brought the ore out of the mines and people into the territory. Mining corporations based in Europe or on the East Coast, such as Phelps Dodge and United Verde, spent large sums of money developing mines, so they pressured lawmakers to keep taxes on corporations low. It is estimated that in 1900 Arizona's mines were worth $100 million but were valued officially at only $2 million for tax purposes. The general public resented this favoritism toward large corporations because the tax revenue could have financed much-needed roads, schools, and other public projects. By most accounts, mining companies and railroads liberally bribed Arizona's politicians to ensure that their investments were not jeopardized by adverse actions of the territorial legislature. Corruption scandals involving the legislature were routinely reported in local newspapers, and the working population grew increasingly resentful of the power concentrated in the corporations, especially when the economy of Arizona was considered among the poorest in the nation.[25]

In the 1890s, disgruntled Arizona voters, both Republicans and Democrats, increasingly turned to the Populists for remedy. Their national platform pledged to help the average worker by passing legislation for government ownership of utilities and railroads, a graduated income tax, an eight-hour workday, and the right for unions to organize. But their most popular cause was direct democracy. Arizonans felt that the initiative and referendum could be effective tools in battling the large corporations in the territory. The state Populist movement was led by William "Buckey" O'Neill, a Republican from Boston who started his career in Arizona as a journalist, served in several county positions, and switched parties to become the Populist mayor of Prescott from 1894 to 1898. O'Neill's popularity in Arizona stemmed from his strong beliefs in democratic rule and egalitarianism. He argued that Republicans and Democrats promoted policies that divided "the people into two classes—a pauper class, who are laborers and producers, the workers in the field and the mines, and a moneyed aristocracy who are drones in our body public." He denounced the corporate interests that controlled half the territory's property as "the little gods who control railroad corporations," and he advocated radical changes in government.[26]

In 1886 O'Neill married a young Catholic schoolteacher, Pauline Schindler, in Prescott. By all accounts Pauline was a remarkable woman and an anchor for the effervescent Buckey. She had been born in 1865 in San Francisco, the only child of Prussian immigrants. Her father was a career army officer who was transferred around 1884 to Fort Whipple, near Prescott, where the first territorial WCTU chapter had been founded the previous year. Although Pauline became dedicated to the temperance movement early in her life, Buckey was, by most accounts, a drinker and a gambler. His nickname supposedly originated from the card game he favored, "Buck the Tiger." One can only speculate what brought a teetotaler schoolmarm and a frequenter of Whiskey Row together, but from all evidence Buckey adored his wife, and it was a harmonious marriage.[27]

Although suffrage was an intrinsic part of the Populist agenda in the Midwest, many Arizona Populists were more interested in direct democracy for men than votes for women. Despite the reluctance of his fellow Populists, O'Neill, probably encouraged by his wife, helped usher a bill through the territorial legislature in 1897 that gave taxpaying women the right to vote in municipal elections. After Governor Nathan O. Murphy signed the bill into law, however, it was challenged in the courts. In March 1899, Arizona Territorial Supreme Court Justice Richard E. Sloan wrote a decision invalidating the suffrage law, ruling that it gave the vote to all taxpayers, including minors, aliens, felons, and incompetents, in violation of the Organic Act governing territorial government. Unfortunately, the bill's champion, O'Neill, was killed in battle in 1898 as a volunteer with Theodore Roosevelt's Rough Riders in the Spanish-American War. Suffrage leader Frances Munds later opined that had O'Neill lived, he would have "straightened out the tangle for us" and successfully given women the right to vote in city elections. Without a charismatic leader, the Populist movement in Arizona died with Buckey O'Neill in 1898. His widow, Pauline, would continue to work for suffrage in the decades to come and would convince other Populist leaders, including George W. P. Hunt, Kean St. Charles, and Albinius Worsley, to support her cause.[28]

The link between Populism and suffrage is important to understanding victories for suffrage in several western states. In 1893 Colorado suffragists managed to get a bill through their legislature asking for a referendum on the vote for women, and the Populist governor signed it. Carrie Catt was able to exploit the popularity of the People's party in Colorado by linking woman suffrage with support for free silver and economic reform. Her campaign included working-class women, not just elites, and won over a majority of state newspaper editors and labor unions with its support for Populism. The weakened Republican and Democratic parties were forced to reassess their view of woman suffrage. Political leaders could no longer afford to ignore the potential female voter, and the Populist success, according to Suzanne Marilley, "provided a context that prepared and enabled white men to see the political exclusion of women as unjust. . . . The men in the state who had campaigned vigorously for the remonetization of silver but had experienced the rejection of their demand for economic relief also began to see the injustice of women's political exclusion." After voters in Colorado narrowly approved the suffrage referendum in 1893, Catt brought her winning ways to Idaho, a territory that resembled Arizona in many ways, with its significant Mormon and mining populations. In 1896 she was able to garner the support of Populists, Mormons, and WCTU members to win more than two-thirds of the popular vote for a woman suffrage referendum. By linking suffrage with Populism, Catt turned suffragists into pragmatic politicians rather than just idealistic reformers.[29]

When Catt arrived in Arizona in 1899, she implemented the aggressive campaign strategies that had succeeded in Colorado and Idaho. With

Pauline O'Neill, the widow of Buckey O'Neill, was a leader in the Arizona suffrage movement and a representative to the state legislature.

woman suffrage, she promised, "there would be more cleanliness, less corruption, better officials, and better life in every way." She spoke at outdoor rallies for mine workers, promising support to Populists, and she selected Pauline O'Neill, the widow of Arizona's greatest Populist leader, to lead her new organization, the Arizona Territorial Woman's Suffrage Association. O'Neill was not just the wife of a famous war hero and Populist leader but had her own unique qualifications as a politician.[30]

Although Pauline O'Neill quit teaching after her marriage to Buckey, she was active in numerous civic organizations before becoming president of the Arizona suffrage movement. After the loss of her only child at the age of two months, she plunged herself into club work. She played a large role in the charitable Women's Relief Corps of the Grand Army of the Republic and found intellectual stimulation in literary clubs. From 1895 to 1899 she served as a member of the Yavapai County Board of Examiners, overseeing teacher certification. She was an early member of the Prescott Women's Club, later renamed the Monday Club, which was part of the General Federation of Women's Clubs. Prescott was the territorial capital from 1865 to 1867 and then again from 1877 to 1889, so the Monday Club included the wives of prominent Arizona politicians and businessmen such as governors Frederick A. Tritle and Nathan O. Murphy, Yavapai County sheriff George Ruffner, and Prescott mayor and Democratic party leader Morris Goldwater. Some female members viewed suffrage as a positive measure, and Pauline formed lasting friendships with like-minded reformers including Frances Willard Munds, who would serve as her corresponding secretary for the suffrage association.[31]

After working with politicians in Prescott and forming suffrage clubs throughout the territory, Pauline O'Neill traveled with Carrie Catt, Mary Hay, and Frances Munds to Phoenix to lobby the legislature for a suffrage amendment in 1899. They successfully steered a bill through the lower house, and O'Neill had lined up "a strong favorable majority" in the upper house, or council, but a filibuster kept the bill from coming to a vote. According to Catt, suffragists "heard the popping of corks and the clinking of glasses that accompanied the barter and sale of senatorial votes to the proprietors of the prosperous saloons of the State." The president of the council, Morris Goldwater, had promised his mother he would vote and work for suffrage, but because, as Catt recounted, "the saloons of Prescott had elected him and had made him their attorney," they threatened to "'break him' completely if he dared to vote for woman suffrage." Catt claimed that other members of the council also received threats from saloon interests, and so the bill died in committee.[32]

Not everyone agreed with Catt's assertion that the legislature was bought and paid for by the saloon interests. C. P. Leitch, editor of the *Arizona Daily Gazette*, a progressive newspaper that supported woman suffrage, wrote that he did not believe an "undue influence" was at work to defeat the suffrage bill. "We certainly do accredit the opponents of the bill with honest motives," he wrote. Those "honest motives" included the concern of territorial leaders that Arizona would not be admitted to the union with a law giving women the vote. Few members of Congress supported suffrage, and most of them discouraged territories from applying for statehood with constitutions that gave women the right to vote. The chairman of the Senate Committee on Territories, Republican Albert Beveridge of Indiana, also believed Arizona was unsuitable for statehood because it had too many Mexicans and Mormons, and granting women the vote would only enlarge those "undesirable populations" of voters. President Theodore Roosevelt agreed with Beveridge's assessment. Together they held up Arizona's admission to statehood because they believed it was a backward territory, "not equal in intellect, resources, or population to the other states in the Union."[33]

Despite the opposition to woman suffrage in Congress, Pauline O'Neill decided to try to convince territorial leaders that suffrage was desired by members of the growing labor movement in Arizona. Nationally, the Populist movement died as an independent movement in 1896, when the economy made a strong recovery and Democrats adopted many of the movement's ideas and ran its leading candidate, William Jennings Bryan, for president. In Arizona the labor movement took up where the Populists had left off, demanding political reforms that would help workers. When the economy improved and mining profits increased, skilled miners still received poor wages and worked long hours under dangerous conditions, so many of them joined the Western Federation of Miners. Like the Populists, this radical western labor union, headquartered in Butte, Montana, demanded increased political representation for citizens to combat corporate greed and influence.[34]

Labor leaders believed that because corruption was so pervasive in Arizona politics, the only way to reduce the power of the corporations was with direct democracy. Organized labor took up Populist causes such as the initiative, referendum, and recall of judges as devices to balance the scales between the needs of average citizens and the might of corporations. The appeal of direct democracy extended beyond labor union members to other progressive reformers. Former Populists such as George W. P. Hunt and Kean St. Charles became prominent members of the progressive wing of the Democratic party. Others, such as Albinius Worsley, became active in the Socialist party. These men began working with labor union organizers such as Joseph D. Cannon, president of Arizona's division of the Western Federation of Miners, to introduce reform in the territory. Businessmen, professionals, and women's leaders saw that their concerns often overlapped with labor's concerns, and the diverse groups forged their first coalition in 1903 to work for progressive change.[35]

The leaders of the national suffrage movement observed these political changes in Arizona and renewed their efforts to pass a suffrage bill in the territory by sending out field organizer Dr. Frances Woods of Kansas in 1903. Pauline O'Neill had moved to Phoenix in 1899, after Buckey's death, and married his younger brother, Eugene Brady O'Neill, a Democrat in the territorial legislature, in 1901. She continued her work for the movement as its legislative coordinator, monitoring events at the state capitol through her husband. Lida Robinson replaced O'Neill as president of the territorial suffrage organization. Little is known about her background besides the facts that she was the wife of the adjutant general, had been president of the Phoenix suffrage club for years, and published a well-written suffrage newsletter. With the help of O'Neill, Frances Munds, and Frances Woods, Robinson held a suffrage meeting in Phoenix in 1903. Mary McClintock, a local suffrage worker and wife of Rough Rider and Arizona historian James H. McClintock, equated the convention with an earthquake in the desert, an "almost unheard of occurrence." Frances Munds acknowledged that this was the "first really hard fight for suffrage that was made in any legislature."[36]

The new suffrage organization certainly did shake things up. Instead of pleading politely for the men of the legislature to pass their bill, the women worked with labor to force a suffrage bill to a vote. The lobbying team of Munds, O'Neill, Robinson, and Hattie Talbot, wife of the mayor of Phoenix, lined up a representative from the mining town of Jerome, labor leader T. J. Morrison, to make sure all bills in the lower house were tied up until the suffrage bill was taken out of committee and voted on. The strategy worked, and the bill passed sixteen to seven. The *Arizona Republican* noted that "most of the democrats looked uncomfortable while the motion was being read, and the republicans smiled," because they suspected the council would easily defeat the bill.[37]

Throughout the 1903 campaign with the legislature, NAWSA stayed in the background, letting the local women take the lead, because this was not the kind of campaign the national movement encouraged. Carrie Chapman Catt, who had assumed the presidency of the national suffrage movement in 1900, believed that the "trading" and "selling" of votes in politics was something women should campaign against, not a tactic to use in their fight for suffrage. She argued that political decisions should be reached strictly on their merits, not because a deal had been worked out between parties. NAWSA leaders hoped to purify politics with women's presence, not lower women to the level of corrupt male politicians, and they believed the just nature of their cause would eventually win over politicians. Frances Munds, Arizona's suffrage association's corresponding secretary, thought the NAWSA strategy was naïve. "They [the national suffragists] can talk all they want to about educating the dear public but a little political strategy will overbalance all the education you do in a thousand years," she later recalled. What women needed was political clout to force the hands of recalcitrant politicians.[38]

After their success in passing a suffrage bill through the house, Robinson, O'Neill, and Munds lined up Kean St. Charles, a Mohave County senator, to introduce their bill in the territorial council, where it was debated for two weeks. St. Charles was a former Populist turned Democrat who used his position as editor of the Kingman newspaper *Our Mineral Wealth* to promote the cause of suffrage. There were too few votes in the council to get the bill out of committee, so on orders from O'Neill and Munds, St. Charles held up a labor bill popular with the majority of lawmakers until enough legislators agreed to support the suffrage bill. The suffragists crowding the council gallery were jubilant when their bill passed eight to four. The bill then went to Governor Alexander Brodie for his signature.[39]

The governor was swamped with messages from supporters and detractors of suffrage, and he assured women's leaders "that he would not go against the wishes of a majority of the legislature." Despite his promise, Brodie vetoed the bill, stating that "it was not consistent with the Constitution of the United States and was beyond the constitutional limitations of the Legislature." The governor, a Republican appointee, told close political friends that he vetoed the bill because it would have increased the Mormon vote, granting them too much power in government. The pro-suffrage women were angry but convinced they had enough votes to override a veto, so "a hundred suffragists had congregated to enjoy their triumph" in the galleries of the state capitol. The council, under Kean St. Charles's direction, upheld its support of the bill, but it went down to defeat in the house, eight to fourteen, a dramatic reversal of the earlier sixteen to seven vote. The women in the gallery, in unladylike fashion, greeted the negative votes with hisses.[40]

National suffrage leaders again blamed the 1903 defeat in Arizona on the liquor interests. "To-night the saloons of Phoenix are the centre of rejoicing on account of the stand Governor Brodie has taken on the suffrage bill, claiming that they are on top and that the Governor is with them. As a prominent citizen said to-night: 'The gamblers and saloons win, the women lose.'" But Arizona citizens knew that explanation was too simplistic. The *Arizona Republican* editorialized that it was wrong to blame saloon interests, and instead women should fault the territorial constitution. Twice—once in Judge Sloan's 1899 decision regarding municipal suffrage for women and again with the Brodie veto of 1903—the Organic Act was cited as a legal barrier to woman suffrage because it did not allow territorial legislatures to determine voting rights. Even many supporters of suffrage argued that given Arizona's territorial status, it would be difficult to pass a suffrage law.[41]

Munds and O'Neill disagreed with the idea that the Organic Act was to blame, because the territorial legislatures of Wyoming and Utah had already passed suffrage laws and had been admitted to the union as states in 1890 and 1896, respectively. Also, in Arizona the legislature had granted women the right to vote in school elections in 1883, and no one argued that this action violated the Organic Act. Instead, Munds blamed the defeat on poor execution and politics. "We do not blame the saloon men for this, for while they are always against us and were loud in their protests when they found we had passed our bill, their work was not necessary for our defeat. A few political tricksters did it." At first suffragists believed they had been double-crossed by legislators, but as Munds later recognized, most members of the legislature had never intended to pass her bill. They voted on suffrage simply to clear the path for other bills, knowing that the governor would never allow it to become law. St. Charles, according to Munds, had failed to hold up the house labor bill that Brodie wanted until after the governor signed the suffrage bill, and "it served our man right for being such a fool." Her political education was just beginning, and in the future she would allow no such mistake to happen again.[42]

Following the Brodie veto, Munds wrote a telling letter to her cousin in which she expressed the suffragists' profound anger at the governor, saying, "We were so vexed with him we almost felt like doing him violence. Just to think that after all our hard work to have an old fool a federal appointee sit up there and undo it all." Though frustrating, the Brodie veto taught Arizona women a valuable political lesson that would help them in future campaigns: the majority of Arizona's politicians, especially those in the Democratic party, would not support a woman suffrage bill even if they professed sympathy to the cause. Although Carrie Catt wrote in glowing terms of the popular support she saw for suffrage in Arizona during her visits, that support did not necessarily translate into votes in the legislature.

Party bosses believed female voters would not exhibit the same loyalty to political parties as their fathers and husbands. When Pauline O'Neill canvassed the wives of key legislators in 1909, she found the situation unchanged, noting that "their husbands are *afraid* of the *independent* vote" of women.[43]

Although NAWSA continued to send workers to the territory, they were unable to find local women who were willing to spend scarce resources on a lost cause. Lida Robinson followed her husband to another military appointment in California in 1907, leaving the movement in the hands of Frances Munds and Pauline O'Neill. These women knew that the composition of the legislature remained unchanged and that antisuffrage governors continued to run the territory. Any hope for victory was with the gaining of statehood and a new constitution, events that would not occur for several years. Rather than continue to fight a losing battle, the two women retired to their personal lives—Pauline to raise an adolescent son she had adopted shortly before Buckey's death and Frances to care for a third child born in 1905—and waited for the right moment to reorganize.[44]

CHAPTER 2

The Battle Is Won

Statehood and Suffrage, 1909 to 1912

In 1909, six years after the devastating Brodie veto, Arizona's suffrage leaders began to rally again, but this time with a new strategy often at odds with that of the National American Woman Suffrage Association. The first territorial suffrage leader, Josephine Hughes, had focused on lobbying the legislature with the message that if women could vote they would clean up government, a policy that reflected Carrie Catt's and NAWSA's strategy. Frances Munds and Pauline O'Neill learned during the early suffrage battles that women would never be taken seriously if they pursued politics for strictly altruistic reasons. Few incumbent politicians had the incentive to clean up government or wanted changes in the electorate, especially if granting women the vote might jeopardize their control of government. National suffrage leaders warned Arizona women to remain nonpartisan, but O'Neill and Munds grew tired of the repeated defeats suffered under this approach and shifted course to focus instead on male voters who were more inclined to view "votes for women" in a favorable light. They formed coalitions with third parties to force Democrats and Republicans to embrace suffrage. They found success not when they remained genteel and ladylike, pleading for the vote, but when they leveled the playing field and employed the same tactics used by male political leaders.[1]

In 1909 it was clear that Congress soon would be forced to admit Arizona as a state because its population had increased dramatically. Women's leaders knew it was always easier to win the vote when a new constitution was written than it was to amend an existing constitution. NAWSA, now headed by Anna Howard Shaw, sent field worker Laura Clay to Arizona to convince an initially reluctant Frances Munds to revive the movement. The two women spent six weeks in the spring of 1909 working to get a suffrage bill through the legislature, but it failed in both houses, defeats Munds had expected. Three legislators told Munds and

Clay that they personally supported the measure but refused to go on the public record as suffrage supporters because they feared repercussions from mining companies, saloon interests, and male voters who opposed the bill. Munds fundamentally disagreed with NAWSA that suffrage could be won in the legislature, because she knew that even progressive politicians who favored suffrage on principle would not vote for it. In 1909, the actions of the territorial legislature confirmed what Munds and O'Neill had known for years — they were waging a losing battle trying to convince the existing group of Arizona lawmakers to support suffrage. They had worked hard to get a suffrage bill through the legislature in 1903, only to see it vetoed by the governor. Now, in September 1909, Sharlot Hall, a celebrated writer and historian from Prescott, was appointed territorial historian by the governor, only to be denounced by some legislators.[2]

Hall had lobbied to create the office of territorial historian, and when her close friend Governor Richard E. Sloan appointed her to the post she became the first woman to hold an appointed, salaried government office in the United States. Hall had strong support for the position not only because she had done extraordinary archaeological work documenting Arizona's native history but also because she had written and distributed to Congress a pivotal poem titled "Arizona." To the dismay of most Arizonans, in 1905 Congress had seriously considered combining the territories of New Mexico and Arizona, but Hall's poetry lobbying efforts were effective in convincing a majority of members to allow Arizona's admission as a separate state. Despite Hall's credentials as the most qualified person for the job of territorial historian, and despite her enormous support among the public, especially territorial women's clubs, vehement opposition arose because she was a woman. Several prominent male politicians wanted the plum job as historian for themselves and questioned whether it was legal for a woman to hold office in Arizona. Patronage and partisanship were deeply engrained in the political system, and Munds and O'Neill recognized that the current batch of legislators was unwilling to share its hard-earned power with a woman, no matter how well qualified.[3]

Munds was more hopeful about the upcoming constitutional convention, for which delegates would be decided by the growing progressive labor vote, which was more open to suffrage than the existing political establishment. Munds and Clay reorganized and revitalized the local

Frances Willard Munds led the
victory for woman suffrage in
1912 and was elected to the state
senate in 1914.

suffrage clubs throughout the territory, and at their suffrage convention,
members chose Frances Munds as president of the new Arizona Equal
Suffrage Association (AESA).[4]

Frances Willard Munds's speaking talent, ability to rally diverse elements
to the cause of suffrage, and close acquaintance with Arizona political elites
made her a natural choice as leader of the suffrage movement at this decisive
moment. Her experience as corresponding secretary for the Arizona suffrage movement in 1903 convinced her that NAWSA did not always have
an accurate assessment of local conditions, and although it provided her
organization with vital speakers and financial support, she disagreed with
the national movement when it came to campaign tactics. Munds was more
aggressive, willing to engage in partisan politics and trade votes to get her
victory. Despite their differences, NAWSA field workers convinced Anna
Howard Shaw that Munds was an effective leader, so NAWSA gave her
financial and organizational support but kept enough distance to allow her
to win. Munds used this juncture to develop a new organization that relied
less on NAWSA and more on local women.[5]

Like Pauline O'Neill, Frances Munds had a strong political background, but the two women's personalities could not have been more

different. Pauline was reticent, studious, and serious, perhaps a result of her military family upbringing and the loss of her first husband and infant child. Frances was outgoing, had a boisterous sense of humor, and rarely held her tongue. Above all else, she was a gifted politician. She was born in 1866, the eighth of twelve children, near Sacramento, California, into a prominent and politically active family. Her maternal grandfather, Colonel James Russell Vineyard, had freed his slaves in 1827 in Kentucky and was active in the abolitionist cause, which enabled him to build a political career first in Wisconsin and then in California. He died shortly before he would have received the California Democratic party nomination for the U.S. Senate. Munds's paternal grandfather, Alexander Hamilton Willard, had been a member of the Lewis and Clark expedition. The two grandfathers had fought together under General Winfield Scott during the Mexican-American War and were neighbors in Platteville, Wisconsin, where their offspring, Joel Willard and Mary Grace Vineyard, met and married. The couple honeymooned in 1852 on the Overland Trail, accompanied by forty-nine other members of the two families as they made the long trip in wagons from Wisconsin to the Sacramento Valley in California.[6]

Frances Munds's father, Joel Willard, was a civil engineer, occasional miner, and rancher in California and Nevada, where Frances grew up riding horses bareback and playing ball games with her five older brothers. Joel, who suffered from tuberculosis, began to move his family and cattle to Arizona in 1878 in search of a better climate for his ailment. He died of pneumonia en route, but his sons continued the journey with the herd and settled in the Cottonwood region. Initially, Mary Willard stayed in Nevada with the younger children, including Frances, while the older boys established a cattle business in Arizona.[7]

Mary Willard was a Baptist who strongly influenced her daughter to support both temperance and suffrage. Frances was also distantly related to Frances Willard, the leader of the Woman's Christian Temperance Union. As a married adult, Frances insisted that her maiden name, Willard, appear on all official publications to demonstrate her relationship to a woman she revered and who served as a dynamic leader to hundreds of thousands of American women in the temperance movement. As "Frances Willard Munds" she garnered more respect and notoriety in WCTU and suffrage circles than she would have simply as "Mrs. John Munds."[8]

As a young child Frances Willard was a bit wild and stubborn and developed traits that would serve her well during her future campaigns against male politicians. She desired a good secondary education, something that was hard to find in the rural areas of the West, so she badgered her mother endlessly until Mary agreed to send her away to school in the East. Frances was the only child in the large family to receive an education beyond grammar school. At age fifteen she boarded a train for the Maine Central Institute, a Free Will Baptist, coeducational preparatory school. She roomed in a boarding house, visiting her older married sister, Nellie Richter, who lived in Maine, on holidays, and did not return home to Nevada during the entire four-year period. Initially, her brother-in-law tried to advise her about how to manage her finances and where to live, but Frances quickly rebelled and demanded control over her own expenses. Dubbed "the Nevada Wild Cat" by her classmates, she showed early signs of becoming a confident, independent, even cocky young woman.[9]

While Frances was away at school in the East, her mother and younger siblings moved to join the older boys in Arizona. The family eventually built the first brick home in the area known later as Willard Springs. When Frances finished her eastern education in 1885, she was reunited with her family in Arizona. Shortly after her arrival in the territory, she met John Munds, a rancher and miner whose family had done business with the Willard family and had homesteaded Munds Park, just south of Flagstaff. Frances and John courted for four years, postponing their wedding until John could finish his studies at a business college in California.[10]

While waiting for John to complete his education, Frances was hired to teach in Yavapai County, where she met Buckey and Pauline O'Neill. She began her teaching career in the Mormon community of Pine and later taught in Payson. When she first arrived in Pine and saw the primitive living conditions, her instincts told her to return home, but her brother, who had brought her over the rough roads by buckboard, said, "Oh Sis, you have to face many hardships here in the west. Sure you can take it, I know you can." So she decided to stay and lodged with a family of six in a one-room log cabin. The only light came from the large fireplace and a single kerosene lamp. Her private space was curtained off and contained only a rough bed, some hooks for clothes, a wash basin, and a cracked mirror. It was difficult to get any sleep between the snoring and the baby's crying, but she managed to adapt and learned to respect the

Mormon families she lived with at a time when anti-Mormon sentiment was still strong in Arizona. Later in her life, as leader of the Arizona Equal Suffrage Association, Munds would note that her work in Mormon communities had left her with tremendous respect for those "serious, hard-working, economical people, devoted to their church, its members and their activities."[11]

She was less impressed with the behavior of some inhabitants of the mining town of Jerome, where she taught in 1889. Her class was located in a former saloon, nestled between two active saloons, so that "intoxicated characters frequently entered the school room by mistake, which caused considerable disturbance among the pupils until the drunk staggered out on his own or was ejected by the police." She finally quit this teaching position when two students drew knives during an argument in her class and the school board refused her request to expel them. Her experiences in Jerome reinforced her already strongly held belief, instilled in her by her mother, that the consumption of alcohol was dangerous and sinful.[12]

By the time Frances and John were married in 1890 in the Willard home in Cottonwood, Frances Willard Munds had become an independent woman. She had grown up with tremendous freedom to roam the countryside in California and Nevada, and she had been educated in the East without male control over her life. She loved the fact that western women were more outspoken than eastern women and recognized that in the West a woman's opinion was valued more highly than it was in the East. She cut her hair short so she did not have to fuss with it and often rode her horse alone in the Arizona countryside. Frances admired women she met in northern Arizona, especially Helen Duett Ellison, the future wife of George Hunt. Duett had been born in Texas and moved to Arizona in 1885 when her family relocated its cattle ranch. The family herd was taken by train to Bowie, Arizona, and Duett and her sister drove the cattle the remaining distance to the Tonto Basin. An expert horsewoman, Duett was foreman of the Ellison ranch. She could rope, tie, and brand long-horn cattle as well as any cowboy and was a "crack shot." Despite her toughness, she was always a lady and never allowed cowboys to "curse, chew tobacco, or wear chaps or spurs in her home." In Frances's estimation, Duett was as feminine and refined as any eastern woman but could also do a man's work. This ideal of western womanhood would guide Munds as the leader of the Arizona suffrage movement.[13]

Helen Duett Ellison Hunt
was the foreman on her
father's ranch before her
marriage to Governor
George W. P. Hunt.

After her marriage to John Munds, Frances continued to teach, even after the birth of their first child, because her husband was just starting out in the cattle business and the young family needed the extra income. Later, after John's stock business and his career in politics began to blossom, Frances could afford to stay home with her two oldest children, William and Sally. She quickly became involved in local civic organizations, including the Order of the Eastern Star, the Monday Club of Prescott, and the territorial suffrage association. John entered politics, first as deputy sheriff and county assessor, and then was elected sheriff of Yavapai County in 1898. The two were established as prominent local figures, known to most people in northern Arizona in the 1890s.[14]

As suffrage leaders, Pauline O'Neill and Frances Munds complemented one another: O'Neill had an excellent knowledge of the behind-the-scenes maneuverings of the legislature, and Munds was the public face of the movement. Although she was only five feet tall, Munds stood out in a crowd with her red hair and flamboyant hats. She loved to engage in discourse with male politicians about suffrage, both in private and on the front pages of the local newspapers. She was never timid and truly believed she could outwit most male politicians. Laura Gregg, a NAWSA field worker who spent considerable time working with Munds, described her as "a one-woman show . . . as efficient a head to the work [as] in any of the western states. . . . She is full of practical ideas, and knows the people and the political situation, and is an indefatigable worker."[5]

In 1909, as Arizona approached statehood, Frances Munds emerged as one of the most prominent politicians in the territory. Newspapers featured interviews with her, and her correspondence with NAWSA was reprinted regularly in the *Woman's Journal*, the official publication of NAWSA, closely linking her name to Arizona suffrage throughout the country. She understood that Arizona was undergoing tremendous political change at the time, and if she played the game right, she could tie suffrage to the statehood movement, which was looming on the horizon. She made sure the suffrage movement stayed on the side of progressivism and the labor unions so that women would benefit from the rising power of those groups. Male voters would be accorded more rights when Arizona became a state, able to elect the governor and vote directly for laws through ballot initiatives, and Munds hoped to convince them to share this new power with their wives, sisters, and daughters.

Under Josephine Brawley Hughes, the early Arizona suffrage movement was closely aligned with temperance, and women's leaders used conservative arguments that women wanted the vote primarily to improve laws for women and children in Arizona. Under O'Neill's brief tenure and Munds's control, the movement was led by a younger generation of more radical women who felt strongly about equal rights and turned the movement in a new direction. As early as 1903 Frances Munds expressed her frustration with woman's traditional role in society: "So many noble women have been crushed beneath conventionality and through their fear of doing something out of their sphere have allowed a superior intellect to become dwarfed from misuse. When I think of the narrow limits of the so called 'woman's sphere' my blood boils to think of the opprobrium she meets when she dares to step over the limit. I have studied this question of 'woman's sphere' until I feel a wild impulse to do something awful, to defy the world." Although her campaign rhetoric would continue to emphasize women's maternalism and the purifying effects they would have on politics, it increasingly incorporated egalitarian arguments that reflected her belief that women were equal, if not superior, to men. The only "awful" thing she did to "defy the world" was to create a powerful political campaign that overwhelmed all the entrenched forces opposing suffrage in Arizona. In the process, she proved that a woman could beat male politicians at their own game.[16]

Munds's first step as president of the Arizona Equal Suffrage Association was to make sure the future of the state was placed in the hands of the "right kind" of men, so she put together a campaign to ensure that only delegates who supported suffrage were elected to the upcoming constitutional convention. Her plan was to exclude or minimize the number of voters who would not support suffrage and to elect pro-suffrage delegates. Toward this end she worked to exclude non-English-speaking Mexican American voters and to elect Mormons, labor union organizers, and progressive reformers to the convention.

In 1910 an estimated 10 to 15 percent of the territorial population was Mormon. Unlike former suffrage leader Josephine Hughes, who had used her editorial influence at the *Arizona Star* to persecute Mormons in the territory, Munds held Latter-day Saints in high esteem and worked to include them in her organization. At least fourteen of the thirty-two Arizona Equal Suffrage Association campaign committee members were Mormon, including Mary J. West of Snowflake, Rose G. Randall of Payson, and Elizabeth Layton and Inez Lee of Thatcher. These women were active in the Mormon Relief Society and worked exhaustively for suffrage in their communities.[17]

After recruiting Mormon women leaders, Munds moved to activate the support of the Latter-day Saint masses. Because she could not afford domestic servants but still had young children at home and was caring for her elderly mother, Munds could not travel extensively for the campaign. At her request, NAWSA sent a field organizer, Laura Gregg of Kansas, to tour the territory in the winter of 1909–10. Gregg had experience working on suffrage campaigns in other states, but she quickly recognized the immense obstacles to organizing local suffrage clubs in Arizona—vast deserts, mountain ranges, limited and expensive railroad lines, and a dispersed rural population. She spent the early part of the winter in the

Laura Gregg Cannon spent time in Arizona campaigning for the National American Woman Suffrage Association.

Mormon strongholds of Apache and Graham counties, where travel was difficult. Some settlements lay twenty-five miles from the nearest rail line, and roads became impassable on rainy or snowy days in the White Mountains. Gregg noted that about two-thirds of her meetings could be reached only by buckboard or stage, and sometimes it took all night to thaw out from the long day of travel in the open air.[18]

Despite the hardships, Gregg enjoyed her work. She stayed in the primitive cabins of Mormon families and held meetings in schoolhouses. She was heartened by the overwhelming hospitality and warmth of the people she met, but she was also shaken by the extreme poverty they lived in and felt awkward about accepting their generosity. Over the winter of 1909–10 Gregg met with thousands of people in northeastern Arizona, collecting 1,500 new members for the Arizona Equal Suffrage Association. She was able to report to the NAWSA leadership that she had found "a larger proportion of sentiment in favor of suffrage than in any other state in which I have worked." Her letters to Anna Howard Shaw gushed so effusively about Mormon qualities that the NAWSA president worried that Gregg might marry into a polygamous family and become "the twenty-fifth of the thirtieth fraction of a Mormon household [before] we get suffrage in Arizona."[19]

The polygamy issue raised by Anna Howard Shaw was still relevant in the Arizona territory in 1909. By courting Mormon voters, suffrage leaders exposed themselves to criticism, not only because some Mormons still practiced plural marriage illegally but also because few supported the progressive labor reforms of the Democratic party. As Munds pointed out, the Democrats "will make a howl about woman suffrage increasing the Mormon vote, they always do that. That would not bother the Democrats one bit if they were sure the women would always vote the democratic ticket." Most Mormons in Arizona remained Democrats but tended to support the corporation wing of the party, which often sided with Republicans. Opening up the franchise to include Mormon women would increase the number of conservative Democratic voters in the state, something progressive Democrats and labor supporters feared. Despite this dilemma, Munds stood her ground and encouraged Mormon participation in the movement.[20]

During her travels in the Mormon communities of Apache County, Laura Gregg met an unexpected group of suffrage supporters. One day she was approached by two young Mexican American men, who asked her, "When are you going to speak to *our* people?" Mexican American communities existed side by side with Mormon communities in the remote parts of the White Mountains, and the two groups often provided services for each other. Gregg told the men who approached her that she could not speak Spanish, to which they responded, "Many of us can understand English." Suffrage workers like Gregg were surprised and unprepared when Mexican Americans showed interest in their cause, but they responded by providing suffrage literature, posters, and speakers when goaded.[21]

Among Arizona suffragists it was believed that the average Mexican American worker opposed giving women the vote. As one suffrage worker put it, "the Mexicans are opposed to woman suffrage because they are ignorant. The Americans are opposed because the Mexicans are ignorant—and there we are!" This bias was common among western woman suffrage leaders, who often worked with labor unions and political parties to neutralize the votes of what were deemed "uneducated" voters. Arizona was no exception. The decision to exclude Mexican Americans from the

Arizona suffrage movement was made with the advice of NAWSA field worker Laura Clay in 1909. Clay was descended from the prominent Kentucky family of Henry Clay and was a veteran of two southern suffrage campaigns, in which she encouraged racist policies to exclude African American women from voting. The population of African Americans was small in Arizona, so they did not threaten the existing Anglo political structure, but Clay was able to convince Arizona suffragists that Mexican American voters did.[22]

After Arizona became a territory of the United States, a small number of Mexican Americans from established landowning families in southern Arizona became leading members of society. Dr. Rosa Goodrich Boido, who served as president of the Equal Suffrage Club of Pima County, was one of the few registered female physicians in the territory at the time and was also the superintendent of scientific temperance for the WCTU. In medical school in California she met and married classmate Norberto Lorenzo Boido, who had been born in Nogales, Mexico. After medical school the couple lived in Central America for several years before returning to Arizona. They homesteaded in Benson in 1899, and Lorenzo became the physician for the Southern Pacific Railroad and headed the second largest Mexican American benevolent society, La Liga Protectora Latina, in the 1910s, while Rosa opened a medical practice specializing in the treatment of women and children. The Boidos quickly became prominent members of both Anglo and Mexican American society in Tucson.[23]

The Mexican American community in Arizona at statehood was led by doctors like Lorenzo Boido, businessmen such as John Lorenzo Hubbell, and newspaper editors like Carlos Velasco. Hubbell ran a successful trading post in Ganado, providing American Indian art, rugs, and jewelry for sale in Fred Harvey's tourist emporiums. He was also a leading Republican who became head of the state party in 1912. Carlos Velasco was a former state senator and judge in Sonora, Mexico, and an attorney in Tucson who edited the largest Spanish-language newspaper in Arizona, El Fronterizo. In 1894 Velasco founded the largest mutual aid society in the Southwest, the Alianza Hispano-Americana. Mutual aid societies, which provided insurance in case of illness or death, emerged in the 1890s and became the most important organizations for Mexican Americans in the Southwest. Although Boido, Velasco, and Hubbell all supported woman suffrage, few other Mexican American leaders did.[24]

Pro-suffrage women had a difficult task trying to sort out how the Mexican American community would vote. Throughout the campaign, Munds and her followers reached out to prominent members of the educated Mexican American business and political community, holding meetings in their homes and publishing suffrage material in Spanish. At the same time they tried to neutralize the votes of working-class males, whom they believed were antisuffrage. Historian Joan Jensen has commented that in New Mexico, "Hispanic males did not uniformly oppose women's political participation, nor did Anglo males uniformly support it," and suffrage leaders recognized that this was the case in Arizona as well.[25]

Frances Munds agreed with Laura Clay's decision to exclude non-English-speaking Mexican American males from voting, believing that recent immigrants would be less likely to vote for suffrage. This was also a popular idea among Democrats, because Mexican Americans registered predominantly in the Republican party during the territorial period. With the support of the Arizona Equal Suffrage Association, labor unions, and the Democratic party, the territorial legislature passed a literacy test for voters in 1909. Registration was denied to anyone who was unable to write his name or read a paragraph of the United States Constitution. The first Arizona State Legislature passed a similar requirement into law in 1912, which resulted in an estimated 30 percent decrease in eligible Mexican American voters. Even those who could read English sufficiently to pass the test were intimidated by nativist poll workers, so many Mexican Americans avoided voting. In Cochise and Pima counties the Mexican American voting population was so affected by the law that there were too few registered voters to hold primary elections in half the precincts in 1912. Although Mexican Americans made up 20 to 25 percent of the population, citizenship requirements and the literacy test reduced them to approximately 13 percent of eligible voters. Munds commented after the suffrage campaign that the state "vote was small, as most Mexicans were disenfranchised by an educational requirement." In the words of historian Katherine Benton, "this was Southwestern-style Jim Crow."[26]

As Frances Munds secured the votes of Mormons and found success in excluding the portion of the Mexican American population that she feared would not support suffrage, she turned her attention to capturing voters from a new third party movement. In 1910, Arizona voters began to rally around the labor movement in sufficient numbers to create a new Labor party. Laura Gregg, who was a labor activist as well as a suffrage organizer, and Munds attended the Labor party convention that summer in Phoenix and induced its delegates to promise to include an equal suffrage plank if elected to the convention. In exchange, suffragists vowed they would support Labor's demands for direct primaries, the initiative, the referendum, and recall of judges, an agreement that stirred up controversy.[27]

The mining corporations were shocked by the news of the partisan alliance and retaliated with a smear campaign in the newspapers, alleging, falsely, that the suffragists had pledged $1,500 and 2,000 members to the new Labor party. Laura Gregg explained that the corporations made these allegations "as a ruse to get us to come out and deny the story, so that they could say in big headlines that the Suffragists had thrown the Labor Party down." Mining companies did not want women to vote, according to Pauline O'Neill's husband, council member Eugene O'Neill, because they might jeopardize corporate control over the legislature. "They use the saloons as channels through which they reach the voters in order to elect the men who shall look after their special interests in the legislature; and in return for this service the liquor interests demand that their representatives shall vote for what the saloons want." No self-respecting woman would be found in a saloon, so how could the corporations keep control of state politics if women voted?[28]

The national suffrage organization had warned Frances Munds and her leadership to remain independent and above party politics so that they would not antagonize powerful politicians. By boldly aligning themselves with a third party, the Labor party, Arizona suffragists came face-to-face with both the negative and positive aspects of partisanship. They gained pro-suffrage delegates to the constitutional convention through the Labor party but antagonized conservative Democrats and their corporation supporters. Despite the controversy, the die had been cast, and the Arizona movement would continue to use political deals rather than persuasion to pursue its goal.

On the surface, a relationship between labor unions and suffragists seemed unnatural. Miners rarely supported the prohibition, anti-gambling, and anti-prostitution measures championed by female reformers. Why would they want women to vote if they might eliminate vice and usher in a dry era in Arizona? In fact, by 1910 many of those old attitudes were changing, and most labor leaders supported local option laws to ban drinking because they conceded that liquor hurt productivity. Alcoholism contributed to absenteeism, accidents in the workplace, and domestic violence. Temperance laws were gaining popularity among a wide range of the territory's electorate, even miners.[29]

More important, miners believed they were underdogs engaged in labor battles with employers for better pay, working conditions, and representation, and they saw women as natural partners in the fight. Women worked in Arizona and needed fair representation in government, the same as men. As union leader Joseph Cannon stated in the 1912 campaign, the vote for women "is not a matter of sentiment, but a necessity. Not a question of ethics but one of economics. From the point of labor unions, the ballot for women is not desired as a means of diversion but as a weapon by which they can obtain better conditions in industry and greater opportunities for the home. . . . The ballot is the most potent weapon that can be given to them."[30]

The newfound strength of the Labor party created panic in the Democratic party, which was split between conservatives who backed the corporations and progressives who backed the unions. The popularity of the Labor party among Arizona voters finally tipped the balance in the progressive Democrats' favor, because the party did not want to concede delegates to the Labor party. The progressive faction took over the leadership of the Democratic party when it became obvious that there was "such an insistent demand for the initiative and referendum that the whole state was alive with the sentiment." The Labor party dismantled itself, and its members pledged their support to the Democrats. Republican President William Howard Taft had advised Arizona to hold out for "a safe and sane constitution," which did not include the initiative, referendum, or recall. But as Frances Munds observed, the Republican candidates who backed Taft "were overwhelmingly defeated in nearly every county in the state." The result was a strong coalition of labor supporters and progressive Democrats that would elect forty-one of the fifty-two delegates to the constitutional convention. The coalition was a setback for suffragists, however, because the Democrats, unlike the Labor party, could not be convinced by Frances Munds and Laura Gregg to commit to a suffrage plank in the new state constitution.[31]

After the loss of her Labor party coalition, Munds renewed her effort with county political leaders to quietly make sure the "right men" were elected to the convention through the Democratic party. "I am writing our friends or the leaders among them in all the counties to watch the candidates for the Constitutional Convention and see that the right men are sent, and in instances where I could do so have warned them who not to send." Communications from suffragists to political leaders implied that "the women of this territory will not forget their friends." She understood that this kind of political activity was, in her words, "risky business." After all, when she had made a partisan deal with the Labor party, the negative publicity had been enormous. She knew that if her efforts were exposed in the newspapers she would be criticized as a meddler in political affairs. But in the end she was comforted "by the fact that men think that women are such fools. We have done all we could to keep up the appearance at times, and have let them think that they can fool us, but we are keeping the game in our own hands and when the time comes they will find out who gets 'stung.'"[32]

While Munds wrote letters and met with influential leaders, NAWSA field worker Laura Gregg returned to the territory and toured mining towns in the spring of 1910, talking to union organizers and gathering more than 3,000 new male and female AESA members' signatures to take to the convention. Gregg had begun her career as a labor organizer and during the Arizona campaign met and married the president of Arizona's Western Federation of Miners, Joseph Cannon, so she was a respected and qualified speaker for mine worker audiences. In trying to win the miner vote, Gregg believed that "when we get the people behind us the politicians will only be too glad to come to us."[33]

Given her past experience with Arizona politicians, Frances Munds was less sure than Gregg that politicians would line up behind popular sentiment for suffrage. She knew that many of the delegates chosen to the convention were personal supporters of suffrage but had voted against it in the legislature—including George W. P. Hunt, the president of the convention. Hunt was a close friend of Munds's and a former Populist turned progressive Democrat. Since his arrival in the territory in 1881 as a young man searching for mineral wealth, Hunt had become a strong advocate of the working class. He had only a few years of formal education and was forced to support himself working odd jobs during his early years in Globe, but he had a knack for retail sales and for politics, so he quickly found success. He served in the legislature during much of the 1890s and early 1900s and then became the Populist mayor of Globe in 1904. By the time the 1910 constitutional convention opened, Hunt epitomized what the progressive wing of the Democratic party stood for in Arizona — a defender of labor rights and direct democracy — and therefore was chosen to preside over the convention.[34]

Hunt's position on suffrage was a conundrum for Munds and the movement. He personally supported the issue but publicly backed away from it. In 1897 Hunt laid out his stance on suffrage in a speech when he asked, "Why is taxation without representation tyranny for man and justice for woman? Why do men declaim against monopoly and perpetuate the greatest and most unjust monopoly on earth, the monopoly of the ballot?" But as president of the territorial council, he had voted against suffrage in 1909, so Munds had mixed emotions about his selection as president of the constitutional convention. After labor unions asked Munds her opinion of Hunt, she wrote to him asking if he would support suffrage at the convention and warning him that "there is considerable dissatisfaction in suffrage circles over your candidacy because you voted against the measure in the last legislature." He responded that the issue of woman suffrage was too important to be decided upon by elected officials and instead should be put before the voters — that was why he had voted against the measure in the previous legislature. He strongly believed that the voters should have a voice in all important issues, and therefore the initiative, referendum, and recall of public officials were the three most important items on his agenda for the constitution, not suffrage. Hunt and his followers continued to be "lukewarm at most" on woman suffrage, according to political scientist David Berman. The progressive Democrats dominated Arizona politics at this point and had "little to gain and a great deal to lose by extending the franchise."[35]

Hunt knew that Arizona voters desired statehood above all else, so he argued to Munds that President Taft would reject a state constitution if it granted women the vote. Munds responded, "You say you think it is unwise to put a suffrage plank in the constitution and then you go on to say that it should contain the initiative and referendum and recall by all means. Either you think that we women are very dense or else you are not sincere. You know as well as can be that there is nothing that Mr. Taft will so seriously object to as that very thing [the recall] that you are advocating so strenuously. On the other hand you have no authority whatever for saying that he is opposed to woman suffrage." When Hunt tried to calm Munds by telling her that the initiative and referendum could be used to obtain suffrage, she replied, "I cannot close without referring to the injustice of your statement that with the initiative and referendum the rights of all will be conserved. What benefits will it be to us women to have such laws when we have no voice in their exercise?" Hunt was unable to respond to this stinging retort.[36]

Munds knew that suffrage was likely doomed without Hunt's support at the constitutional convention but decided to make a show of it anyway. Suffragists deluged the convention with petitions and speakers, hoping to put the issue to a public vote. On November 2, 1910, the Committee on Elections was called to order and the chairman turned the proceedings over to Frances Munds. Supporters filled the gallery of the council chamber. Munds introduced her first speaker, Mrs. J. A. Hopkins from the Gila County mining town of Miami, describing her as "one of the large number of persons designated by the census officials as without occupation; that is, she was nothing but a housekeeper." Hopkins argued that granting women the vote "would be better for the women, better for the men and better for the state." Dr. Agnes Wallace of Prescott, who represented the working women of the state, argued that both female wage earners and professional women were handicapped in obtaining jobs because they were "without votes and consequently without political influence." Pauline O'Neill, adopting an equal rights stance, argued that women should not be taxed without representation. The final speaker was Ernest Liebel, formerly of the Labor party, who "presented his prayer for the emancipation of women in the form of a more or less imperious demand," warning politicians that women were sure to be given the vote soon and would then turn antisuffrage men out of office. Suffrage "was coming anyway and those who contributed to its delay would find themselves stranded political hulks." Despite the persuasive testimonies and forecasts of political suicide, delegates rejected the suffrage plank by a vote of thirty to nineteen, agreeing with Hunt that woman suffrage was "a dangerous and radical thing" to include in the constitution because it might prevent ratification by President Taft.[37]

If the defeat of suffrage was not disappointment enough, constitutional convention delegates then attempted to bar women from holding public office. Many male politicians were angry that Sharlot Hall was still territorial historian, and although they were unable to generate enough votes to keep women from all public offices, they inserted an article into the constitution that kept women from running for state executive positions. Suffragists worried that school suffrage, a right enjoyed by women in the territory for almost thirty years, might also be annulled by the new constitution, so Munds wrote to Hunt asking if this were the case. In her letter Munds stated that she believed the right to vote in school board elections was preserved, but she added sarcastically that "as I haven't sense enough to cast an intelligent ballot, I may not be able to express a correct opinion on a matter of such importance." In the end, women were allowed to continue participating in school board elections, but the behavior of the delegates was so insulting to suffragists that they would hold a grudge against Democratic leaders for the next twenty years.[38]

An outraged Munds concluded that many delegates to the constitutional convention were not as "progressive" as she had hoped. "We labored long and well with that Convention, but it was useless, for we soon found that although the majority was labeled 'Progressive' that only a few were the genuine article." Delegates had "insinuated that suffrage was a dangerous and radical thing to put into the constitution and that it would endanger its acceptance both by the people and by President Taft. But we soon came to see the difference between machine politicians and the rule of the people." Historians of the constitutional convention agree with Munds's assessment of the delegates—they were not so much progressive or pro-labor as they were anti-corporation in their outlook. During the campaign for delegates to the convention, the Democrats assumed a progressive agenda to capture the Labor party's vote, but once elected to the convention or to office, many turned out to be less interested in truly reforming government than in preserving their own power. Munds knew that her only hope for success was with the male voters of the state of Arizona, who now held the power of the initiative to introduce legislation.[39]

Statehood came for Arizona on February 14, 1912, but there were no valentines for women when the first election was held. Not only were women barred from voting by the new constitution, but most of the same men who had defeated suffrage at the convention were elected to prominent positions in the state capitol, including George Hunt as governor. In her message to NAWSA's newspaper, the *Woman's Journal*, Munds issued a thinly veiled threat to state legislators: it was "hardly probable that this Democratic Legislature would deliberately alienate the women by refusing to submit the suffrage amendment since we have the power to initiate it by petition." Privately, Munds felt that a suffrage referendum had little chance with the current group of representatives.[40]

Suffragists bombarded Governor Hunt with requests and petitions to recommend a suffrage amendment to the new constitution, and he obliged them in his message to the first state legislature. John Hughes, the son of Josephine Brawley Hughes and a newly elected senator from Tucson, introduced a suffrage referendum during the first session. The bill passed in the house but failed by one vote in the senate, a scenario all too familiar to Munds and her supporters. Labor unions denounced the legislature's failure to pass the referendum. The Chloride Miners' Union sent a resolution demanding action to the state's newspapers and to the *Miners Magazine*, the voice of the Western Federation of Miners. The article outlined labor's reasons for supporting the issue, arguing that "our mothers and sisters are already entered into all lines of all professions and industries and are the independent owners of property and taxpayers, and no democracy can be truly such when any portion of its moral membership is denied the right to participate in its governmental affairs."[41]

Even before the bill failed in the legislature, Munds began to circulate suffrage initiative petitions. She had lost faith in the legislature but knew that, as the *Graham County Guardian* put it, "if the people ruled, victory would be with the women without a doubt at the earliest possible moment." NAWSA chose not to participate in the initiative campaign because criticism surfaced that outsiders were meddling in Arizona politics, so Munds had only six weeks and local resources at her disposal to collect the 3,342 signatures necessary to place an initiative on the November ballot—a daunting task in the summer heat of Arizona. Privately, Anna Howard Shaw worried that the Arizona organization would fail because of its limited resources. AESA efforts were concentrated in Maricopa County, the most populous county, because organizers lacked the volunteers to collect signatures in the rest of the state. The Civic League of Phoenix was formed and led by Pauline O'Neill to circulate petitions in Maricopa County, and Maie Heard, wife of *Arizona Republican* newspaper publisher Dwight Heard, was named treasurer of the league. For six weeks more than fifty male and female volunteers, many of whom belonged to the Socialist party, canvassed the male electorate, asking for their support for suffrage. Corsets were loosened, sun hats were worn, and more than 4,000 signatures were collected in 100-degree heat by the July fifth deadline, a "remarkable feat." Signers of the petitions came from all classes and ethnicities and included Mexican American, Chinese American, and African American registered voters.[42]

With the successful completion of the petition drive, Frances Munds opened her state campaign headquarters in the Adams Hotel, the unofficial meeting place of the state legislature in downtown Phoenix, in September 1912. She hired her son's fiancée, Madge Udall, a young University of Arizona college student, as her secretary and first paid employee for the campaign. Munds now faced her ultimate political test. She had long believed that even though Arizona's politicians were hostile to her cause, male voters would support her. She was about to find out whether she was right. She benefited from recent suffrage victories in other western states, especially the narrow win in California in 1911. Popular support was building, and NAWSA returned to help with the final campaign, sending Alice Park fresh from the California campaign with hundreds of pounds of leftover suffrage literature. Park, a veteran of numerous state suffrage campaigns, was amazed at the positive attitude of Arizona voters. "I never saw anything like the attitude of the Arizona people. The passing of the amendment on Nov. 5 is so taken for granted. There is no opposition. I have argued suffrage, written it, distributed its literature for years, and I find this the most extraordinary experience of my career." Park and Munds were both naturals at generating publicity, and rarely a day went by without a pro-suffrage editorial or interview in the local papers. NAWSA provided roughly half the $2,200 it cost to run the final phase of the campaign. The other half was raised by Arizona supporters—including large financial contributions from Munds and Governor Hunt. In addition to providing financial support, NAWSA president Anna Howard Shaw made seven speeches in the state, drawing large and enthusiastic crowds.[43]

Munds launched a comprehensive suffrage barrage to win over voters, declaring that "every precinct will be organized. Every chance to spread the suffrage gospel will be grasped. Every woman will be urged to take her part in securing equal suffrage for Arizona. Society women, club and business women, and the unassuming housewives will all unite to give their best efforts to obtain the ballot." A week before the election she set up a booth at Arizona's first state fair, held in Phoenix. Festooned with yellow bunting, a suffrage flag, posters, and a twelve-foot "Votes for Women" banner, it was declared "the most conspicuous on the grounds." The fair was the single most important event of the year in Arizona and the only occasion when cattlemen, sheep growers, miners, and farmers came into town from remote parts of the state, so this was the perfect opportunity to reach the voting public. Munds and other suffragists gave many impromptu speeches. They hired boys to hand out suffrage material at the train stations as people headed home from the fair. Suffragists ended up handing out more than 20,000 buttons, badges, and leaflets, enough for one of every four eligible voters in the state.[44]

Munds was especially effective at working with state newspapers, which tended to be progressive during this period. She had recruited many of the wives of prominent editors to the movement, and their husbands responded with positive endorsements in all the major newspapers. Munds asked Josephine Hughes to write an editorial, which was widely reprinted throughout the state. Hughes argued that because women had pioneered Arizona, suffering hardship and deprivation, they should be rewarded with the ballot. "I do not believe there is a fair-minded man, especially of our pioneers, who will not concede that the women of Arizona during the last forty years did equally as much as the men in the building of the state of Arizona." She also wrote personal letters to individual legislators, reminding them that their own wives and daughters were intelligent women who had no influence in government. Almost all state newspapers printed positive editorials about the suffrage amendment. A. D. Nelson of the *Parker Post* wrote, "In the home woman has the same to face as the man. At times she has the greater burden there to bear. She is fast winning her way to a parity with man in the business and professional world. . . . From a standpoint of twentieth century democracy, woman of a right, should have the ballot: for the freedom of the race will, perforce, always be measured by the freedom of the women, not of the men."[45]

In interviews with state newspapers, Munds continued to argue that votes for women would usher in an era of clean government and social improvement for the new state. Citing Colorado as an example, she claimed that where women voted, the most scientific and progressive laws on the books could be found. She chastised the constitutional convention delegates and the first state legislature for failing to include women in the great progressive experiment they were embarking upon. She wrote a press release that was printed in most state newspapers urging women to talk to the men in their lives and convince them to vote for suffrage. "We know many men who say that they would willingly vote for the amendment if only the woman of their household and their women friends would ask them to. Obviously then, the thing to do is ask."[46]

Munds also made the egalitarian argument that women had a right to vote based on the notion set forth in the Declaration of Independence that "governments derive their just powers from the consent of the governed." As taxpayers subject to the law, women were justified in demanding the vote, an argument that appealed to working men and women. Munds had received letters from working women across Arizona who, like newspaper editor Angela Hammer, wanted to know why "low class men, drunkards and inebriates of all descriptions who will sell their vote either to the highest bidder, or for a drink, can vote, but such women as myself among thousands of others, who are taxpayers, and identified with the business life of our commonwealth, have been denied the privilege of a voice in the affairs in which we are so deeply interested."[47]

Once again, Laura Gregg Cannon, back from the successful campaign in California, was a powerful spokesperson for the cause as she began an extensive state tour with her new husband, labor leader Joseph Cannon, and Socialist state senate candidate Albinius Worsley. Rallies were held all over the state, and the Cannons addressed "monster gatherings" in the mining communities of Cochise, Gila, Greenlee, and Pima counties. Worsley told labor union crowds that the "female portion of the race has the same rights as the male. Who will dare to say that the woman has not as much interest or as many rights in this world as the man?" Henry A. Davis, state senator from Maricopa County, agreed, telling his constituents that "every argument in favor of granting the privilege to any man of whatever attainments applies with the same force to every woman who possesses equal attainments. To hold otherwise is to maintain that there is a fundamental inequality in intellect as between the sexes, a proposition most emphatically denied by everything in reason and in nature."[48]

The labor strategy paid off. By October 1912, 95 percent of the state's labor unions had endorsed a woman's right to vote, including the Western

Federation of Miners, the American Federation of Labor, and the United Mine Workers of America. Munds and O'Neill had cultivated the unions for years, and labor leaders appreciated the way suffragists had supported them prior to the constitutional convention. Although the Labor party had dissolved and the progressive Democrats were a disappointment to many union men, the Socialist party continued to demand the initiative, referendum, and recall, the direct primary, an eight-hour day, social insurance for workers, a graduated income tax, public ownership of railroads, a federal department of labor, a corrupt practices act, and equal rights for women. Joseph Cannon was the most popular Arizona Socialist candidate, and his presence at rallies in heavy mining counties was important to the subsequent suffrage victories in Cochise, Gila, Mohave, Yavapai, and Yuma counties. Socialist presidential candidate Eugene V. Debs toured Arizona in 1912 and asked miners to support the suffrage issue. Debs's popularity—he received 13.4 percent of the vote in Arizona, more than double the vote he received in the country as a whole—was key to inspiring a large Socialist turnout at the polls. When the campaign was over, Munds concluded, "There is no doubt that our large majority was contributed by the labor men and the Socialist Party and that they each gave us almost their solid vote."[49]

The Arizona suffrage movement also benefited from the endorsement of Progressive Bull Moose presidential candidate Theodore Roosevelt, who toured the new state in the fall of 1912. Roosevelt appealed to the state's leading progressive businessmen and politicians, many of whom had served with him as Rough Riders in the Spanish-American War. He was an enormously popular figure and was the leading presidential vote getter in Arizona that year. Roosevelt's support of suffrage forced the Democrats to reevaluate their opposition to the measure. The Democrats' presidential candidate, Woodrow Wilson, did not support suffrage, but the party's base in the state was splintered by the Socialist and the Bull Moose Progressive candidates—Debs and Roosevelt together captured 40 percent of the Arizona vote that year—so Democratic bosses had no choice but to invite Munds and O'Neill to speak at their conference that fall. The women told Democratic leaders that if they did not support suffrage, the Arizona Equal Suffrage Association would be unable to keep its campaign nonpartisan, and they would "feel obliged to help the party that helped us." Although women could not vote, they could encourage male family members to support the party that supported suffrage. Popular support for the measure was so great that Arizona Democrats responded to the threat by including suffrage in their platform. After years of work, suffrage leaders finally had gained the leverage they needed to force the state's dominant party to back their cause.[50]

Munds and O'Neill sent a similar message to the Republican conference, which was led by John Lorenzo Hubbell, chairman of the party. Munds had courted Mexican American leaders, including Hubbell, a long-time supporter of suffrage, and her strategy paid off when he brought his Republican party around to support the women. "I am in favor of equal suffrage and believe that the republican party should come out strongly for justice to the women," Hubbell told the press. By early October 1912, the women had the endorsement of all five political parties in the state: Democrats, Republicans, Progressives, Prohibition, and Socialists. As Munds put it, "The shrewdest thing that was done during the whole campaign was the obtaining of a suffrage plank in both Democratic and Republican State platforms. . . . When the party conferences were held for the purposes of formulating the party platform for the State campaign, we women went before the Democratic and the Republican conferences and beat the reactionaries who had again gained control of the machinery. We had a battle royal, but we won by the simple play of wit which taught me that man's wit is no match for woman's in point of keenness." By threatening to pledge the woman's vote to the national party that endorsed suffrage—the Progressive Bull Moose party—Munds played the state parties against each other and ended up with the endorsements of all of them. "The Republicans and Democrats were too wise to give the Bull Moose an advantage of that kind," recalled Munds.[51]

With all political parties backing suffrage, and with strong support from labor, newspaper editors, and Mormons, the movement was on solid ground for the fall initiative election. A "Votes for Women" banner was hung across Central Avenue in downtown Phoenix and was stolen at least once as a high school prank, but Munds did not mind the theft because it became front page news, promoting her cause further. Politicians observed that the tide was changing, and it was time to publicly support suffrage. An *Arizona Gazette* editorial noted, "There are democrats and republicans alike, who at heart are in favor of equal suffrage, but who do not have the courage of their convictions to express themselves as they honestly believe, through fear that they might offend someone." Munds benefited from the support of Democratic U.S. Senator Henry Ashurst, who spoke at rallies, stating, "It has been urged that the women do not need the ballot, the ballot needs the women." Other leading Democratic politicians, including Governor Hunt, Congressman Carl Hayden, whose mother and wife were both suffragists, and U.S. Senator Marcus A. Smith, also endorsed the initiative.[52]

On November 5, 1912, election day, Frances Munds spent a busy morning distributing suffrage materials outside Phoenix polling stations. She found that the saloon interests, working with Democrats, had hired men to intimidate voters planning to vote for the suffrage initiative. Munds may have convinced the party's leaders to give lip service to her cause, but rank-and-file party operatives continued their opposition to suffrage. When she tried to hang pennants outside a polling location she was threatened by a poll worker, so she quickly hunted down one of the Democratic bosses she knew and issued a threat of her own. "I told him that if he didn't get busy, I would telegraph all over the state what the democrats were doing in Phoenix. He said, 'you keep still, you little girl, and I'll fix it up.'" Within an hour he had done the job, and suffrage workers were allowed to work outside the polls. Munds later reported: "The saloon men were almost crazy and tried their best to line up the working men, but men who stood in line and heard them trying to tell the working men to vote against the suffrage amendment told me that they heard ever so many say 'Oh you go to h — —l.'" The liquor interests had lost their influence to a five-foot-tall redhead in heels.[53]

After working the polls all day, Munds finally went to bed exhausted, slept until ten o'clock the following morning, and then headed down to the *Arizona Gazette* newspaper office to watch the returns with Pauline and Eugene O'Neill. Eugene tried to cheer up a worried Frances, telling her they might get lucky and eke out a small victory. By evening it was clear, however, that the victory would be substantial. Sixty-eight percent of Arizona voters supported the amendment, the largest popular vote for suffrage in the nation (table 2.1). Every county returned a majority. Graham and Apache counties, with large concentrations of Mormon voters, gave the highest percentages for suffrage, 81 and 72 percent, respectively. The important mining counties, such as Mohave, Gila, and Cochise, where Laura Gregg Cannon and union organizers had worked so diligently, returned 70 percent or more of their votes for the amendment. Maricopa County, with more than 20 percent of the state's voters, had been the biggest source of concern for suffrage leaders during the campaign. There they had appealed to Progressive voters and were happily surprised with their solid majority of 66 percent. Munds gave much of the credit for the victory in Phoenix to Henry A. Davis, Democratic state senator from Maricopa County, who had given many speeches during the campaign and worked at the polls passing out "votes for women" cards on election day. Davis was one of Munds's strongest allies, arguing that "nobody thinks of questioning a man's right to the voting franchise just because he is a male. . . . Just why women should be classed with children, the uneducated, criminals and idiots in the division of the human family who are denied the suffrage privilege has always surpassed my comprehension." In exchange for the many votes Davis won with his campaigning, Munds hoped that the new women voters would reward him with a U.S. Senate victory in 1914.[54]

Arizona's victory stunned Anna Howard Shaw and the national suffrage leadership, who expected the initiative to fail because of a lack of resources. Although Munds and her organization operated on a shoestring budget with limited personnel, they enjoyed enormous popular support. Arizona historian Will Robinson summarized the suffrage battle best in 1919 when he said, "The truth is that the politicians were afraid of the women—afraid they would vote the state 'dry'—which they did; and afraid they would do all sorts of other unreasonable and revolutionary things—which they did not—or certainly no more than the men. . . . Here it may be said that the only surprising thing about granting the women of Arizona the franchise is that it wasn't given them sooner. Undoubtedly they would have voted years earlier if the politicians had been of the same mind as the average citizen." David Berman's recent analysis of the 1912 election demonstrates what Munds and her followers already knew: the measure was supported strongly by Mormons, Socialists, farmers, and miners. Progressives voted for suffrage, but not as strongly as expected, and Democrats and Republicans were more likely to vote against suffrage than for it. Western-born voters were much more likely to support the measure than voters born in the East, the Midwest, or Mexico.[55]

The final initiative campaign benefited from the pro-labor, progressive climate in Arizona politics and from a well-run campaign organized by

TABLE 2.1 Woman Suffrage Vote by Arizona County, 1912

County	Total votes	Percentage of votes for woman suffrage	County's percentage of all voting-age males in state
Apache	217	72	2.8
Cochise	3,941	73	17.3
Coconino	712	68	4.4
Gila	1,737	70	9.9
Graham[a]	878	81	10.4
Greenlee[a]	1,071	55	—
Maricopa	4,539	66	22.4
Mohave	525	70	2.8
Navajo	612	66	3.0
Pima	1,318	65	6.4
Pinal	678	65	3.3
Santa Cruz	431	65	2.1
Yavapai	1,991	69	10.3
Yuma	994	66	4.9
Total	19,644	68	100.0

Sources: Berman, Reformers, Corporations, and the Electorate, 199; U.S. Bureau of the Census, Population of the United States, 1910, 585, 587.
[a]In 1910, when census information was collected, Greenlee was still a part of Graham County. Graham and Greenlee counties together accounted for 10.4 percent of the total male voting-age population.

women who appealed to the many disparate interests of the new state. Their egalitarian message—that as taxpayers and workers, women were entitled to equal representation with men—struck a chord with many working-class Arizonans. In a few short years, local suffrage leaders had become astute political observers and adopted tactics generally used by male politicians to win campaigns. When Laura Clay first arrived to revitalize the suffrage movement in early 1909, she agonized over women's inferior position when dealing with the Arizona legislature. "As Mrs. O'Neill and I sat there day after day watching for some stray chance to speak for a moment to the members about our bill, and saw the floor crowded with men lobbyists who had the ear of the members every moment . . . I realized profoundly that we were engaged in a most unequal contest." But by election day 1912, Frances Munds had leveled the playing field considerably and was commanding a Democratic boss to do her bidding, make him run "from ward to ward like a chicken with its head cut off." After the election Munds concluded that "if there were any Antis they had not a word to say." At the last moment, "the saloon men tried to fight us as they always do, but when they found how the labor men were lined up for us, they took a very philosophical view of it and said, 'Well if we let them alone they will perhaps let us alone. We can't beat them anyway.'" In its three short years under Munds's direction, the Arizona Equal Suffrage Association had become a force to be reckoned with. Munds commanded the support of important politicians and labor unions and dragged the major parties reluctantly to her side. Her political savvy, the force of her personality, and her undying dedication to women's rights made Munds the perfect choice to lead the women of Arizona.[56]

Through trial and error, women's leaders like Frances Munds learned to harness the different facets of Arizona's political landscape—a strong temperance movement, significant Mormon and Mexican American populations, and third party movements such as the Populists, the Labor party, the Socialists, and the Progressives—to win a decisive victory. In the process, they established a precedent for women's participation that extended far beyond just marking a ballot. Unlike many eastern suffrage leaders, Munds was not content with simply gaining the right to vote. She argued that the striking victory in Arizona was a mandate for women's full political participation, not just as voters but as office holders. "That the men of Arizona need and want the help of our women in solving the problems which confront us, is shown by the overwhelming vote they gave in granting us the ballot."[57]

On primary election day in 1914—the first statewide election that included female voters—the streets of Prescott were busy from early morning until late afternoon as voters stopped to talk with one another after casting their ballots. Frances Munds noted that on this occasion the scene was quite different from that in years past. "The polling places have heretofore been places that we women instinctively shunned, and, although it has been against the law to sell liquor on that day, there has always been more or less drunkenness and many street fights. Not so this time." The town's saloons closed at six o'clock the night before the election and did not reopen until the polls closed, so the rowdy behavior traditionally associated with an election was absent. Munds was jubilant as she stood on a downtown street corner watching automobiles transport men *and* women to vote. After more than two decades of toil by suffrage workers, women were turning out in large numbers to cast their ballots for the first time in an election in Arizona.[58]

Frances Munds believed that granting women voting privileges would have a transformative effect on the new state. Reflecting on that first election day for women, she wrote in the *Woman's Journal*, "There was no evidence whatever that politics had degraded or lessened in any way the womanliness of our women, and there was every evidence in the world that women had elevated and purified politics mightily." Arizona women had begun the suffrage battle to eliminate corruption, alcoholism, and vice in the territory, but by the time the vote was won they had become convinced that much more was at stake: full political participation on an equal basis with men.[59]

Although Munds had won the suffrage battle, the war was not over. She knew it was going to be difficult to work with all those men who had fought against suffrage for the past thirty years. Throughout the campaign, her power had grown as she formed alliances within the labor unions and the progressive wing of the Democratic party, but she had also made many enemies along the way. Established politicians had much to fear from the new women's leader who could command her followers to do her bidding.

CHAPTER 3

The War Is Not Over

Political Parties and Women's Clubs

In May 1913, NAWSA staged a massive parade in New York City to celebrate the three new suffrage states of Arizona, Oregon, and Kansas. Tens of thousands of people cheered Arizona's standard bearer, Madge Udall. Back in Arizona, suffrage leader Frances Munds predicted that the advent of women in politics would mark a distinct era in the progress of civilization and would result in the "erection of the ashes of the past of a real, true democracy." But not everyone in Arizona agreed that suffrage was a universal elixir. State political party leaders brushed aside Munds's rhetoric and worried about more practical issues, such as which political party women would join and whether they would vote along party lines or be independent. Would they try to form a female voting bloc to unseat the legislators who had rebuffed their efforts to gain the vote and replace them with women? Members of the Arizona State Legislature, shaken by the large suffrage victory, moved quickly in January 1913 to pass an emergency law that opened the registration books to women, and Maricopa County party leaders held a banquet for the new members of the electorate "to welcome them in royal fashion." But beyond the initial hoopla, most male political leaders silently hoped that women would vote their conscience and elect the "right men" to office, leaving the business of running the state to the existing leadership. State women's leaders, however, believed their resounding suffrage victory was a referendum for full participation. Clearly, the battle would continue even after suffrage was won.[1]

The national political parties quickly devised mechanisms to incorporate women as they gained the right to vote. In late 1917 the Democratic National Committee created women's divisions in fifteen of the sixteen suffrage states. The Republican National Committee responded with its own women's division, called the Republican Women's National Executive Committee. These organizations were staffed and run by women, but the male members of the state central committees controlled funding

Madge Udall represented the new suffrage state, Arizona, in a 1913 suffrage parade in New York City.

and chose the leaders. The parties recruited some talented women from suffrage organizations to run the divisions at the national level, including national suffrage leader Harriot Taylor Upton and the daughter of Republican leader Mark Hanna, Ruth Hanna McCormick, and these women convinced Democratic and Republican male leaders that only women knew how to reach out to the new female electorate. The women's divisions appealed to women by emphasizing their responsibility to pass legislation concerned with children, education, and health. They were primarily responsible for producing campaign materials, educating women on party issues, encouraging female campaign volunteers, and registering women to vote.[2]

Women's leaders such as Upton and McCormick were initially hopeful that women would be integrated into the party system. As it became evident from the early voting of women in western states that a female voting bloc would not emerge and that women would not threaten party leadership, Democratic and Republican leaders became less supportive and kept women from assignments that wielded power. The suffrage movement had united women behind a single issue, but when the vote was won, women pursued a variety of causes and lost much of their political clout. Democrats and Republicans expected women's leaders to register female voters and drive them to the polls, not to run for office or demand political appointments. Women's political ambitions and legislative agendas were effectively silenced as they joined the party ranks.[3]

After the ratification of the Nineteenth Amendment in 1920, national Democratic and Republican leaders "expressed disappointment that women did not at once enter the party campaigns with the same zeal and consecration they had shown in the struggle for the vote," wrote Carrie Chapman Catt and Nettie Rogers Shuler in 1923. "These men forgot that the dominant political parties blocked the normal progress of woman suffrage for half a century. The women remembered." Just as women's demands for the vote had been ignored for decades, so female candidates and party leaders were not taken seriously, and former suffragists were usually given roles as social hostesses at Democratic and Republican gatherings. Emily Newell Blair, the vice chair of the Democratic National Committee from 1922 to 1928, observed that women's roles were as "mere stage furniture, belittling to one's reputation and insulting to one's self-respect. . . . The doors to political success are guarded by men." Others, including Eleanor Roosevelt, commented that widespread male hostility existed toward sharing control of the parties with women. Male-dominated county committees chose female committee members on the basis of their bank accounts or the status of their husbands within the party, not according to their political abilities. Susan Ware's study of the life of Mary Dewson, the highest-ranking female Democrat in the 1930s, reveals that "the traditional structures in both parties were too formidable for individual women to make a difference without the collective support of their sisters. And even then breaking in was far from easy." There were notable exceptions, such as Jeannette Rankin, congresswoman from Montana, and first lady Eleanor Roosevelt, but for the most part women rarely penetrated the chambers of national party politics before the 1970s.[4]

As bad as the relationship between political parties and women was at the national level, it was decidedly worse in Arizona. The antagonism created during the suffrage battle between Republicans, Democrats, and female leaders lingered after 1912 and left Arizona lagging behind most of the nation in incorporating women into the existing political parties. Frances Munds and Pauline O'Neill, the state's leading suffragists, were not even offered positions on committees of the Democratic party, as was customary in other states. Democrats belatedly asked Munds to be an elector to carry the Arizona vote to Washington, D.C., in 1912, but when they could not locate her immediately, they sent a male representative instead. Munds was irate. When the national party asked Munds in 1913 to create a women's organization in the state, she declined, noting that she "could not name more than half a dozen who could be depended on to work for the entire democratic ticket" and that she feared the state party would be unwilling to fund a women's division. The project languished until the 1930s. Pauline O'Neill was chosen as a presidential elector for Democrats in the 1914 election only after women's groups demanded it.[5]

Arizona was the only early suffrage state in which Democratic leaders failed to organize a women's division and one of only eight states in which no provision was made by either law or party regulation to incorporate women on state political committees after suffrage was granted to all women in 1920. In 1922, ten years after suffrage was won in Arizona, the state Democratic central committee finally resolved to choose a female vice chairman of the state party—Theodora Marsh, a former state legislator. By 1924, thirty states had female vice chairs at all levels of state party committees, but not until 1958 did Arizona pass a law requiring that women serve as county vice chairs of the parties. In 1936, James Farley, chair of the Democratic National Committee, scolded state party chairman William P. Stuart for not establishing women's committees in Arizona, but neither the Democrats nor the Republicans attempted to create separate women's divisions until the 1940s.[6]

As the minority party, Arizona Republicans saw an opportunity to widen their voter base in the state with new women voters and made a better effort to include women than the Democrats. In 1916 Grace Forbes Alexander and Freeda Marks undertook the job of organizing women in Republican clubs. In Phoenix the Woman's Republican League conducted a house-to-house canvass of precincts to get out the woman's vote that year and met weekly to discuss issues on the ballot. In 1920 women were appointed as regional vice chairs to travel the state and register women in the GOP, with resounding success. In some towns registered Republicans outnumbered Democrats for the first time in history, because of the organizational work of women.

For example, in the town of Williams in Coconino County, eighty-seven more Republicans than Democrats were registered, thanks to the efforts of the Woman's Republican League. In the house, Republicans won nineteen of the thirty-nine seats, and in the senate they gained a one-seat majority over Democrats. Governor Thomas Campbell, a Republican, was careful to praise the efforts of women in 1920 for his election and the GOP's capture of state government. He forced the reluctant Republican state central committee to grant women's demands for female representation on the state and county central committees. Party leaders delayed implementation until 1924, and even then female representation on Republican committees increased only slightly, to 10 percent. In 1924, state figures revealed that 64.2 percent of women were Democrats and 33.1 percent were Republicans, in comparison with 66.4 percent of men who were Democrats and 30.6 percent who were Republicans. Republican women such as Grace Forbes Alexander and Freeda Marks believed they were doing the bulk of the registration work and were responsible for increasing the Republican vote, especially among new female voters. But according to Alexander, they received "little encouragement" from male party leaders.[7]

The Democratic party was so strong in Arizona before World War II that it did not need to curry favor from women. In turn, female politicians were not beholden to the Democratic ticket. Upon entering the state legislature in 1916, Pauline O'Neill declared, "I am not tied to anyone. No one can dictate to me for I am not pledged to the corporations nor the labor unions and recognize that both have a right. I mean to be guided solely by my own conscience." When Nellie Trent Bush first ran for the legislature in 1920, she also asserted her independence, proclaiming, "Why, I'm a Democrat, but I don't believe in party politics to the exclusion of all else. I intend to vote for the measure which will serve the greatest interests of the state, regardless of party lines." Polly Rosenbaum admitted that she switched to the Democratic party when she first arrived in Arizona in 1929 because "there wasn't a Republican in sight." She remained a Democrat "but never considered herself a slave to any party."[8]

Female nonpartisanship infuriated Arizona's politicians. Governor Hunt's Democratic machine was legendary during his lengthy reign over state politics, and his control over state agencies and unions was comprehensive. Democrats elected to the legislature were expected to back up the administration and the unions. When they did not, political retaliation was swift and public and often made the front pages of local newspapers. Representative Nellie Bush of Yuma County often found herself at odds with Hunt but "had gone into the Legislature with a determination to represent my county as seemed best to me. Actually I'd given small thought to the Governor's opposition. I knew he liked complete power, that he expected 'his people' to stand solidly behind him. I'd even support him whenever I could convince myself that what he wanted was for the public good. But I never considered myself 'his person' . . . and when it was necessary I stood up to be counted against him." Frances Munds had to fight the local saloon interests and the United Verde Copper Company in Yavapai County while campaigning for the state senate in 1914. In 1930 Jessie Bevan waged a close primary race for the legislature against a male candidate in Cochise County. Bevan later recalled that the Phelps Dodge mining company opposed her in the election, and the "county Democratic machine did not expect to have opposition in the general election [but she] had the backing of women's clubs throughout the county and they turned out the vote." She was so thankful for the work of the local Business and Professional Women's Club that she joined it and served as an officer. Long before Barry Goldwater was heralded as a maverick politician, many female Arizona politicians defied their party. Although some historians have characterized Arizona politics during these years as under the complete control of the mining companies and railroads, too many independent women were successfully challenging male candidates backed by corporations for that to be a completely accurate assessment.[9]

Prominent suffrage leaders such as Frances Munds and Pauline O'Neill quickly emerged to challenge leading Democrats in 1914. Munds boldly stated that she no longer trusted the men running Arizona. "It amuses me to hear the men who have opposed us bitterly for years saying now that they always did believe in suffrage. When I went back to Prescott those old vagabonds that I have scrapped with for fifteen years all came rushing up and congratulated me and told me what a smart woman I was and gave me all kinds of taffy. . . . They think I have forgotten all about the past." Munds angered Democratic leaders in 1914 when she crossed party lines and came out in favor of a Socialist superior court judge in Yuma County over the Democratic candidate, who had not supported suffrage. Political journalist John Dunbar denounced the suffrage leaders for hounding antisuffrage candidates. He argued that women "now have the right to vote in Arizona and it is high time they were realizing that the WAR IS OVER. . . . The fact that a man opposed equal suffrage a year ago is no fit reason for the suffrage leaders to jump into the fight against him now." Dunbar went on a virulent crusade against Munds and O'Neill, characterizing them as "unscrupulous short haired women who posed as political bosses." In the reform climate that permeated Arizona at this time, many hoped that women voters would crusade against political bossism and corruption, so when Dunbar accused suffrage leaders of becoming political bosses themselves, he was attacking them for forsaking their clean government campaign for political ambition.[10]

During the 1914 campaign Munds further angered politicians when she placed a letter in newspapers throughout the state addressed "To the Women of Arizona," urging them to support incumbent Marcus A. Smith over challenger Reese Ling in the Democratic primary for U.S. Senate. Neither candidate had a sterling record on suffrage. Smith had originally failed to support suffrage legislation in the U.S. Senate but changed his mind in 1912 when he saw how popular the measure was, and in October 1914 he asked the national Democratic party council to adopt a plank pledging to a national woman suffrage amendment. His opponent in the primary, Reese Ling, contended in the press that he had "worked untiringly to help the women gain the ballot." Munds countered that he was printing lies and that as Democratic national committeeman he had been discourteous to her when she asked him to support the suffrage platform in 1912. She told female voters that Ling would be "dangerous indeed, not only to the national suffrage bill which is now pending in the United States senate, but to other legislation in which women are vitally concerned." Ling was one of the most conservative members of the Democratic party and therefore would never be viewed as an asset to women. Furthermore, he was a rival of Eugene O'Neill's for the position of Democratic national committeeman in 1912, so Pauline O'Neill and other suffrage women also worked for his defeat in 1914.[11]

An editorial in the progressive *Arizona Republican* denounced the suffragists for supporting Smith, condemning them for intervening in the election and making suffrage an issue, especially because neither Ling nor Smith could be considered a "good suffragist." John Dunbar wrote in an editorial that he believed Pauline O'Neill had become part of the Democratic machinery and was directed by high-ranking party officials, an idea that must have seemed outrageous to Munds and O'Neill, given the clashes they experienced with Democratic leaders. Every time a woman expressed her political opinion in public, she was tagged a "political boss," and a female political boss was worse than a male one. "Male political bosses are a lot of cheap hirelings and vandals, but when it comes to the female of the species, we cannot find language to describe them," wrote Dunbar. Like many other political observers, Dunbar could not tolerate the nonpartisan behavior of women, alleging that "if Mrs. Munds is to remain in politics in Arizona she will ascertain that one of the prime requisites to success is party loyalty." What Dunbar and most men in party leadership did not understand was that because male politicians had repeatedly rejected suffrage and now rejected integrating women into the party system, the war was not over but just beginning. Frances Munds and many other local suffrage leaders continued to endorse candidates on the basis of their attitudes toward suffrage, insisting that pro-suffrage candidates offered the best hope to voters interested in laws benefiting women and children.[12]

Almost a century later, it is difficult to determine exactly how much influence suffrage leaders had on female voters in Arizona. What is known is that in 1914, only four of the nineteen senators who were members of the first state legislature, which rejected the suffrage referendum, were reelected. In 1916 many people suspected that new female Mormon voters were responsible for George Hunt's loss of the governorship, because they rejected his platform to abolish capital punishment. Whether women were voting to punish antisuffrage politicians or simply were more conservative than most men, it is clear that female voters had a strong effect on these early elections. Male candidates were forced to say repeatedly that they had been supporters of woman suffrage. As late as 1930, George Hunt was still running advertisements in the state federation of women's clubs newsletter, *Arizona Woman*, claiming that he had been an "Outstanding Advocate of Woman's Suffrage." By injecting suffrage into Arizona campaigns from 1914 to 1930, Munds and other suffrage leaders continued to try to direct women voters and challenge the leadership of the Democratic party.[13]

Although women were often at odds with Democratic bosses, they did step up and support their party when an outside threat appeared in 1914 and again in 1916. Alice Paul, the radical young eastern suffrage leader, sent her Congressional Union representatives to Arizona as part of a national campaign to "Defeat the Democrats" in suffrage states. She reasoned that because Democrats controlled Congress and the White House, they were responsible for blocking the national suffrage amendment and should pay the highest political price: removal from office. Originally Paul organized the campaign within the National American Woman Suffrage Association, but NAWSA leaders grew increasingly uncomfortable with her militant, partisan stance. Anna Howard Shaw cultivated supporters from both parties and did not wish to antagonize either side, so Paul left NAWSA in 1914 and set up her own suffrage association, the Congressional Union, which later became the National Woman's Party, headquartered in New York City. After Arizona became a suffrage state in 1912, Paul targeted state Democrats for removal, even though the state party had endorsed suffrage, albeit reluctantly, in its platform.[4]

When Congressional Union organizers Josephine Casey and Jane Pincus arrived in Arizona in 1914, they campaigned against two Democrats pledged to woman suffrage: U.S. Representative Carl Hayden and Senator Marcus A. Smith. Former suffrage leaders Josephine Hughes, Pauline O'Neill, and Frances Munds made public statements condemning the "Defeat the Democrats" campaign. Hughes characterized the Congressional Union women "as political meddlers, creating discord and strife," while Munds thought they were "militant suffragists" who "had been repudiated by the regular woman suffragists of the country."[5]

Although the Congressional Union found some support in the state, notably among radicals such as labor activist Rosa McKay, the majority of Arizona women viewed Alice Paul's "Defeat the Democrats" workers as outsiders and extremists. They responded by forming Woodrow Wilson Leagues in 1916 to show their support for the president and their disdain for "the impertinence of Eastern women, who seek to direct the women voters of Arizona how to vote." No Democrats lost their seats because of the campaigns, and the stressful six-week 1916 campaign caused the National Woman's Party representative, Edna Latimer, to seek a complete rest in a sanitarium at its completion. Yet the "Defeat the Democrats" campaigns of 1914 and 1916 did have an important effect on state politics. Democratic candidates were forced to make public statements in support of suffrage because, as Congressional Union worker Jane Pincus said, "every candidate who was running, even for state or county offices, felt it

A controversial National Woman's Party banner hung across downtown Tucson in 1916 for three weeks before it was torn down.

necessary to declare that he had always believed in woman suffrage, that his mother had believed in woman suffrage, and that his grandmother believed in it." In many ways the Congressional Union's battle in Arizona continued the antagonism between male and female political leaders as they vied for the support of women voters. By keeping the suffrage issue alive long after the 1912 election, the fight continually reminded voters that the majority of the state's male politicians had not supported suffrage and perhaps were unqualified to represent women's interests.[16]

After passage of the Nineteenth Amendment in 1920, the National American Woman Suffrage Association dissolved itself and created a new organization, the nonpartisan League of Women Voters, which was dedicated to female voter education. But in states such as Arizona, where suffrage was achieved before 1920, local women were left to create their own voter organizations. Some nonpartisan clubs, such as Pauline O'Neill's Phoenix Civic League, were started in 1912 to collect signatures during the petition drive for suffrage, and after victory they refocused on female voter education. Frances Munds established a nonpartisan club in Prescott in 1914 "dedicated to educate the female voter into properly exercising her privilege of suffrage." These clubs sometimes pushed the boundaries of female voter education, setting up committees that investigated conditions at the state correctional schools, prisons, and mental hospitals. For example, Munds's Prescott club endorsed Governor Hunt's program to eliminate the stripes on inmate clothing and the shaved heads that stigmatized prisoners.[17]

Frances Munds hoped that issues, not parties, would compel female voters and immediately set about planning "how we shall band ourselves together in a non-partisan body for the carrying out of plans for ideal legislation, for women and children especially." Editorials concurred with Munds that female voters would remain independent. The *Bisbee Daily Review* asserted that "the moral standard of women is so firm that election choice will be much dictated by 'what is right.' In their own minds if a man is better than his opponent, the better man will receive the vote." Governor Thomas Campbell echoed this sentiment in 1917: "The very nature of the matters in which women are interested precludes partisanship."[18]

Numerous female nonpartisan organizations focused on another progressive issue that had attracted so many women to Arizona politics to begin with: prohibition. In Cochise County women formed a Political Victory Club in 1914 to support prohibition candidates. Although this club's stated purpose was to hear each candidate's position on the issues, its underlying aim was to endorse candidates "standing for the best as regards moral advancement and public good." The female members of this club interviewed all candidates for county and state office about their views on prohibition and published a list of their candidate endorsements, without reference to political party, in the local newspaper.[19]

Although prohibition had strong backing in Arizona by many progressive groups, and local option laws allowed towns to outlaw drinking, in the minds of activist women the legislature had done too little to discourage alcohol consumption. Now that women had the vote and the initiative was an option, organizations rallied to place a prohibition amendment to the state constitution on the ballot in 1914. The Arizona WCTU launched a successful campaign to register female voters, and although all-male anti-prohibition leagues appeared in Arizona to combat the amendment, they were greatly outnumbered by prohibition supporters, especially among recently enfranchised women. Although neither the Democratic nor the Republican party endorsed it, the prohibition amendment of 1914 passed with 53 percent of the vote. Contemporary observers such as Grady Gammage, secretary of the Arizona Temperance Federation, believed that about two-thirds of the supporters of the measure were female, and without them it would have been "swamped by the men's negative vote." The *Christian Science Monitor* "conceded that the votes of women contributed largely to carrying through the amendment to the constitution eliminating the liquor traffic in Arizona." Frances Munds told readers of the *Woman's Journal* that the passage of the prohibition amendment was evidence of how women could purify politics.[20]

The presence of female voters changed the political landscape in Arizona after 1912. Suddenly a woman counted for something because she voted, and she had even more power if she belonged to an organization that challenged male leadership. In Prescott before 1912, women had spent years petitioning the city council to enforce local drinking ordinances, without much success. Local law enforcement ignored the laws until women were granted the vote and club women began to agitate for compliance, and only then were elected officials and saloon owners forced to act. Not only did they enforce the existing laws, but they also passed new laws to make sure saloons would be closed after midnight and on election day. In 1914 female voters were critical to the passage of the prohibition amendment, and when it became apparent that the law was not being enforced, women throughout the state formed the Woman's Law Enforcement League to identify and oppose candidates who did not support prohibition and to monitor officials who were lax in upholding the law. Membership included 3,500 women in Maricopa County alone, almost 16 percent of the women of voting age. Women also championed clean government. When civic leaders in Phoenix in 1912 appointed an all-male commission to investigate the implementation of charter government to fight corruption, they were asked to appoint "a generous number of women" after receiving a "gentle reminder" from women who wanted a voice in city government.[21]

Although local nonpartisan clubs were effective in forcing city councils to respond to issues, many women sought a more united effort to influence the state legislature. Munds and other suffragists hoped to use their collective female talent to increase agitation for progressive change through the Arizona Federation of Women's Clubs. Family size was decreasing and education levels for women were rising throughout the United States, and women's clubs were founded in the 1870s to meet the needs of the growing middle class of women who craved intellectual stimulation, which was denied to women confined to the domestic sphere. Some clubs were social, exploring literary and cultural themes, others were active in reforming the community, and still others became places for women to hone their political skills. In the 1890s these disparate clubs began to affiliate in the General Federation of Women's Clubs, the largest organization of women's clubs in the United States. It attracted 20,000 members when it was founded in 1890 and grew to a million women by World War I. Members took on a variety of civic and philanthropic endeavors, raising money for schools and libraries, town beautification projects, and child welfare, which reflected the interests of their middle-class, educated backgrounds. Women often used their local women's clubs to lobby state legislatures or Congress, asking for child labor laws, mothers' pensions, vocational education, increased funding for schools and libraries, and a variety of other reform measures. Historians have characterized the activities of these clubs with terms such as "organized motherhood," "virtuous womanhood," and "maternalism," because members believed that mothers were best suited to understand the needs of women and children. Most women chose to use this form of indirect influence in clubs rather than engage directly in male-dominated electoral politics. The degree of political activity varied from club to club and from state to state, but overall, historians agree that women's clubs created a separate political culture that appealed to women.[22]

The General Federation of Women's Clubs pursued a racist policy that barred minority women from membership, so African American women founded the National Association of Colored Women (NACW) in 1896 with the motto "Lift as we climb." Most Anglo settlers in the Arizona territory had been immigrants from the American South who incorporated racist laws and customs in the state. The 1909 territorial legislature passed a law permitting school segregation, and the best neighborhoods in Phoenix had "whites only" covenants that kept Mexican Americans, Asians, American Indians, and African Americans out. Companies hired minorities only for the lowest-paying jobs, if at all, and public buildings often had signs reading "Mexicans and Negroes not welcome." In 1910, only 764 African American males, about 1 percent of the voting population, lived in Arizona. The small community of approximately 200 black women in Phoenix started a movement to create the Arizona Federation of Colored Women's Clubs (AFCWC) as early as 1915, dedicated to fighting racism, improving educational and economic opportunities in their community, and educating voters on the issues and the candidates.[23]

In 1916 the president of the AFCWC, Ella S. White, led a protest by club members and church leaders of the showing of *The Birth of a Nation*, a movie that gave a favorable view of the Ku Klux Klan and negatively portrayed African Americans in the South following the Civil War. White argued that the "terrible effect of that picture, which is not historically correct, has been demonstrated. It has created prejudice against the colored man. . . . we do not ask for social equality—that has never been our aim, but in a time like this we want fair play. We are good citizens, property owners and taxpayers." Her actions convinced the Phoenix city commission to ban the movie, but a local theater manager ran it for twenty weeks in defiance of the ban, until he was arrested and fined. In 1917 the president of the Phoenix City Federation of Colored Women's Clubs, Mrs. Jessie James, sponsored successful legislation to create Carver High School in Phoenix to accommodate black children, who were barred from white schools by legislative action. She was also responsible for a law that allowed African Americans to attend Arizona Teachers' College in Tempe, where her own son became the first black student to enroll.[24]

The Ku Klux Klan began threatening Phoenix residents in 1921, raiding Sunday services at African American churches and kidnapping, assaulting, and threatening black citizens. In response to the racial violence, the Arizona Federation of Colored Women's Clubs, under the leadership of James, collected funds to buy a building for the Phyllis Wheatley Community Center in 1927 in Phoenix to provide a meeting place for African Americans. In this atmosphere of virulent racism following World War I, the Klan also attacked other minority groups, including Catholics, Jews, Mormons, Italians, and Mexican Americans, burning crosses on lawns and threatening people with violence.[25]

During and after World War I, Arizona Anglos were concerned that too few immigrants could speak English and were familiar with American customs and laws. As published reports of high illiteracy rates among immigrant populations surfaced in Arizona in the 1910s, many Anglo leaders sought methods to Americanize Mexican immigrants. The Arizona

Federation of Women's Clubs began to fund night schools for recent Mexican immigrants in Phoenix. As a result of this Americanization effort, local clubs, according to historian Janet McFarland, "could no longer justify not having Mexican women in its clubs and club women realized the exclusion of Mexican women only hindered their transition." In 1919 the Central District Federation of Women's Clubs, which included Phoenix, resolved that Mexican American women could join their organization, although there is no evidence that they chose to do so. In 1921 Friendly House, a settlement house, was established in Phoenix as a place where Mexican immigrants were taught English and American government, hygiene and homemaking. Placida Garcia Smith served as its director for decades.[26]

Unlike African American and Anglo women, Mexican American women did not create separate female-only organizations but instead were involved in male-led mutual aid societies such as the Alianza Hispano-Americana and La Liga Protectora Latina or in Catholic church organizations such as La Junta. The Alianza's motto was "Protection, Morality and Instruction," and women and children had their own auxiliaries in the organization. Women such as Trinidad Lopez, Dolores Gallardo, and Belen B. Garcia served as officers in La Liga, helping to provide financial support for the unemployed, disabled, and ill. Although they did not run for public office before 1950, they were involved in politics indirectly, supporting organizations such as the Alianza and La Liga as they worked to improve the conditions of Mexican American workers during copper mining strikes.[27]

The first Anglo Arizona women's club, the Monday Club, had been founded in Prescott in 1895. Phoenix followed with a club in 1897, and Tucson in 1898. A state federation, the Arizona Federation of Women's Clubs (AFWC), had been created in 1901, with member clubs in all the major towns of the territory. The AFWC's agenda mimicked that of the national movement: the Douglas club established a public kindergarten, the Yuma club maintained a public reading room, and most clubs contributed to the AFWC's Girl's Scholarship Fund. The AFWC offered women in communities "cut off from many avenues of culture and intellectual enjoyment" an opportunity to socialize and study important issues. By statehood, the federation had a membership of more than 800, with local clubs in ten of the state's fourteen counties.[28]

The Arizona Federation of Women's Clubs was also interested in stimulating voter education and was especially effective at voter registration drives aimed at women. Prize money was awarded to the local club that registered the most women to vote, and as a result, female registration increased from 35 percent of all eligible voters in 1916 to almost 41 percent in 1924 and 43 percent by 1928. The proportion of registered males correspondingly decreased during this period, from 50 percent of all eligible voters in 1924 to 47 percent in 1928. Women's clubs were such powerful instruments for organizing and educating Arizona's female voters that a state federation of the League of Women Voters, the most important organization for educating women voters in the country, was not convened until 1950 because it seemed redundant.[29]

Some former suffrage leaders hoped that the Arizona Federation of Women's Clubs would become a powerful conduit for the voices of women. Frances Munds wanted women to rally to pass laws to improve the morality, education, and public welfare of the new state. In 1913 the organization effectively lobbied the Arizona State Legislature to enact legislation establishing an eight-hour workday for women, creating pensions for mothers, and raising the age of consent. Munds commented, "It does make a difference whether we are disfranchised idiots or not."[30]

Other club women were skeptical about involving their organizations in politics. When women achieved the vote in Arizona in 1912, the Arizona Federation of Women's Clubs was under the leadership of Dr. Agnes McKee Wallace, a Prescott physician. Wallace had testified for suffrage on behalf of professional women and wage earners at the constitutional convention in 1910, but she was adamant that the AFWC stay clear of political issues during her presidency. She agreed with the majority of club women that they should remain above the political fray, avoiding partisanship and the unseemliness associated with campaigns. Frances Munds, on the other hand, wanted the AFWC to take a stand on issues and asked the organization to support Governor Hunt's campaign to abolish capital punishment in Arizona. After deliberating, the AFWC declined to oppose the death penalty because it was a "political question" that should not be allowed on the club program.[31]

The Arizona Federation of Women's Clubs became even more resistant to political action in 1914 under its new president, Margaret Wheeler Ross, wife of the chief justice of the Arizona Supreme Court. In that year, Pauline O'Neill's Phoenix Civic League investigated the local cattle industry, demanding that a new slaughterhouse be built in Phoenix in accordance with state provisions, and asked the legislature to ensure that higher standards for milk inspection be maintained. O'Neill's work angered city fathers, and Ross took their side, admonishing "women to be conservative along the line of legislation they undertake. Because we have the ballot and two members of the legislature [Frances Munds in the senate and Rachel Berry in the house], we should not allow our heads to be turned by making an effort to revolutionize the laws of the state. We are not yet ready for that."[32]

The state federation then passed a resolution stating that individual clubs could not endorse legislation without the approval of the AFWC, a clear slap on the wrists of Munds and O'Neill for lobbying the legislature. A legislative department was established to review all submissions for legislation by individual clubs. Local clubs could still initiate local reform, but they could not appeal directly to the state legislature to back bills without prior approval of the state federation. Only initiatives that were acceptable to the majority of members would be endorsed, and individual clubs that worked at cross-purposes with the state federation could lose their affiliation with the state organization.[33]

By creating these constraints on local clubs, the state federation effectively put a halt to local political initiative. The amount of legislative work done by the Arizona Federation of Women's Clubs dropped precipitously after 1915. The organization's legislative department advanced only three items in 1917: the expansion of the state library system, legislation aimed at curbing immoral behavior, and an endorsement of a minimum wage law for women. But even this limited agenda met with increased criticism from the majority of members, as Grace Forbes Alexander, chairman of the legislative department that initiated these issues, quickly recognized.[34]

Grace Alexander was a pragmatic, intelligent politician who, like Munds and O'Neill, hoped to unite women in the club movement to study and generate legislation that would benefit women and children in the state. As the Arizona Federation of Women's Clubs' legislative chair, Alexander worked to overcome the apathy and outright antagonism of leaders and members from 1915 until 1920. Her credentials were impressive: she had been involved in the suffrage movement and the Woman's Christian Temperance Union and had co-founded the Woman's Republican Club in

Arizona in 1916. An independent streak had appeared in her youth. Grace's mother died shortly after her birth, and when she was sixteen she lost her stepmother and subsequently ran away from home. Eventually she landed a job as a secretary to Mark Hanna at Carnegie Steel. After a short marriage that produced a daughter but ended in divorce, Grace traveled across the country to Phoenix in 1905, where she started her life over working as a clerk in the United States Attorney's office. There she met and married her boss, John Alexander, the former Rough Rider and chairman of the Progressive Party in Arizona, in 1912 and became involved in state politics as a member of the Arizona Federation of Women's Clubs.[35]

Alexander faced vocal opposition from her fellow club women when she tried to address the female vice problem, because they thought the topic was indecent. She countered that "it certainly cannot be unwomanly for us to consider legislation" that would protect girls from prostitution and venereal disease. When the AFWC refused to help, she turned to a club member on the Public Health Committee in the state legislature, Maricopa County representative Pauline O'Neill. Alexander and O'Neill worked to introduce several bills that would help protect young girls. House Bill 62 raised the age of consent for women from fourteen to sixteen and for men to eighteen, and it legitimized children born of parents barred from marriage because of immaturity.[36]

Despite these successes, Grace Alexander was embarrassed and frustrated by the unwillingness of club women to endorse measures in the legislature. In 1919 the AFWC passed a resolution outlawing lobbying by club members and mandated that bills be "allowed to stand or fall on their merits." AFWC president Emma Guild was adamant about not mixing club business with politics, stating, "We should stress the literature and art departments and so-called more womanly activities of the club." Alexander was angered that the majority of members believed it was unfeminine to take part in male politics and wanted to exert only influence "derived from their elevated moral standards, altruism and strict nonpartisanship." Alexander condemned this attitude, arguing that women had the obligation to support laws they felt were beneficial, and she launched a heated debate within the AFWC over lobbying. The attitude of the AFWC was similar to that of other state federations. In California, women's club members believed that partisan politics had corrupted state government, so they distanced themselves from it. According to historian Gayle Gullett, this stance "gained a moral citizenship that placed them far above the power struggles of men" but also kept them from obtaining "an equal distribution of power." Linda Van Ingen concurs that the goal of California club women "was to clean up politics and to raise the political standard, not to join in the fray of dirty politics."[37]

The final indication that the AFWC would not tolerate involvement in politics came in the spring of 1919 when Grace Alexander published the names of state senators who had voted against a law that would have raised the age of consent for women to eighteen and enforced laws against prostitution. Even though the federation of women's clubs had not endorsed the bill, because of its prohibition on political activities, Alexander felt that "as women" the members should look at her list of names to guide their decisions in casting future ballots for the legislature. She was reprimanded by the AFWC president for "dipping into politics." It was clear that the state federation was ignoring her recommendations and that she had become impotent within the organization. In 1920 she left the AFWC and turned her full attention to Republican politics in the state.[38]

The AFWC was successful in registering large numbers of female voters, and it produced effective leaders, many of whom became successful politicians—more than half of all female legislators between 1914 and 1950 were AFWC members. The organization endorsed many important measures enacted by the legislature in the 1910s and 1920s, such as the introduction of state kindergartens, an improved compulsory school law, and the provision of health care for infants. Some individual clubs, especially in Phoenix, influenced local legislation, but after 1915 the AFWC carefully avoided divisive issues at the state level that would have deviated from woman's traditional role, and therefore the organization played a limited role in state politics. Women's leaders such as Munds, O'Neill, and Alexander envisioned the Arizona Federation of Women's Clubs as the logical vehicle for the transformation of public policy, but they were disappointed.

In 1920, C. Louise Boehringer, a Democrat from Yuma, took over Alexander's position as legislative chairman of the AFWC and steered the organization away from controversial issues such as prostitution. She teamed up with Vernettie Ivy, a representative in the legislature from Maricopa County, to sponsor a state child welfare law. The 1917 legislature had passed a new widowed mothers law that created county welfare boards to assess the needs of women with dependent children, but several county superior court judges refused to authorize the boards or release funding. Boehringer and Ivy ushered a law through the 1921 legislature that mandated state money for the boards, and by the end of the year all counties were in compliance. When the county welfare boards were finally up and running, a majority of the women chosen to serve on them were members of the AFWC. Despite her victory, Boehringer was as frustrated as Alexander had been with the recalcitrant leaders of the AFWC and quickly moved to form a new organization, the Arizona Federation of Business and Professional Women's Clubs (BPW).[39]

In many ways the work of BPW women mirrored that of AFWC women, and many women in the state belonged to both organizations. They sometimes shared a common newsletter, *Arizona Woman*, and both groups developed community programs, sponsored voter registration drives, and were generous in donating college scholarship money for girls. The two federations briefly debated the idea of merging but decided to remain separate because of their different views of a woman's role in business and politics. Margaret Wheeler Ross, AFWC president and historian, described her members as well-educated women married to professionals, businessmen, politicians, and ranchers. BPW women defined themselves not in relationship to their husbands but by their own professional accomplishments.[40]

The first meeting of the National Federation of Business and Professional Women was held in St. Louis in July 1919. Lena Madesin Phillips was chosen to lead the new organization to demand equal pay for equal work for women. Members of the fledgling organization complained that men consistently were chosen for promotions over women in companies and women were excluded from male business clubs. Over the years the national organization developed an agenda that supported female jury service and the Equal Rights Amendment and sought to defeat protective legislation it believed impaired a woman's success in the job market. These positions set the BPW apart from most mainstream, moderate women's organizations, whose members believed women were different by virtue of their biology and therefore entitled to special protection under the law. Because women were smaller, weaker, and bore children, moderate women's leaders argued, they required legislation that would exempt them from heavy lifting, long hours, and some of the hazardous work conditions that maimed or killed thousands of laborers each year. This protective legislation gave preferential treatment to women over men, but BPW women understood that ultimately these laws would hurt women in the workplace.[41]

Few women in the 1920s supported the notion that men and women should be treated as equals, and there were thousands of laws on the books that discriminated against women. The Equal Rights Amendment, introduced to Congress by radical feminist Alice Paul in 1923, stated simply, "Men and women shall have equal rights throughout the United States and every place subject to its jurisdiction." Its passage would have eliminated all protective legislation favoring women. Paul reasoned that if a woman was prohibited by law from working more than eight hours a day or lifting an object that weighed more than twenty pounds, and a man was not, he would be hired instead of her. Protective legislation did not help women, in Paul's opinion, but rather hindered them in their quest for equality in society. But most moderate women's organizations, including the League of Women Voters, the General Federation of Women's Clubs, and the Women's Trade Union League (WTUL), opposed the Equal Rights Amendment. In an era with few government controls on employers, they believed it was better to have some protections for women working in factories. On the East Coast, organizations such as the WTUL fought to unionize women, especially garment workers, to protect them from unsafe working conditions. In Arizona, almost no women worked in industrial settings, and most female workers were middle-class businesswomen or educated professionals—who were hindered more than helped by protective legislation—or manual laborers who were domestics or worked in the fields and were rarely covered by labor laws.[42]

After suffrage was won, Alice Paul's National Woman's Party dwindled from 35,000 members in 1920 to a mere 1,000 in 1930 as she single-mindedly pursued the Equal Rights Amendment. The National Federation of Business and Professional Women's Clubs grew rapidly during the same years as it adopted a broader agenda, which included the ERA, but reached out to a larger group of educated working women faced with employment discrimination. The accomplishments of the National Woman's Party and the WTUL, which catered to poor working girls in the urban Northeast, have been well documented by historians, but there are no in-depth studies of the role of the national BPW, even though this organization worked tirelessly to earn equality for women in the workplace and in politics. BPW leaders argued that as long as women were outside of the major male organizations where power resided—political parties, chambers of commerce, and business organizations—they would always face discrimination. Women who were teachers, doctors, attorneys, or in business competed with men daily but were paid less, denied advancement, and sometimes even kept from practicing their professions because of discriminatory attitudes. Their goal was to break down the barriers facing women at work and in politics and create a world in which women were not placed on pedestals but treated as "human beings," equal to men. National BPW president Lena Phillips believed that "wifehood and motherhood are as legitimate a part of the life of any woman as husbandhood and fatherhood are a legitimate part of the life of any man. But they are only a part. . . . The picture I see of future America is woman working side by side with man," a radical departure from woman's traditional role in the 1920s.[43]

Business "girls" clubs, as they were first called, appeared in Arizona towns between 1912 and 1915. C. Louise Boehringer represented Arizona at the first convention of the National Federation of Business and Professional Women's clubs in 1919 in St. Louis, Missouri. She was a teacher in Yuma who became the first woman elected to office in Arizona in 1913. After returning from the BPW meeting in St. Louis she reported that "a group of business and professional women, seeing things that needed doing and un-doing for themselves and other women, caught a vision of what might be accomplished through the mobilization of the millions of women who daily follow trades and professions in every city and hamlet of our land. They saw standards for themselves lifted, barriers broken down, laws changed, opportunities opened, conditions equalized through a mass movement of women." Following the convention, Boehringer returned to Arizona and spent weeks riding on trains to convince the existing businesswomen's clubs in Douglas, Nogales, Prescott, Tucson, Yuma, and Phoenix to affiliate into a state federation in 1921. She was rewarded for her hard work when the Arizona organization selected her as its first state president.[44]

C. Louise Boehringer was the first woman elected to public office in Arizona, served in the state legislature, and organized the Arizona Federation of Business and Professional Women's Clubs.

The Arizona Federation of Business and Professional Women's Clubs attracted members from the state's unusually large number of working women. Arizona's BPW women were lawyers, social workers, journalists, stenographers, doctors, teachers, and businesswomen. Overall, members were more likely to be single than married, and a substantial proportion was widowed or divorced, with the sole responsibility of supporting themselves and their families. They often owned their own homes and businesses, more than half had college educations, and almost 30 percent had postgraduate degrees.[45]

Angela Hutchinson Hammer is an excellent example of the type of woman the Arizona Federation of Business and Professional Women's Clubs attracted. Hammer, a divorced mother of three boys, supported her family as a newspaperwoman in early Arizona, running papers in Wickenburg, Casa Grande, and Phoenix from 1905 until the late 1930s, often competing with men who tried to drive her out of business. Over the years she used the editorial columns of her newspapers to champion the suffrage movement, to challenge graft and corruption in government, and to boost the local economy. Although she lost a close race for Pinal

County representative in 1918, Hammer was chosen as the county delegate to the 1922 Democratic convention in Tucson, receiving support for both efforts from her local BPW club. The BPW gave working women like Hammer, who were isolated in the male-dominated business world, a sense of solidarity with other women facing similar hardships.[46]

Working women have an obvious vested interest in the laws passed by government, so it is not surprising that more than 85 percent of Arizona's BPW members stated they voted, without fail, in every election. In contrast, only 50 percent of the general population was even registered to vote in the 1920s. Alice Birdsall, one of the first female attorneys in Phoenix and a delegate to the 1920 Democratic convention, advised her fellow BPW members to continue their involvement "by active means, not passive ones." She urged women not to shrink "from the word 'political' as tho' it were poison." In a clear jab at the Arizona Federation of Women's Clubs, Birdsall complimented the BPW's legislative chairman, Harriet Jean Oliver, for printing the names of public officials and legislators who did not support BPW-endorsed issues. "My theory is that these actions and records should be carefully watched and the facts all collated long before a political campaign begins — not only by this but by other women's organizations." Where Grace Alexander was condemned for her attempt to inform the AFWC membership about where public officials stood on issues of interest to club women, her counterpart in the BPW, Harriet Oliver, received only praise. As Louise Boehringer later commented, women were learning that the "hand that writes the ballot rules the world."[47]

The state BPW grew quickly in the 1920s. Six clubs formed the initial state federation, but by 1924 three more, Globe, Jerome, and Miami, had been added, and total membership topped 400. In 1926 the club had grown to 500, and in 1928 membership increased 65 percent over the previous year. The list of well-known Arizona female politicians who led the BPW from the 1920s through the 1940s is long and impressive. Louise Boehringer represented Yuma County in the state legislature while serving as the state's first BPW president. She also served on the Democratic State Central Committee, along with her successor as BPW president, May Belle Craig. Craig began her political career as a secretary for both houses of the state legislature and went on to become the head of various state agencies from the 1920s to the 1940s. Wilma Hoyal, BPW president in the late 1920s, rose through the ranks of the Republican party from president of the Douglas Woman's Republican Club to Arizona national committeewoman, and she played important roles in the national party in the 1940s. Annie Campbell Jones presided over the state BPW in 1938, just after completing four consecutive terms in the Arizona legislature representing Yavapai County. Harriet Jean Oliver, president from 1933 to 1934, began her career in the secretary of state's office, where on several occasions she became acting secretary of state and even, by some accounts, acting governor when all the top-ranking government officials were out of the state. Beyond this list of women were many other BPW officers who served in pivotal local and state positions.[48]

In 1937 Earlene White, president of the National Federation of Business and Professional Women, conducted a survey of women in public office, the results of which were discussed by White and first lady Eleanor Roosevelt during a radio broadcast by the National Broadcasting Corporation. Roosevelt told the audience that "there is a great need to increase the number of women in public office. . . . Just as in the home and in business, the work of men and women supplement each other, so in government, each one supplements the other." White hoped that the survey results would "be a reminder to those in charge of the great political parties of the country that women are available and equipped to hold public office." Arizona BPW newsletters from 1921 to 1950 also urged women to seek office and asked members to support female candidates with donations and their votes. State officers toured the state and encouraged local clubs "to sponsor some qualified woman for an office, either state, county or city," to combat the discriminatory laws that women faced.[49]

The importance of the partnership between Arizona's female candidates and the Business and Professional Women's Clubs is especially apparent when comparisons are made with California. Following a narrow suffrage victory in 1911, California women ran for the state assembly with some success, but by 1926 they had experienced severe setbacks, and very few were elected even though they were well qualified and well funded. From 1912 to 1970, 300 California women ran for state or national office, but only 17 won. During the same period, 61 women served in Arizona's legislature. An important difference between California and Arizona seems to be that the California BPW did not endorse female candidates until 1951. Before then women won election to only 1 to 2 percent of California State Assembly seats. After the BPW involved itself in campaigns, women experienced substantial increases in their success rate, doubling their numbers of candidates and victories. Clearly, women needed organized support to win elections, and in early Arizona that support came most often from the Business and Professional Women's Clubs, not from Democrats or Republicans.[50]

Arizona BPW members agreed with early suffragists that men could not adequately represent their interests and actively campaigned for women to run for office. They were not middle-class housewives but working women who paid taxes and had a large stake in the economy. Too many laws were on the books that discriminated against them, and the only way to fix the problem was to make sure women themselves rewrote the laws. As Frances Munds said, she wanted "the women to realize that they will have to make a concerted demand for the things they want, and not merely present a bill and ask someone to put it through for them. I want them to get into the battle themselves."[51]

CHAPTER 4

"A Woman for a Woman's Job"
Female Candidates, 1914 to 1927

On January 19, 1915, the junior senator from Yavapai County, Frances Willard Munds, banged her gavel on the podium, called the Arizona State Senate into session, and announced, "We are here for business." The press had eagerly anticipated this moment and wondered how Munds, reportedly the first woman in the world to preside over an elected body, would act. Most observers assumed she would make a lofty speech to commemorate the occasion, but instead, "she simply informed the senate that she did not propose to waste any time in preliminaries 'or that sort of thing'" and attended to the business at hand. After interviewing her, a reporter revealed that "her highest purpose in seeking the office she now fills so capably, was to make it easier for talented members of her sex who may come after, to live up to their possibilities for good."[1]

Most early female office seekers in the United States were former suffragists like Munds who had picked up political skills during the campaigns for "votes for women." When they ran for office they promised to purify politics, and they viewed candidacy as a way to enact laws assisting women and children. They agitated for improved education, social welfare legislation, and labor laws. Suffragist candidates tended to be idealistic volunteers, uninterested in recognition. Yet candidacy, as political scientists define it, is "an inherently egotistical act." They categorize office seekers who are unwilling to compromise as altruistic and "amateurs," whereas "professional" politicians as those who are intent upon winning. It is difficult to win an election if a candidate does not enjoy campaigning or the attention that comes with office holding. Women who ran solely for idealistic reasons appealed only to a narrow portion of the electorate and angered political party leaders, who wanted to win elections above all else. Men were considered more outgoing and ambitious, more partisan, and more knowledgeable about business and legal affairs, making them better candidates in the minds of career politicians. If women did not emulate their male competitors, they would struggle to win elections.[2]

Initially, the national political parties supported the candidacies of suffrage leaders, hoping to attract the new female voters. Progress stalled in the mid-1920s, however, when male politicians discovered that women's interest in politics had peaked and diminished and they were no longer a unified force. The national suffrage movement had held together a diverse group of women—moderates and radicals, Democrats and Republicans, working class and middle class—all striving for a common goal. After the Nineteenth Amendment passed, women dispersed, pursuing a variety of interests. Many turned their attention to the growing international peace movement, a few joined Alice Paul's fight for the Equal Rights Amendment, and a handful became political party activists or ran for office. Political parties lost interest in running female candidates when they felt those candidates could not help the ticket, and women won election to only about 2 percent of all state legislative seats in the United States from 1920 to 1928.[3]

Mary Rothschild and Pamela Hronek pointed out in 1992 that "women have been accepted more readily as politicians in the West than in any other region, continuing the momentum they had gained in early suffrage campaigns." Contemporary political observers also noted that western women enjoyed greater respect than eastern women. A New Yorker told Arizona politician Isabella Greenway in 1928, "The political power of the right kind of woman in your part of the country is enormous. Here it amounts to very little." Colorado, Washington, Oregon, and Arizona consistently sent more women to their state legislatures than other states. In Utah and New Mexico, too, above-average numbers of women initially won election.[4]

In Colorado, after women won the vote in 1893, Republicans, Democrats, and Populists all competed for the support of newly enfranchised females, allowing women the opportunity to participate in state party committees and as candidates. Three women, all Republicans, were the first ever elected to a state legislature: Carrie Clyde Holly, Frances Klock, and Clara Cressingham. They proved themselves capable legislators, unintimidated by men, and quickly introduced bills concerned with public morality, prohibition, and capital punishment, and even an early equal rights amendment. But public office holding was not a goal of the suffrage movement, and Colorado women's leaders told voters that women wanted the vote only to "raise the education of the electorate, clean up polling places, improve candidates, and insure that politicians paid more attention to the public welfare." Voters believed that only some seats in the legislature should be reserved for women, leaving the majority under continued male control. Often women ran against women for these select seats, granting them "the status of genuine political actors but perpetuat[ing] the sense they were nevertheless different sorts of political actors from men." Despite their difference, Colorado voters continued to send women to the legislature in greater-than-average numbers over the decades to follow.[5]

New Mexico is another state in which surprising numbers of women were elected to the legislature, especially considering that the state suffrage movement was unsuccessful and women did not gain the vote there until the Nineteenth Amendment was ratified in 1920. Unlike in Arizona, where Mexican Americans were a minority population and faced a literacy test for voting, in New Mexico Hispanos outnumbered Anglos and were guaranteed the right to vote by the state constitution, even if they spoke only Spanish. The Republican party struggled to maintain its control of state politics against an insurgent Democratic party just as women were entering the electorate. To attract female voters, both parties invited Anglo and Hispanic women with strong ties to politically powerful men to run for office. After gaining the right to vote, women ran for school superintendent in twenty-one of the twenty-nine counties, winning in nineteen. Hispanic women were sometimes hampered by proscribed behavioral limits. Soledad Chávez Chacón, for example, ran for secretary of state in 1922 only after asking permission of her husband and father. Elizabeth Salas comments that Hispanic women "were subject to the will of their fathers before marriage and [were supposed to] seek their husband's consent in making decisions after marriage." But even with these constraints, women such as Adelina Otero-Warren, who ran an unsuccessful primary contest for the Democratic nomination for Congress in 1922, received strong support in heavily Hispanic precincts. Women continued to find electoral success until the party balance shifted in the 1950s and competition for their votes tapered off, and then they lagged behind other states in representation.[6]

The Mormon population of Utah is also considered culturally conservative, but female politicians there experienced early success. Although the Utah territorial legislature granted women the vote in 1870, women were not allowed to run for office until statehood was achieved in 1896. Utah elected the first female state senator in the United States that year, Dr. Martha Hughes Cannon, and two other women were elected to the house. Female office holding in the legislature was meager before 1912 but increased and averaged between 5 and 6 percent before dropping off in the 1950s. Most of Utah's early female legislators were well-educated professionals, Mormons, club women, and Republicans. In Arizona, female candidates also tended to be well-educated professionals and club women. Some were Mormons but almost all were Democrats. In Colorado and New Mexico, the major parties ran female candidates to attract women voters, but in Arizona the major political parties were uninterested in women. Instead, women pursued public office on their own name recognition as suffragists or as members of prominent pioneer families.[7]

Almost half of all women in Arizona running for county office and the state legislature before 1928 had been born or raised in a western state or territory. By comparison, only about a quarter of Arizona's male legislators were western born, whereas 43 percent came from the Midwest and 29 percent from the South, statistics that mirrored the origins of the state's overall population. Women who held elected office often noted that their experiences growing up in frontier conditions had prepared them for public service. As a young teacher, Frances Munds had lived in rural communities and taught in mining towns. State representative Nellie Bush shelled almonds to pay for her clothes as a child in grammar school and milked cows and plowed fields to earn enough money to attend Tempe Normal School. Many worked with their fathers, brothers, or husbands on farms or ranches, in mining, or in other businesses. They understood the problems facing their young state and were willing to roll up their sleeves and join the men in finding solutions. In campaign advertisements they were quick to include their pioneer status among their qualifications for office, assuring voters that they were from well-established Anglo families that had a stake in Arizona's growth.[8]

The early stories of Arizona are filled with the exploits of famous male sheriffs such as Wyatt Earp and Harry Wheeler in Cochise County and George Ruffner of Yavapai County, but occasionally women also became law enforcement officials. Ora Matthews, a policewoman, was appointed deputy sheriff by the Maricopa County board of supervisors in 1915, and in 1914 Lucretia Roberts, an attractive young widow, was elected constable in the small town of Canille in Santa Cruz County. Roberts visited New York City in 1915 to raise money for an Arizona sanitarium and caused quite a stir when she showed up at a downtown hotel dressed in cowboy boots and a tan riding suit, carrying a .45 Colt revolver and a lariat. She thrilled the New York press with stories of her work chasing horse thieves through the desert for days and shooting a pack of wolves that had attacked a neighbor's cattle. Back home, the local Santa Cruz County newspaper, *The Oasis*, was unhappy with the publicity Roberts generated, because it gave easterners the impression that Arizona remained an uncivilized place where women had to carry guns to protect themselves.[9]

The majority of women in Arizona held less exciting positions in government. They served on administrative boards for education and child welfare, or they ran for county offices that were considered appropriate for women, such as school superintendent and county clerk, where their teaching or clerical skills were used. More ambitious female politicians ran for the state legislature. All these races were inexpensive to conduct, rarely costing more than $50, and candidates were chosen in primaries in which the political parties were forced to remain neutral. It was more difficult to compete with male political veterans for seats in the state senate, for statewide office, or for federal office before 1928. Women were still untested candidates, statewide campaigns were much more costly, and candidates for state and federal offices were chosen not in primaries but rather by male-dominated political party committees, which gave women a distinct disadvantage. In the years following suffrage, women quickly sorted out which political roles they would be welcome in and which would remain male strongholds of power.[10]

Few women in the United States ran for city councils prior to the 1970s. Merchants and large property holders who had local influence and knowledge of economic development usually ran for these positions, and the candidates with those qualifications were overwhelmingly male. In Arizona, mayors and city councilmen tended to be well-known businessmen with knowledge of construction and machinery. They approved bids for sewers, lighting, and new buildings and ordered vehicles and equipment used by the towns. Merchants understood what improvements were necessary to promote growth, and men who owned construction businesses understood the costs and work required for new projects. When W. N. Lester ran for town council in Nogales, his campaign advertisement told voters he was "a builder in concrete and if elected will be in demand on the committees that will have construction work to consider. His technical knowledge of how concrete should be handled will probably save the town a good many dollars in building work." Although many women worked in business, they often toiled at clerical or accounting work, rarely were well versed in engineering or construction, and with the exception of a few wealthy widows and heiresses, were not influential property owners. Nor did women exhibit much interest in running for city council positions. A survey of elections for municipal office for Graham, Yavapai, Cochise, Santa Cruz, and Maricopa counties from 1914 to 1950 uncovered only a handful of female candidates for town council. The only time women became involved in municipal politics was when charges of corruption or rampant vice erupted in towns and women were called in to help remedy the situation.[11]

Hattie L. Mosher, a prominent Phoenix resident, was the first woman to run for the Phoenix city commission in 1923, and her campaign illustrates the obstacles women faced at the municipal level. Mosher urged voters to "have four men and one woman in the City Commission of Phoenix. Wake the old town up!" The *Arizona Labor Journal* endorsed Mosher's candidacy even while noting that "in some quarters there is a prejudice against placing a woman on a body like a city commission." The newspaper argued that Mosher was well qualified for the job because she was a large property owner, which gave her the "same interests which every other taxpayer has. She long has taken a direct and active interest in the government of the city, attending commission meetings and studying the work and the reports of the various departments." Mosher was the daughter of Phoenix businessman Samuel Lount, who had made a fortune with the first ice production plant in the city, and she inherited from him significant property along Phoenix's main thoroughfare, Central Avenue. Despite her qualifications as a leading citizen and property owner, Mosher lost the election. The first woman to obtain a town council seat in Arizona was Marion Blakely, elected in the town of Gilbert in Maricopa County in 1926. Fannie B. Gaar of Casa Grande became Arizona's first female mayor in 1928.[12]

Although few women were elected to municipal positions, that did not mean they were uninvolved in local affairs. For example, Grace Sparkes, who served as secretary of the Yavapai County Chamber of Commerce from 1913 to 1945, was the region's biggest booster. She promoted funding for good roads, a first-class hotel for Prescott, and the veteran's hospital at Fort Whipple. She was also instrumental in creating the Arizona Pioneers' Home and the Sharlot Hall Museum, ran Prescott's Frontier Days Association for thirty years, and was an advocate for self-determination by the Yavapai nation. Many more women like Sparkes quietly promoted the welfare and economy of local communities, but few received much attention for their accomplishments.[13]

The most important contribution women made to local politics was as members of various county boards. The 1883 territorial legislature granted taxpaying women the right to vote in school board elections and the right to serve on those boards. Women's clubs lobbied for the creation of county child welfare boards in 1917 and made sure they were well staffed with knowledgeable women to oversee the distribution of funds to poor women and children. By 1929, forty-five of the fifty child welfare board members were female. Women also dominated state nursing and cosmetology boards, professions that primarily employed women. Some women even served in nontraditional areas: Antoinette Barrett was appointed assistant state attorney general in 1921, and Jane Rider became director of the state board of health laboratory at the University of Arizona in 1923. The first woman to earn an engineering degree at the University of Arizona, Rider was one of only two women in the country to run a state laboratory. Her work led to her appointment as chairman of the state board of health in 1947.[14]

Women quickly won numerous elections for county office after suffrage was granted in 1912. An editorial in the *Arizona Republican* in 1914 supported the election of Sara Whitfield, Progressive candidate for county school superintendent, because "it would show that the citizens not only acknowledge a woman's right to vote but to hold office and consequently advance woman's position. Miss Whitfield realizes that defeat will retard the feminist movement and for that reason has sought the support of women especially." Many women viewed candidacy as a way to achieve equality, but it was also a way to provide a steady income either to support themselves or to contribute to their family's income. More than three-quarters of county candidates were single, widowed, or married with children, living in small towns where the economy was dominated by mining or agriculture and where few jobs were available to educated women. In the five counties surveyed for this study, all female county candidates were Anglos before the 1950s.[15]

Women served as assistants and deputies in the offices of the county recorder, court, treasurer, and superintendent of schools in large numbers before 1912, but with the passage of suffrage they began to run for their bosses' jobs. Five women were elected county officers in 1914, and by 1918 women held nineteen county positions in the state: eight county school superintendents, five recorders, four court clerks, one treasurer, and one assessor. Additionally, three women were selected as justices of the peace in Yuma County in 1918, and many other women served in that capacity over the years. Results were similar in other western states, such as Colorado, Utah, and New Mexico, where women quickly dominated the county school superintendent, county recorder, and court clerk positions, but in the East women won only a small percentage of these jobs. Women rarely challenged men for positions as county sheriff or county attorney or for seats on boards of supervisors until after the 1960s in any part of the United States, including Arizona. In this way, county seats were fairly equitably distributed between men and women along gender lines, with women dominating the educational and clerical fields and men dominating the law enforcement, legal, and policy-making jobs. At the county level, women generally remained in their prescribed sphere of influence between 1914 and 1950, administering schools and safeguarding the honesty of local government, often employing the campaign slogan, "A Woman for a Woman's Job."[16]

Women often downplayed partisanship and emphasized their independence in politics, which made them good choices for voters seeking unbiased county officials. As county treasurers, women tracked property taxes and dispersed all county funds. As county recorders they registered voters, oversaw local elections, and recorded all public and private property transactions, liens, and mining claims. As county clerks they recorded all court cases, issued licenses, safeguarded legal papers, and collected legal fees. And as school superintendents they were responsible for the development of the public education system. These positions required candidates to be efficient, nonpartisan, and honest, because voting irregularities plagued early Arizona politics. The *Nogales Daily Herald* claimed that Republicans were underrepresented in the county because "practically all of the county recorders in the state are Democrats. That they and their Deputies have been urging Republicans to vote as Democrats is well known." When Alice Birdsall tried to vote in a Phoenix municipal election in the 1930s, someone else had already voted in her name. To combat voter fraud and safeguard legal transactions, voters increasingly looked to female county officers. Before 1928 women usually ran against men for these county seats, but gradually voters came to prefer female over male candidates because they were viewed as more trustworthy and less partisan. By the 1930s women were running against women for the majority of these posts—few men dared to challenge them—and had established themselves as capable public servants in their local communities.[17]

Most women who ran for court clerk, recorder, or treasurer had some education or training in accounting or legal work, and most were married or widowed. Just over 20 percent of women in these three positions were widows, and of those widows, more than a quarter had children under the age of eighteen. In 1916 Eli Perkins, a Republican candidate for Yavapai County recorder, unexpectedly dropped out of the primary race. According to the local newspaper, Perkins decided not to run because "he could not conscientiously make a fight for the office, in the event that Mrs. Edith Ruffner, a widow with several children, should be his Democratic opponent." Perkins conceded the race to Ruffner because he felt there were "plenty of opportunities for me, as a man, to make a living, which do not readily offer themselves to a woman."[18]

County office gave widows an opportunity to support their families with a respectable job. Olive Failor ran for Pima County superior court clerk in 1918 after her husband died and she was left to raise their three young children alone. Although Failor was an attorney, the only work she could find in Tucson at the time was in the county courthouse. After serving four consecutive terms she was able to build a private law practice based on her reputation as county clerk. Mrs. C. E. Gentry ran for Yavapai County recorder in 1930 and 1932, asking voters to support her candidacy and noting that she was "doing what she [could] with her limited means to put her four daughters through school." Grace Genug Chapman had "the traditional incentive of a really successful business woman, she was left with two small children to support, and faced the world because she had to," according to a campaign profile. Chapman started out as many women had, serving as a deputy in the superior court clerk's office and then as deputy in the recorder's office in Yavapai County, before winning election as county recorder with the support of the local Business and Professional Women's Club.[19]

The office of county school superintendent was the most popular choice for female candidates because so many women were certified teachers, a requirement for the job. According to historian Elinor Kyte, "the general feeling was that a woman should fill the position, because it deals largely with young women, many of whom are far away from home, and because this was the first opportunity to recognize woman in an elective position since Arizona granted suffrage to its women." The office primarily attracted married women, who were barred by custom, though not by law, from working as schoolteachers in Arizona. Counties often discriminated against married women, offering them positions only in remote schools at low pay, forcing them to live away from their families for long periods of time. Approximately two-thirds of the county school superintendents were married, just over a quarter were single, and 14 percent were widows. For many married teachers, the superintendent's position was a way to prolong their professional careers and help support their families.[20]

Newspaper editors often endorsed women for school superintendent, criticizing male candidates as unqualified or as politicians who ran to collect a paycheck rather than as professionals willing to fulfill the obligations of the office. C. Louise Boehringer became Arizona's first female school superintendent in 1913 when the Yuma County incumbent, John Hess, was recalled in an election orchestrated by the Yuma women's clubs. Hess, a husband and father, was accused in the recall petition "of undue familiarity with one of the female teachers . . . visiting her at her apartments, and carrying on an improper correspondence." Boehringer beat Hess and three other candidates to become the state's first female elected official. By 1924 women held eleven of the fourteen county school superintendent positions.[21]

Women who undertook the demanding job of school superintendent often received bipartisan support from voters. About half of all female candidates for school superintendent were Democrats, and the other half were Republicans or third party candidates, despite the fact that Democrats outnumbered Republicans two to one in the state. Women such as Bessie Kidd Best and Elsie Toles were Republicans who served multiple terms in Democratic counties. Best noted that "she received bipartisan support over the years because people had confidence in her and she never violated that trust." An editorial endorsing Toles's reelection in Cochise County noted that voters should not mix politics with the handling of the school systems and encouraged them to cross party lines. Toles was an exceedingly popular public official who was able to use her experience as county school superintendent to run successfully as the first female state superintendent of public instruction in Arizona in 1920.[22]

County school superintendents logged long hours on Arizona roads to inspect schools, fill vacancies on school boards, and conduct exams for teaching certificates. Elsie Toles discovered she spent most of her time visiting rural schools. Because there were so few cars on the roads in those days and even fewer female drivers, when Toles's "little model T went buzzing along a country road, everyone knew that the Superintendent was on her rounds." Bessie Kidd Best started her forty-five-year career as Coconino County school superintendent in 1928, traveling in a "Chevrolet over roads that were often no more than rutted, boulder strewn trails through rugged mountains and high desert country." It took a dedicated and adventurous woman with the ability to fix a flat tire or an overheated engine to survive as school superintendent in rural Arizona.[23]

School superintendents played important roles in the development of local education systems. They hired teachers in the rural districts, were responsible for the condition of school buildings, issued warrants to pay expenses, and served as liaisons between school districts and the State Department of Public Instruction. The county superintendents oversaw budgets and therefore were required to appear before the county board of supervisors to explain their expenditures and to request funding for new schools and supplies. They also traveled extensively to supervise rural schools, which were often one-room log buildings heated by pot-bellied stoves, sparely furnished, and lacking supplies. School superintendents not only fought for capital improvements but also tried to enrich the lives of children living in remote areas, sending them on field trips into the larger cities, where they could view a movie, use a telephone, or eat in a restaurant for the first time. Superintendents such as Elsie Toles argued for higher pay and better conditions for their female teachers,

Elsie Toles of Cochise County was the first female state superintendent of public instruction in Arizona.

who were often relegated to the lowest-paying jobs in rural schools while men reaped significantly higher pay in plum urban settings. Successful superintendents were rewarded with reelection. Of those women elected as school superintendents, 78 percent were reelected to two or more terms. Many, such as Bessie Kidd Best and Gwyneth Ham, served for decades, becoming well-respected, integral figures in their communities and supervising the growth of the state's schools as they transitioned from one-room cabins to large, modern school districts.[24]

While county offices offered women respectable jobs, women interested in public policy ran for the state legislature. From 1914 to 1950, thirty-five women were elected or appointed to the house of representatives or senate from ten of the fourteen counties in Arizona (tables 4.1, 4.2). Some counties simply were unreceptive to female candidates. A Greenlee County Democratic chairman told national committeewoman Isabella Greenway in 1930, "We are somewhat old-fashioned here and the women do not take an active part in politics." Travel conditions also made it difficult for women in distant places to reach the state capitol. For example, when Rachel Berry was elected to the state legislature in 1914 from Apache

TABLE 4.1   Number of Women Elected and Appointed to the
Arizona Legislature, by County, 1914–1950

County	Number	County	Number
Apache	1	Navajo	1
Cochise[a]	3	Pima	1
Coconino	0	Pinal	0
Gila[a]	3	Santa Cruz	2
Graham	0		
Greenlee	0	Yavapai	2
Maricopa	18	Yuma	5
Mohave	0	Total	35

Source: Legislative files, ASLAPR.
[a]Rosa McKay was elected from both Cochise and Gila counties.

County, she had a full day's journey on a buckboard just to reach the nearest train station for travel to Phoenix. No other woman from Apache County was elected during this period. Although Arizona remained a rural state before 1950, 78 percent of all female candidates to the legislature came from urban areas with populations greater than 2,500. It was simply easier for women in the larger towns with railroad lines and major roads to get to the legislature.[25]

Women's clubs were established in all the major cities, providing another catalyst for female candidates from urban areas. The two counties that consistently produced the most female legislative candidates were Yuma and Maricopa, where women's clubs were especially active. The Arizona Federation of Women's Clubs led registration drives in the major towns, encouraging women to vote, and the Arizona Federation of Business and Professional Women's Clubs sponsored female candidates. A BPW woman represented Yuma County in every legislative session from 1918 until 1950, except in 1924, when no woman served in the legislature. Maricopa County, where the state capitol was located, attracted the most female candidates for the legislature. Between 1914 and 1950, 90 women ran and 18 women were elected or appointed from Maricopa County. Starting in 1927, a woman from that county sat in every legislative session.[26]

TABLE 4.2 Number and Percentage of Women in the Arizona State Legislature, Elected and Appointed, 1914–1950

Year	House — No.	House — Percent	Total members of House	Senate[a] — No.	Senate[a] — Percent	Total members of legislature	Overall percentage of women
1914	1	2.8	35	1	5.3	54	3.7
1916	3	8.6	35	0	0.0	54	5.6
1918	4	11.4	35	0	0.0	54	7.4
1920	2	5.1	39	0	0.0	58	3.4
1922	4	8.5	47	0	0.0	66	6.1
1924	0	0.0	47	0	0.0	66	0.0
1926	3	5.8	52	0	0.0	71	4.2
1928	6	11.1	54	0	0.0	73	8.2
1930[b]	9	12.7	63	0	0.0	82	9.8
1932	6	9.4	64	0	0.0	83	7.2
1934	1	2.0	51	1	5.3	70	2.9
1936	2	3.9	51	0	0.0	70	2.9
1938	2	3.8	52	0	0.0	71	8.5
1940	6	11.5	52	0	0.0	71	8.5
1942	4	6.9	58	0	0.0	77	5.2
1944	3	5.2	58	0	0.0	77	3.9
1946	4	6.9	58	0	0.0	77	5.2
1948	3	5.2	58	0	0.0	77	3.9
1950	4	5.6	72	0	0.0	91	4.4

Source: Arizona Capitol Times, 15 November 1996; legislative files, ASLAPR.
[a]There were 19 members of the Arizona State Senate in each year.
[b]Although nine women served in 1930, six were elected, two were appointed to replace men, and one woman was appointed to replace an elected woman, so no more than eight women, or 12.7 percent of the House, served at any given time that year.

Almost two-thirds of the thirty-five women elected to the state legislature between 1914 and 1950 had some level of college education, and just under a quarter had some form of postgraduate education. Thirteen taught school prior to their election, three had legal training, seventeen worked in business—as clerical workers, journalists, or business owners—and only 23 percent identified themselves solely as housewives. From 1914 to 1927, most female legislators were former teachers, such as Frances Munds and Nellie Bush, but these women also worked in other capacities. In a campaign advertisement for the state senate, Munds pointed to her experience helping with her husband's cattle business: "My training has been largely in the business world, and I am proud of being able to call myself a business woman." Nellie Trent Bush operated a ferry service, a hotel, and numerous other enterprises with her husband in Parker.[27]

Possibly because so many women were experienced in business and the public was so supportive of suffrage, early female candidates stated that they detected little resistance from male voters. Gertrude Bryan Leeper recounted the words of an elderly male voter in her district in Maricopa County in 1930 who told her, "Danged if I'd ever thought fifty years ago I'd be fixin' to vote a woman into office, but I'm mighty glad I lived to see the day of flyin' machines and radios and a lady in the legislature." Vernettie Ivy, who served three sessions in the legislature in the 1920s, was described in the *Arizona Labor Journal* as "one of the women in the legislature who have justified ladies in politics. The Lord knoweth they could only help, there was no chance to make it worse." When Nellie Bush first campaigned for her seat from Yuma County in 1920, she was surprised that men were so supportive. "I met almost no prejudice against a woman being in government. I remember one man who put it more clearly than most, saying, 'It'd be a good thing for the country. The way I figure it, a woman generally cares more about what's right than a man generally does. It wouldn't be a bad thing to have someone down there who cared about what was right.'"[28]

Nellie Bush might have found "little prejudice from male voters," but that was undoubtedly because she was an Anglo woman. No Mexican American, no Native American, and only one African American woman ran for the Arizona legislature before 1950. However, women candidates represented diverse religious backgrounds. The U.S. Census of 1906 revealed that two-thirds of the Arizona population was Roman Catholic, a reflection of the large numbers of Indians evangelized by Spanish missionaries and of Mexican and Irish immigrants living in the territory. Approximately 15 percent of the population was Mormon, and less than 20 percent was Protestant. These proportions remained fairly stable until the population explosion that accompanied World War II. Among women in the legislature from 1914 to 1950, 14 percent were Mormon, an accurate representation of the LDS population in the state, but 57 percent were Protestant and only 17 percent Catholic. Six women declined to specify a religious preference in their legislative files, and one, Freeda Marks, was Jewish.[29]

Until 1950, the Arizona State Legislature met only during odd-numbered years for a maximum of sixty days between early January and early March, with special sessions following as needed. Members received meager paychecks, and few viewed the legislature as a career. Legislators rarely ran more than once or twice, so there were few incumbents to dislodge, and they only occasionally used the legislature as a springboard to higher office before 1950. Perhaps because the legislature in Arizona was not a prestigious political prize, women felt less resistance to their campaigns than women in states with more powerful legislatures.[30]

Campaigning for the legislature was conducted door-to-door, and the experience was intimidating for some women. Democrat Gertrude Bryan Leeper wrote about her experiences in the Phoenix summer heat in 1930. "July dragged its weary way through the calendar, bringing hot nights and hotter days in its wake. And I dragged my weary way through July, my tired feet lifting me to door steps and my tired hands leaning heavily on door bells which cut the hot silence of midday with shrill, insistent calls. I never knew what adventure lay behind those doors." Sometimes she was met with a friendly face and a cold glass of lemonade; other times she found mothers trying to placate sickly children. She helped to calm crying babies and soothe elderly shut-ins, and she faced hostile Republicans who threw out her precious campaign cards. "I hated it with a growing hatred. I hated asking people to vote for me. I felt that I was infringing on their independence of judgment. But I had to play the game according to the rules; so I rang bells, wilted visibly in the heat—and walked."[31]

Another obstacle to office holding for women was family obligations. It was difficult for mothers with young children to spend the summer and fall months campaigning, and this kept many from seeking office until their families were grown. Ninety percent of all female legislative candidates were married, and three-quarters had children, but only 12 percent had children under the age of sixteen at the time of their candidacy. Frances Munds's youngest daughter, Mary Fran, was in grade school when her mother was in the state senate, and she often completed homework on a stool by her mother's desk in the capitol while waiting for her mother to finish her work. Nellie Bush's son, Wesley, was only five when she first ran for her seat from Yuma County, and she was questioned in an interview about her ability to be successful as both a politician and a mother. The reporter summarized Bush's views: "She says it's all foolishness, this idea that a woman can't hold two positions and do justice to them. The man is the head of the family, and of his business, yet no one accuses him of neglecting the one for the other. Then why put women in the feebleminded class?"[32]

Writing in the 1960s, political observer Irene Diamond contended that women "need strong political cues within the family to drown out or at least modify the cues they receive from the wider environment. . . . A woman is unlikely to become active in politics if exposure to political matters occurs only later in life." Her research revealed that 50 percent of female politicians listed their natal family as critical to their involvement in politics. Only a handful of Arizona's female legislators, however, had fathers or brothers in politics. A much more striking link can be found among spouses: almost two-thirds were married to men with political careers. Female role models were also abundant and undoubtedly played a crucial role in convincing women to run. Lorna Lockwood, who served in the legislature in the 1940s and was a pioneer female justice, cited Sarah Herring Sorin, her father's law partner and Arizona's first female attorney, as her inspiration for running for office. Two of Rachel Berry's daughters, Mary Alice Patterson and Jennie Palmer, followed their mother's example and ran for the legislature. Gladys Walker, a representative from Santa Cruz County, was the daughter of Lucille Walker and sister-in-law of Inez Walker, both county politicians, and Inez Walker's daughter, Fritzi Struckmeyer, represented Phoenix in the legislature in 1936. Elizabeth Rockwell represented Maricopa County from 1965 to 1988 and was the daughter of Republican party leader Margaret Adams Rockwell, a congressional candidate in 1944. Obviously it was much easier for women to enter public office once other women, especially family members or colleagues, had established the precedent.[33]

Although most early female legislative candidates in Arizona were reluctant to tie themselves closely to a political party, party affiliation was important for the success of female candidates. The lack of true party competition in the state between 1914 and 1950 gave all Democratic legislative candidates a distinct advantage. Any candidate who won the Democratic primary nomination for the state legislature was almost guaranteed the party's endorsement and a victory in the general election. The most important qualification for winning was membership in the Democratic party, and the most critical part of the campaign for Democratic women was the primary. Democratic female candidates won just over 50 percent of the primary races they entered but 95 percent of the general elections. In contrast, only four Republican women were elected to the legislature between 1914 and 1950.[34]

In 1922 Freeda Marks became the first Republican woman elected to the state legislature, joining five male Republicans serving in the house that year. As a member of the minority party, Marks was careful to "declare that she did not aspire to the legislature as a partisan" but rather was open to legislation that deserved passage, whether proposed by Democrats or Republicans. Perhaps because of her work organizing women in the party, or perhaps because she was willing to work with Democrats, her colleagues nominated her for speaker of the house. Naturally, as a member of the minority party, she had no chance of winning, but she was selected by fellow Republicans to serve as house minority leader in 1923.[35]

Early female candidates, regardless of party, ran for the legislature as social reformers. During her run for state senate in 1914, Frances Munds told voters that the "laws governing women and children in Arizona are not vicious in any way, but they are by no means ideal. It is my ambition to help make them so." Approximately two-thirds of women's campaign literature printed from 1914 to 1928 addressed what can be called a woman's agenda: education, public health and welfare, children, morality, and working conditions for women. The other third reflected issues generally connected to men, including taxation, finance, and business. Nellie Bush, Yuma County representative in the 1920s and 1930s, believed that "women must live and raise families under the laws of the state, therefore they must protect that sphere in which they move. That is woman's reason for being in politics." When Hattie Mosher ran unsuccessfully for state senate in 1922, she promised voters she would clean up corruption in government.

Hattie Mosher's 1922 state senate campaign advertisement promised that she would clean up politics.

Other female legislative candidates promised to help mentally disabled children, to establish a reformatory for delinquent girls separate from the male facility at Fort Grant, to create county child welfare boards, and to hire a matron for the Arizona State Prison. Not one of these issues was endorsed in the regular party platforms or in any male candidate's campaign advertisements before the 1930s.[36]

Once elected to the legislature, early female representatives left an enduring legacy of work. In 1914, in the first election after winning the right to vote, several suffragists threw their hats into the political ring and ran for the legislature. Two were elected: Frances Munds to the state senate and Rachel Berry to the house. Munds had just become a grandmother at age forty-eight and was only the third woman in the country, after Martha Hughes Cannon of Utah and Helen Ring Robinson of Colorado, to reach the upper house of her state legislature. She commented: "Our friends, the true blue conservatives will be shocked to think of a grandmother

Rachel Berry, a Mormon
from St. Johns, was the
first woman elected to the
Arizona State House of
Representatives, in 1914.

sitting in the state Senate." Munds appealed to both male and female
voters by emphasizing her experience in business and her pioneering
work for woman suffrage, stating that she would "feel amply repaid for
the fifteen years work I gave for equal suffrage in Arizona, if they [the
voters] show their confidence in me by voting for me in the primaries."
Munds won a narrow victory in the Democratic primary against four
male competitors. Once the nomination was locked up, she breezed to
victory in the general election in her predominantly Democratic county.
According to newspaper accounts, women turned out in large numbers to
help Munds, thanking her for her instrumental role in achieving the vote.
After battling male legislators for years to win the right to vote, Munds
must have felt vindication with this victory. She had long believed in
woman's equality with man, if not her superiority to him, and now she was
about to take her seat across the aisle from many of the same men who
had belittled women as unfit for the full rights of citizenship.[37]

Rachel Berry, a Mormon pioneer in Apache County, also received
strong support from women voters when she became the first female member of the Arizona House of Representatives. She had arrived in St. Johns,
Arizona, in 1881 with her husband as part of a group of Latter-day Saints
sent from Utah to establish new Mormon settlements. She worked as a

teacher in St. Johns while her husband was a sheriff in Apache County, and together they raised seven children. Berry was a well-known suffragist and local school trustee who ran unopposed in the primary and defeated the Progressive party candidate, Mary E. B. Farr, in the general election.[38]

Journalists declared the second state legislature the "best looking legislature Arizona ever had," no doubt referring to Berry and Munds, and often trivialized their activities in the legislature. When Munds missed a session, capitol beat reporters for the *Arizona Gazette* wondered if she had been out shopping; in fact she was attending the Arizona Federation of Women's Clubs convention in Phoenix. They pestered Munds to tell her age or to reveal who had sent flowers to her senate desk, questions they would never have asked her male counterparts. Munds used humor to turn the tables on the press, telling newspapermen that on her silver wedding anniversary she had baked a fruitcake for her fellow senate members and employees, "just to show the senators that women can cook as well as legislate."[39]

Although she enjoyed joking with other senators and the press, on the floor of the senate Munds was all business. She knew she was setting a precedent and was determined to show journalists and the voters that women could be qualified public officials. She rarely engaged in debate on the senate floor, but when she did the press observed that "she has the courage of her convictions and when she has anything to say she does not want for words. Perhaps that's the 'woman' of it." Frances Munds had fifteen years of campaign experience sparring with male politicians by the time she entered the senate, but she knew that she was now part of mainstream politics, and her best strategy was to fit in with her fellow senators. When a Phoenix minister asked her to introduce a resolution banning smoking and chewing tobacco on the senate floor, she refused because, as her daughter later recalled, "it would only cause them inconvenience and it would in no way improve their morals and certainly not improve their dispositions." Munds knew she had many battles ahead, and this one was not worth fighting. Even John Dunbar, the political journalist who had criticized Munds during the 1914 campaign, applauded her reluctance to ban smoking. "We commend the tact and good judgment of Mrs. Senator Munds for her refusal to prohibit the senators from smoking. . . . Senator Munds has certainly started her senatorial career along the right lines, and we predict she will be a valuable member of the second Arizona legislature."[40]

Rachel Berry had no experience in the capitol before her election in 1914 and made the mistake of introducing a smoking ban in the house, antagonizing her colleagues in the process. Journalists complained that they were "much disappointed in the representative from Apache [County]. . . . It's mighty tough on the press lads, to say nothing of the members, some of whom aver their inability to think straight without the comforting presence of Our Lady Nicotine." Berry's resolution to bar chewing tobacco and cigarettes was not approved and, by creating an uproar, proved to many observers that women threatened to destroy the traditional ebb and flow of the legislature. In the following years, many female legislators would be asked to reintroduce a smoking ban, but all of them followed Munds's lead and declined. Nellie Bush explained in 1920, "With me, I expect nothing more from a man, in politics, than he gives another man. If he wants to smoke, I say, 'Go ahead and smoke.' And if he wants to swear, I'll sit by and enjoy hearing him do it. If it doesn't hurt him, it certainly isn't going to hurt me." Jessie Bevan outlined her position in 1931, stating that she was personally opposed to the habit but would not deny a man one of life's few remaining pleasures. The decision to tolerate spittoons and smoke-filled rooms was important to female political success: women did not seek to radically alter the way business was conducted but rather tried to achieve their goals by quietly blending into the existing male power structure.[41]

Munds considered two laws aimed at protecting women and children her most important bills: one raised the minimum age for marriage to sixteen for women and eighteen for men, and the other raised the widow's tax exemption. She believed young girls should be protected from predatory older men. The bill also made it a felony for any public school official to abuse the moral and statutory law. Women in the Woman's Christian Temperance Union had been trying unsuccessfully since the 1880s to pass a bill to raise the age of consent for girls in Arizona in an attempt to reign in prostitution. Although Munds's bill did not pass in 1915, it was reintroduced by Pauline O'Neill, with the support of the Arizona Federation of Women's Clubs, in the next session and was finally signed into law in 1919.[42]

Munds's other bill, the widow's exemption bill, was also designed to protect the interests of women. The large number of widows in the state had motivated members of the previous legislature to enact the first old-age pension and widowed mothers law in the United States. The act granted $15 a month and $6 a child to men and women over the age of sixty without visible means of support. Munds proposed to raise the tax exemption for widows from $1,000 to $2,000 on all possessions under $5,000. At a time before universal income tax, most people paid taxes on property and possessions. By proposing to raise the exemption for widows, Munds offered them significant tax relief. The bill passed both houses and was referred to the next election and approved by voters. She introduced other bills that she considered less important, including one to allow unincorporated cities to establish and maintain public libraries, an appropriations bill to purchase Aztec pottery, and several amendments to the penal code. These bills, and one to abolish the school census that would have saved the state $8,000 to $10,000 a year, all failed. In contrast to Munds, Rachel Berry had a much lower profile in the lower house. She introduced several minor bills—to establish a state flower and the state colors—but concentrated on education. She proposed bills to allow the use of the Bible in public schools and to create pensions for retired teachers. Of the nine bills she sponsored, only the bill designating the state colors passed.[43]

How successful were these first two female entrants into politics? The legislative reporter for the *Arizona Gazette* concluded at the termination of their first session that "the women of the legislature have distinguished themselves for their quiet dignity and excellent grasp of affairs. They have justified their selection and advanced their cause of suffrage." The *Arizona Labor Journal* also applauded their work, noting that an "Arizona State Federation lobbyist reported that Berry and Munds 'gave reason to hope that the next election would return more women to the capitol. Labor's cause would not suffer if entrusted to women legislators.'" Munds and Berry had proved to observers that women could be capable legislators. Munds especially wanted to show male politicians that women were equal in intellect and abilities. When she retired from the senate, she said she had entered politics not so much for legislative accomplishments as to set an example for other women "who may come after, to live up to their possibilities of good, rather than achieve special fame herself." If this was her goal, she succeeded ably.[44]

The real work of the state legislature was performed in committees. Committee chairs traditionally belonged to the majority party and had complete power over the disposition of bills submitted to them. Committee assignments usually reflected the personal interests, experience, and relative power of a legislator. All the twelve women who served from 1914 to 1927 had one or more assignments on the Education, Public Institutions, Child Welfare, and Public Health committees, but they were rarely given chairmanships. Frances Munds, a former teacher, was selected to chair the Education and Public Institutions committees and was also a member of the Land, Public Health, and Enrolling and Engrossing committees in the senate. After her arduous trip to the capitol, Rachel Berry showed interest in improving transportation in the state and served as chairman of the Good Roads Committee. She was also a member of the County and County Affairs, Education, and Public Health and Statistics committees in the house. Rosa McKay, a radical labor activist, drew the most nontraditional committee assignments of any woman in this early period, serving on the Rules, Judiciary, Corporations, and Efficient Government committees and chairing the Elections and Suffrage Committee during her three terms. Theodora Marsh, a widow who ran a large hardware and furniture business, also received important assignments, including Accounting and Business as well as Ways and Means. In 1927 Nellie Bush, an attorney, became the first woman to chair the Judiciary Committee. But most early women legislators, like Munds, who refused an assignment to the Judiciary Committee, felt more comfortable reviewing bills concerning the public health, welfare, and education of the state.[45]

The bills introduced by members in legislative sessions between 1915 and 1927 reflected their committee assignments and areas of expertise. Men concentrated on issues concerning business, labor, and economic development, and women focused more on education and public welfare. Although there was some overlap—women occasionally proposed highway bills or tax measures, and men sometimes proposed education bills—it became an unspoken agreement that women were experts in matters concerning the traditional interests of women and children, whereas men would lead in all other areas. From 1915 to 1927, the twelve female legislators introduced 116 bills, 63 of which related to this woman's agenda.[46]

When Pauline O'Neill took her chair representing Maricopa County in the house in 1917, she told reporters that she would introduce "bills that have received the endorsement of the state federation of women's clubs," a continuation of the work begun by Munds. Most of these bills were concerned with protecting young women, and they included laws to prevent prostitution, forced marriage, and the marriage of young women to older men. Nellie Bush introduced a bill to create a children's colony that passed over Governor Hunt's veto in 1927. The bill provided a home for "backward and mentally deficient children" and gave these children special training and attention. The funding of this institution was a favorite project of many other female legislators over the years. Vernettie Ivy sponsored a bill that created a position for police matrons for female prisoners in 1923, and in 1929 she finally succeeded in having a matron appointed to the state prison system. Female prisoners would no longer be subject to searches by male guards.[47]

Education reform was also a favorite issue among female legislators. Former schoolteacher, principal, and county school superintendent Louise Boehringer of Yuma County introduced numerous education bills, including a failed bill that provided for compulsory education. Her bill to provide for the Americanization of foreigners through the education of children and adult immigrants passed in 1921. Evidently, her fellow lawmakers were more eager to Americanize immigrants than they were to have compulsory education for all children. Boehringer also was successful in seeing through a bill that legitimized every child born out of wedlock. "By virtue of this law, parents may be 'illegitimate,' but never the child," was the assessment by the Delta Kappa Gamma Society, the honorary society of female educators.[48]

Perhaps the most important legislation introduced by a woman during this period was Rosa McKay's bill to establish a minimum wage for women. McKay was a native of Colorado with little formal education, elected by a pro-labor coalition to represent Cochise County in 1916. Although she was often described as an "avid socialist," McKay ran as a labor Democrat, dedicated to improving working conditions. The minimum wage in Arizona was designed to provide a decent wage for young women working in department stores and the Fred Harvey House system of restaurants and stores. An eight-hour workday bill for both men and women had already passed, but now McKay hoped to raise women's wages to $12 a week from the prevailing rate, which hovered between $3 and $6 a week. According to the local press, the speaker of the house had "declared the bill was slated for the waste basket, 'where it belonged.'" Republicans, mining companies,

In 1923 Governor George Hunt signed a women's minimum wage bill while the bill's sponsors, Rosa McKay (labeled number 1) and Vernettie Ivy (labeled number 2), looked on.

and the railroads, according to historian Katherine Benton, "saw the law as an opening wedge into men's labor laws" and quickly tried to kill it. By all accounts, McKay fought the bill through both houses with little help from other legislators and was credited with securing, as a compromise, a minimum of $10 a week for women in 1917 with her "thrilling bursts of oratory" on the house floor. Her success was applauded by the pro-labor press as evidence of the importance of having women in law-making bodies. "The rights of the female laborer are better safe-guarded in women-voting States than in non-suffrage States." McKay was characterized as "instrumental in large degree, in removing the objections of people to women entering politics," because of her ample "energy and ability" in championing the minimum wage bill. In subsequent sessions of the legislature, McKay continued to usher through minimum wage laws, raising the weekly rate to $12 in 1919 and $16 in 1923.[49]

Despite her accomplishments, Rosa McKay became a lightning rod during the turbulent years of labor unrest during World War I. On July 12, 1917, the Cochise County sheriff, the Phelps Dodge mining corporation, and leading Bisbee businessmen rounded up 2,000 striking miners at the local baseball park. Six hundred men returned to work, but the rest were put at gunpoint on trains to New Mexico, where they were left in the desert without shelter, food, or water. Phelps Dodge officials and local business leaders believed that radical members of the Industrial Workers of the World (IWW) were responsible for creating labor unrest and were disloyal Americans because they were on strike during a war, justifying their deportation.[50]

Rosa McKay, Cochise County representative, clearly sided with the labor unions. She was knocked down by a gunman as she tried to enter the Western Union telegraph office to send a cable to President Woodrow Wilson and U.S. Senator Henry Ashurst during the deportation incident. Later, when she was finally able to send a telegraph, she told the president and senator, "As representative of state from Cochise County I am asking protection for the women and children before we have another Ludlow, Colorado. They walked men out of town this morning that had not done one thing." Tom Foster, another representative from Cochise County who opposed the deportation, was himself deported from the county by the Workers Loyalty League. McKay organized women to collect and deliver supplies desperately needed by the deportees in New Mexico, where she was cheered by crowds. When she returned to Arizona, however, her train was fired upon by vigilantes at the border. As public outrage against the IWW increased, some voters called for McKay's removal from office because of her militant pro-labor stance. She left the county, saying she feared for her safety, and moved to Gila County, where she was elected to the legislature again in 1918 by more sympathetic voters. In 1919 she sued the *Bisbee Daily Review* for publishing "false and malicious statements" calling her a member of the IWW and an ex-convict. In 1924 she left the legislature to seek nomination as county supervisor but failed to win the Democratic primary for that traditionally male position.[51]

During the early years after statehood, labor issues divided Arizona citizens, both male and female. Many criticized the radicals in the labor movement because they believed the unions threatened the economic health of the state with their demands. Nellie Hayward, elected from

Cochise County in 1918, after the deportation, sponsored a resolution to remove all "slackers," the term used for draft dodgers. Pauline O'Neill proposed legislation to limit the liability of employers in workmen's compensation suits and introduced a resolution denouncing the activities of the IWW in 1917, actions that caused a rift in her relationship with Frances Munds, who remained loyal to the labor movement. After the Bisbee deportation, the public's attitude toward labor turned negative, and according to George Hunt, the progressive movement died. A few women, such as Frances Munds and Rosa McKay, stood steadfastly by the labor movement throughout the anti-IWW hysteria during World War I, but their influence clearly declined in the years that followed as Arizona politics became increasingly conservative.[52]

Perhaps the most satisfying moment for female legislators of this period came on February 12, 1920, when Governor Tom Campbell called the Arizona legislature into a special session to deal with an urgent matter: the ratification of the Nineteenth Amendment to the U.S. Constitution. Although the resolution met with contentious debate in most statehouses, in Arizona the members of the legislature listened to antisuffrage arguments with amusement and quickly passed the Susan B. Anthony Amendment granting women the right to vote, without a dissenting voice in either house. The resolution was sponsored by the four female members serving that year, Pauline O'Neill, Rosa McKay, Nellie Hayward, and Anna Westover, all of whom were former suffrage leaders. That summer, Tennessee became the last state to ratify the amendment after a raucous battle and with only a one-vote majority. Women had already voted in three elections in Arizona, and seven women had already served in the legislature. Now the eastern part of the country was starting to catch up.[53]

Despite women officeholders' early accomplishments, obvious limits to female office holding existed in Arizona before 1928. Women ran most often for positions deemed appropriate for women, in which their clerical skills or teaching credentials were put to use or their knowledge as mothers was essential. Although women were successful in running for the state legislature, most were elected to the house of representatives, which was considered the less prestigious legislative branch. Not until the 1960s and the modern women's movement were women elected in significant numbers to the Arizona State Senate, reflecting a national trend. Some women expressed the opinion that the Arizona State Senate was "undesirable for women," and the public evidently supported this view. Each senate district encompassed an entire county, which meant that candidates had to cover a lot of ground and spend considerably more money campaigning than representatives in the house, whose districts were much smaller. Larger percentages of women lived in urban areas, and women's clubs, concentrated in Arizona cities, often mobilized to help women win seats in urban districts but had less influence in the rural areas so necessary to winning senate campaigns. Frances Munds was the first woman to reach the senate. Nellie Bush ran for state senator from Yuma County against a man in 1928 and lost. She was elected to the state senate only when she beat another woman, Clara Botzum, in the primary in 1934. Three other female representatives ran for state senate between 1914 and 1950: Jessie Bevan, Maxine Provost Brubaker, and Pauline O'Neill, all of whom had successful careers in the lower house but still failed to reach the senate.[54]

Arizona women also found it difficult to reach state executive offices. During her campaign for secretary of state in 1920, Nellie Hayward stated that she believed women were entitled to certain positions in Arizona state government: "The women are not seeking the office of U.S. Senator, Congressman nor Governor, but they ask for the office of Secretary of State, the fourth place on the ticket." When Rose Kibbe Krebs ran as the Republican candidate for superintendent of public instruction in 1914—the first Arizona woman to seek statewide office—she toured the major cities and reported that she "found the women voters very enthusiastic. . . . Mothers who have children in school say they would like to see what a woman could do as state school superintendent and many gallant gentlemen of Arizona have said, 'Well, I think that a woman is better fitted for that place, anyway.'" An *Arizona Republican* editorial concurred with this assessment when it noted during Louise Boehringer's run for superintendent in 1916 that "it is known to many that the trend of the west is in the direction of recognizing the woman of the enfranchised states by electing a qualified woman in the state educational office." Editorials in other Arizona newspapers agreed that the job of the state's top educator should be filled by a woman. Yet despite their qualifications and support from leading newspapers, neither Krebs nor Boehringer won election.[55]

Barriers to women in statewide office were many. State campaigns required more financing than most women could muster, especially at a time when women lacked strong party support. Whereas a legislative race might cost a candidate between $20 and $50, Frances Munds estimated in 1918 that it would require $1,000 to win the primary for secretary of state and another $1,000 to win the general election, sums she was unwilling to spend and the Democratic party was unwilling to help her raise. Not only was it expensive, but it was also technically illegal for women to hold state office. In 1910, delegates to the constitutional convention barred women from holding positions as governor, attorney general, auditor, secretary of state, and superintendent of public instruction. Unofficially, attorneys argued that the suffrage amendment allowed women to hold those positions, but not until 1988 was the state constitution finally amended to allow women to serve in the top executive offices.[56]

At the county and legislative levels, candidates were chosen in primary elections, but state party executive committees chose candidates for the primary ballot for all federal and statewide positions. Of the twenty-five women who ran for state office before 1950, eleven ran on the Republican ticket, six as Socialists, one as a Communist, and only eight as Democrats. Given the acrimonious relationship between early women's leaders and Democratic bosses, it is surprising that any woman managed to win nomination from the party leaders. Only one Democratic woman, Ana Frohmiller, and one Republican, Elsie Toles, achieved state executive office before 1950.[57]

Republicans tried to gain political mileage from the reluctance of Democrats to nominate female state candidates. In 1922 the Republican party nominated Elsie Toles for reelection as state superintendent of public instruction, Jane Gregg as state treasurer, and Arizona Federation of Women's Clubs president Emma Guild for Congress. In an appeal to women voters, an article appeared in the *Phoenix Tribune* under the headline, "Women of Arizona Not Forgotten by Republicans in their Party Councils: Three on State Ticket." By nominating these women, the Republican party stated that it was recognizing "the womanhood of Arizona." Another editorial noted the lack of women on the Democratic ballot, asserting that although the Democrats reminded women that they "now enjoy the inestimable privilege of electing deserving male Democrats to office . . . [the Republicans] assumed that if women are as well qualified as men, they are as well qualified for office." Despite these efforts, Republicans were unsuccessful in electing any of the three female candidates in 1922; even incumbent Elsie Toles lost to the male Democratic candidate. In a state where Democrats outnumbered Republicans two to one, GOP women could easily be nominated but had little chance of winning.[58]

Elsie Toles was elected superintendent of public instruction in 1920, the first woman to hold state executive office in Arizona. She benefited from the Republican wave of the late 1910s, made possible by the registration efforts of Republican women. Republicans won almost half the house seats and a slim majority in the senate in 1920 and, with Thomas Campbell in the governor's office, captured control of state government for the first and only time until 1966. It helped that Toles's opponent was a Mormon, A. C. Peterson, who frightened many non-Mormon voters. Prominent members of Presbyterian, Methodist, Baptist, and other Protestant churches circulated a vicious pamphlet aimed at Peterson, denouncing the influence of Mormon politicians in Arizona. It asserted that the Church of Latter-day Saints controlled all its members, including Peterson, and that he would place the state's school system under the influence of the Mormon church and imperil the education of Arizona's children. In 1914 Mormon legislator Rachel Berry had sponsored a bill to allow the use of the Bible in schools, and some voters feared a Mormon superintendent might impose even more radical religious measures in the classroom. Toles denounced the pamphlet, declaring that she had no part in its publication, and deplored "the intrusion of religious matters in to public schools." Given the choice between two "dangerous" candidates, one female and one Mormon, voters chose Toles. In the following election, Republicans across Arizona suffered serious setbacks and were able to hold onto only six seats in the house and one in the senate. With Hunt's return as governor, Democrats held firm control of politics for the next forty years. The Democrats ran C. O. Case, a Protestant, for state school superintendent, and he defeated the incumbent Toles by a comfortable margin despite her solid record in office.[59]

Although many people believed women were a natural choice to serve as superintendent of public instruction, Toles was the only woman elected to the post before 1950 because many voters had reservations about the broader responsibilities of the position. State office holders supervised many people and controlled large budgets, and the superintendent also sat on the Arizona Board of Pardons and Paroles. Toles acknowledged that sitting in judgment of convicted felons was a difficult part of her job.

After her election in 1920 she received a letter from a death-row prisoner asking her to save him from the gallows. Toles recalled in a 1965 interview, "Receiving that was a terrific shock. For the first time I actually realized that in my new position I would have the power to send a human being to death. I can still remember the expression in the stenographer's eyes that morning when she handed me the mail with this on top. . . . Her silence was eloquent in asking, 'How could you, a woman, want such a job?'"[60]

The Board of Pardons and Paroles remained a barrier to women seeking the school superintendent position before 1950. Louise Boehringer was one of the most eminently qualified educators in the state. She held a B.S. in education from Columbia University, had served as Yuma County school superintendent from 1914 to 1917, and chaired the house committee on education in 1920, yet she was rejected by Democratic voters in the primaries when she ran for superintendent of public instruction in 1916, 1922, and 1940. Local papers denounced the loss by Boehringer to C. O. Case in the 1922 primary, noting that Case's previous record as superintendent "never set the world afire," whereas Boehringer was "one of the most capable and efficient school administrators in the state." In 1940 Boehringer was forced again to address the parole board issue in her campaign material, writing that "those in eastern Arizona [home to Mormon and Mexican American voters] supporting Miss Boehringer said they could see no reason why a woman member of the board of pardons and paroles was objectionable in any way, and said they could think of no decision coming before the board that could not be made by a woman member as well as a man." Despite this claim and her qualifications, Boehringer again lost and subsequently retired from public life.[61]

The office of secretary of state was another likely choice for women, and in neighboring New Mexico numerous women, including Hispanic women, won this largely ceremonial office. Arizona voters were reluctant to choose women for secretary of state, however, because it was considered the back door to the governor's office. Unlike most other states, Arizona has no provision for a lieutenant governor, so the secretary of state is next in line should the governor be unable to perform his or her duties. In 1918 Frances Munds faced Mit Simms, former Graham County recorder and state treasurer, in the Democratic primary for secretary of state and lost. Although Munds was a well-known suffrage leader and a successful state senator, she had underestimated the obstacles to her run for this higher

office. After her defeat in the primary, George Hunt told her, "I believe
if you had ran [sic] for any other office you would have been elected.
The chief campaign material that was used against you was the theory
that when the Governor was out of the State you would act, and that we
could not afford to have a woman in the Governor's chair. That this feeling
should exist is absurd, but nevertheless, the fact remains that it does exist."
Hunt went on to say that soldiers were leaving their homes, children, and
businesses in the care of their wives during World War I, and "a man who
could entrust the sanctity of his home to a woman should have no fear in
entrusting the State of Arizona to a woman."[62]

Although Arizona voters were reluctant to elect women as secretary
of state and school superintendent, they had no qualms about choosing a
woman for the unlikely position of state auditor. From 1926 to 1950, Anastasia "Ana" Collins Frohmiller served as state auditor, the first woman in
the nation to hold this position. Like so many of Arizona's other successful
female politicians, Frohmiller had shouldered tremendous responsibilities
as a young woman. She moved to Phoenix from Vermont with her family
when she was a child and was in high school when her mother died
and she became responsible for the day-to-day care of her seven younger
siblings. She took a job at age twenty-five as a bookkeeper for the Babbitt
Brothers Trading Company in Flagstaff, in Coconino County, bringing
her brothers and sisters with her so that she could raise them.[63]

In 1922 Frohmiller began her political career when she was appointed
by the county board of supervisors to replace the county treasurer after his
death. She was reelected to two additional terms. In 1925 she persuaded
thirty-eight other women to form the Flagstaff Business and Professional
Women's Club because she was dissatisfied with the Flagstaff Woman's
Club's lack of interest in the issues of working women. With the support of
the state BPW, she ran for state auditor in 1926, beating a male opponent
in the Democratic primary. She was unopposed for reelection in 1928
and soundly beat two other women, Quida Cox and May Belle Craig,
and one man in the 1930 Democratic primary. Frohmiller continued to
defeat Democratic challengers handily and until her resignation in 1950
rarely faced Republican opposition in the general election, receiving 70
percent of the vote in ten of her fourteen races.[64]

One of the chief goals of early female candidates was to clean up corruption in government. As state auditor for twenty-four years Frohmiller

earned the title "watchdog of the treasury" because of the close eye she kept on state finances. The auditor was the state's bookkeeper, responsible for the accounting and auditing of all state departments and agencies. According to her biographer, Frohmiller "received, investigated, and passed judgment on all financial claims against the state, including payrolls, expense accounts, contractors' bills, pensions, and relief payments." Over the years she filed numerous suits against state employees and agencies for fraud, malfeasance, and waste of public funds, earning her the admiration of many voters but also the enmity of many state officials with whom she had disagreements.[65]

Frohmiller strongly believed that accountability in government was important, and as state auditor from 1926 to 1950 she engaged in many investigations that uncovered an abundance of fraud and waste in the state. In 1939 she audited and found "malfeasance, misfeasance, nonfeasance and laxity" in the State Tax Commission, the State Corporation Commission, and the State Department of Public Education. Individual targets included Secretary of State James H. Kerby, who was charged with illegally depositing more than $27,000 in state funds in personal bank accounts, and Dr. H. E. Hendrix, state superintendent of public instruction, who was charged with pocketing $32,500 in textbook funds. The frequent irregularities in state finances induced Frohmiller to examine and propose revisions to the state's financial laws, resulting in a new financial code in 1943. Dubbed the "Czarina Law" because of the power it placed in Frohmiller's hands, the new code gave the state auditor comprehensive oversight of the state budgeting process, subjecting all funds to a pre-audit by her office.[66]

The Arizona state auditor's office is an administrative office rather than a policy-making office, but through her numerous lawsuits and investigations and her control of the budget, Frohmiller clearly held policy-making power, and she created many enemies in the process. Her careful stewardship of public finances often brought her into conflict with the governor, state executive officers, the legislature, and state supreme court justices. In 1950, when she ran for governor, Democrats were reluctant to get behind a candidate who had irritated so many male political leaders. Regardless, she stands as an example of the way some Arizona women were able to gain the support of voters when they chose to dedicate themselves to eliminating graft and corruption and steered an independent course in politics.

From 1914 to 1927, most commentators believed that a woman's justification for running for office was to expand her traditional role as mother and housekeeper into the public domain of politics. As one journalist summed up the women in the 1923 legislature, "they still are just plain, old-fashioned wives and mothers, who look forward to the time when they may cease to cuddle the 'baby state' and return once more to manage the affairs of a well-ordered household." At the county level, women would continue until the late 1940s to gravitate toward positions that favored women's experience as clerical workers and teachers, but many suffragists entered politics to prove that women were equal to men in their abilities. By 1927 women had established a solid record in the Arizona legislature with the bills they had introduced and passed affecting education, health, women, and children, but they also showed interest in public works and tax bills. They quickly recognized that they did not represent just the interests of women but had been elected to represent all constituents. They would continue to introduce legislation pertinent to women, but much of the groundwork was laid by 1927. With the onset of the Great Depression, women found it necessary to turn increasingly to the needs of all Arizona residents, male and female, who were suffering under devastating economic conditions.[67]

CHAPTER 5

"Mis"-Representatives

Expanding Representation, 1928 to 1940

When Annie Campbell Jones, representative to the Arizona House of Representatives from Yavapai County, was interviewed in 1930, she joked that "no matter what she did in the legislature, she would always be a 'mis'-representative." Female politicians, in the public's eyes, ran only to represent the interests of women, but Jones argued "that fundamentally all are human beings and that problems which must be met by law-making bodies should be met as human beings and not as men and women." In 1930 the world was changing rapidly, and women's interests would take a back seat to a depression that crippled state and national economies. Issues that had absorbed most of the energy of female politicians, such as education, corruption, and prohibition, became less important as state governments struggled with mass unemployment, drought, crop failure, and sometimes even starvation. In Arizona, ranching, farming, and copper mining were hit hard during the 1930s. Copper mines closed all over the state, precipitating an 80 percent drop in the number of employed miners. The price of cattle and cotton plummeted, and 27 percent of state residents were receiving aid from the Federal Emergency Relief Agency (FERA) by the summer of 1933, second only to New Mexico in the western region. The focus of state government was to try to attract as many projects funded by the federal government as possible, to create jobs and tax revenue. If women wanted to continue to serve in public office, they would have to adjust and become experts in a broad range of laws affecting all voters.[1]

During the Great Depression in Arizona, female candidates continued to campaign on issues important to women but also increasingly touted their business expertise. Although most women's clubs experienced declining membership in the 1930s because women could no longer afford the luxury of paying dues, the Arizona Federation of Business and Professional Women's Clubs actually grew as new clubs opened in Bisbee, Clarksdale,

Kingman, and Williams. As women faced increased competition and discrimination in the job market, the Arizona Federation of Business and Professional Women's Clubs stepped up its campaign to demand equality for working women. The BPW was dedicated to placing "the right kind of women in public office . . . to assure the advancement of our cause and promise the most for our carefully planned forward-looking legislative program." Rather than focusing simply on women's issues, the goal of the national organization was to "assume real leadership in thinking on economic problems."[2]

Since Frances Munds had led the suffrage victory in 1912, Arizona women had remained marginalized by the major parties and been forced to find support from women's clubs. After 1928, Isabella Greenway, who became state Democratic national committeewoman that year, created organizations that for the first time gave women meaningful roles in the party machinery. Under Greenway's direction, Arizona women began the transition from alienated outsiders to veteran politicians integrated into the party system. Whereas the first generation of legislators consisted mostly of schoolteachers, during the 1930s more women came to the legislature with degrees in law or with experience in business. Women increasingly ran for multiple terms, and many were given important committee assignments that had less to do with education and child welfare and more to do with appropriations, the judiciary, and the economy.

The Democratic party solidified its hold on state politics during the Great Depression and the presidency of Franklin Roosevelt. The state GOP had enjoyed a moderate wave of support in the late 1910s, electing Thomas Campbell as governor and briefly controlling government in 1920, but the 1930s were a disaster for the party. Republicans failed to capture a single Arizona senate seat from 1933 to 1951 and never held more than 15 percent of the house. Party registration dropped from 33 percent in 1928 to 14 percent in 1938. The largest newspaper, the *Arizona Republican*, even changed its named to the *Arizona Republic* to distance itself from the negative connotations of the party. Republicans struggled to field candidates in primary elections, and if they were able to induce someone to run, he or she was usually chosen either by a party caucus or as a write-in candidate. Some evidence indicates that Republicans actually paid candidates to run for state office. The dismal condition of the GOP in the 1930s and 1940s led Barry Goldwater later to quip that "a state Republican convention could have been held in a telephone booth." Much of the Republican women's organization that had been constructed by Freeda Marks and Grace Forbes Alexander in the 1910s and 1920s fell into disarray in the early 1930s. As economic conditions worsened, Republican leadership at the national and state levels failed to provide answers, and Republican women became susceptible to dissension, sometimes sacrificing the state party for their personal careers.[3]

Wilma Hoyal served as Arizona's Republican national committee-woman from 1932 to 1940. She had arrived in Arizona in 1921 from Kansas, where her father and grandfather had been Republican leaders, and settled in Douglas, where she was a partner with her husband in a successful jewelry business. Hoyal served two terms as president of the Arizona Federation of Business and Professional Women's Clubs, from 1927 to 1929, and then moved on to become president of the Douglas Woman's Republican Club, working her way up in the party from precinct member to county committee and national committeewoman. She served as a presidential elector in 1928 and became the first woman in the country to chair a national delegation when she led Arizona's group at the Republican convention of 1944.[4]

As Arizona's Republican national committeewoman, Hoyal spent substantial time campaigning for candidates in other western states, probably because she recognized that Arizona was a hopeless cause for Republicans. Her work attracted the attention of national party leaders, and in 1935 she was appointed director of the Women's Division of the National Republican Committee, the highest female party position in the country. Soon she received a promotion to assistant to the chairman of the GOP National Committee, a post she held from 1936 to 1940, the first woman to serve in this capacity. Although Hoyal enjoyed a splendid personal political career, she was often at odds with other Republican women in Arizona, inexplicably refusing to form a women's division within the state party and blocking attempts by Freeda Marks and Emma Parsons to create a statewide organization of Republican women's clubs, work that would not be completed until after Hoyal's departure for Washington, D.C., in the 1940s. Neglect and squabbling among both male and female Republican leaders in the 1930s, combined with the popularity of Franklin Delano Roosevelt and the New Deal, left the door wide open for Democrats to dominate state politics at every level.[5]

In contrast to the Republicans, Democratic women enjoyed unsurpassed leadership and unity under Isabella Selmes Greenway, who became one of the most effective and influential politicians, male or female, in Arizona during the 1930s. Greenway was unique not only because she became so powerful in the state but also because of her national reputation, a result of her close association with the Roosevelt family. She had been raised in privilege and associated with political elites as a young woman, but she had also lived in frontier conditions in the West as an adult. When Isabella Greenway came to Arizona in her thirties, she was both dazzling and down to earth, equally at home with national leaders and with Arizona veterans, miners, and ranchers. Because she was able to cross easily between these worlds, she was an ideal political leader for Arizona, a state that cherished its frontier traditions but desperately required federal assistance during the country's worst economic depression.

Isabella was born in Kentucky in 1886 and grew up on a ranch in North Dakota owned jointly by her father, Tilden Selmes—a Yale-educated lawyer who had worked with Abraham Lincoln—and Theodore Roosevelt. She attended the Chapin School for Girls in New York City, where she met Theodore's niece, Eleanor Roosevelt, and the two women became lifelong friends. Isabella served as Eleanor's bridesmaid in her wedding to Franklin Delano Roosevelt in 1905, and when nineteen-year-old Isabella married Robert Ferguson that same year, the two couples honeymooned together for a while at the Ferguson ancestral estate in Scotland. Later, Eleanor Roosevelt recalled that Bob Ferguson's sisters were responsible for introducing her to the idea that women should take active roles in politics.[6]

Isabella's first husband, Robert Ferguson, was a member of a wealthy, titled, Scottish family and a Rough Rider who had served with Theodore Roosevelt during the Spanish-American War. In 1910 he was diagnosed with tuberculosis, so the couple moved with their two young children to the drier climate of New Mexico for his health. The prescribed cure for TB at the time was outdoor tent living and fresh air, regardless of one's social class, and Isabella's new life in the West stood in stark contrast to the luxury she had experienced in New York. Her biographer Kristie Miller relates that "camp life was primitive. There were outhouses and no running water; water was caught in tubs as it ran off the roofs of the tents. At night their water basins froze. They gathered wood for fuel." Isabella wrote to her friend Eleanor Roosevelt: "Living in scattered tents, fetching and eating

From left to right, Isabella Greenway, Eleanor Roosevelt, and son Elliot Roosevelt on a visit to Tucson in 1933 during Greenway's campaign for Congress.

food a large part of the day, running a garden patch . . . nearly 200 chickens and now a horse—and no man!!! The real frontier spirit creeps in."[7]

Frontier living did not dampen Isabella's interest in politics. Her husband's good friend, John Greenway, a mining engineer, was organizing the Progressive party in neighboring Arizona and often visited with the Fergusons in New Mexico to discuss politics. Bob Ferguson encouraged Isabella's participation in politics, and when Theodore Roosevelt came to Albuquerque to campaign for the presidency on the Progressive Bull Moose ticket in 1912, she delighted in spending time with him at political rallies. She tried her own hand at politics a few years later, serving on the Grant County Board of Education at the end of World War I.[8]

When Bob Ferguson finally succumbed to tuberculosis in 1922, Isabella moved to Arizona and married John Greenway, the popular World War I hero who by that time had become a prominent figure in state politics. After the Progressive movement waned during World War I, the Greenways became Democrats. In 1924 they attended the Democratic national convention in Chicago, where John was nominated, unsuccessfully, for the vice presidency. That same year, Isabella, now thirty-eight, gave birth to a son. Two years later John Greenway died unexpectedly from complications following surgery, and she was once again left a widow, this time with three children. She could have moved back to New York and lived comfortably but chose instead to stay in Arizona.[9]

In the 1920s Greenway devoted herself to helping veterans in Arizona. Both of her husbands had distinguished themselves as soldiers, and she enjoyed a warm relationship with veterans of both the Spanish-American War and World War I. She established the Arizona Hut in Tucson, where veterans made furniture, toys, and novelty items that were sold in stores all over the country. Her close friendship with Eleanor Roosevelt, who at the time was co-director of the National Women's Committee of the Democratic party, coupled with her own work in veterans' affairs in Arizona, led to Greenway's appointment as Democratic national committeewoman for Arizona in 1928. Initially, many believed her appointment was made as a salute to John Greenway's political accomplishments, but it quickly became clear that Isabella took the role seriously and would use it to promote her own political aspirations. Unlike most national committeewomen, who were appointed as figureheads and expected to follow male party leaders, according to Kristie Miller, "it was more apparent than ever that her appointment as national committeewoman was a tribute to her political prospects."[10]

With the old suffragist generation of women retiring from politics, Greenway filled a vacuum in the Democratic party in 1928. She traveled throughout the state, rallying unprecedented numbers of women to campaign for Democratic candidates. As national committeewoman she began to draw many new female members into the party with her dynamic personality and speaking ability, and soon she became known as the "hardest working Democrat in the state." Greenway managed to get the women in Arizona's Democratic party "organized 100 percent throughout the State" by driving hundreds of miles each day. Her itinerary for a ten-day period in October included meetings with women's Democratic clubs in Winslow, Prescott, Tucson, Douglas, Bisbee, Thatcher, Miami, Casa Grande, Globe, Clifton, and Morenci. She joked to Eleanor Roosevelt that campaign aides were planning to buy a stretcher for her the day after the election and charge it to the party. By election day in 1928,

Democratic women's clubs had been established for the first time in a majority of the counties (eleven of fourteen), and a female vice chairman was appointed to serve on each county committee. Even at the precinct level an attempt was made to appoint women to serve with the elected precinct committeemen to "jointly analyze every registered vote to the best of their knowledge." Women had finally been brought into the party at every level."

Although a handful of Democratic women's clubs cropped up in Arizona cities during the 1910s and 1920s, Frances Munds and other Democratic women had refused to organize these clubs into a statewide network because they believed women had insufficient interest in working for the party, and they knew that male leaders would not fund such organizations. Greenway understood that the current generation of women entering politics was no longer driven by distrust of Democratic leaders as the suffragists had been, so she rallied women to clubs just as Democratic women's leaders had done in other states in the 1910s and the early 1920s. The Arizona Federation of Democratic Women's Clubs, created in the spring of 1933, grew out of discussions between Greenway, vice chairman of the state central committee Gertrude Bryan Leeper, and state party chairman Sidney Osborn, but it was really the product of Greenway's 1928 campaign to organize women in the party.[12]

Even with an effective women's organization, Greenway faced a daunting challenge in the 1928 election. Al Smith was the Democratic presidential candidate, and he did not appeal to most Arizona Democrats because he was Catholic and did not embrace prohibition. The *Arizona Republican* forecast in August that only about 60 percent of the state's Democrats would vote for Smith, with the remainder sitting out the election or going over to Herbert Hoover. Women voters who had worked so hard for prohibition were especially reluctant to get behind Smith. Even Greenway initially had reservations about his candidacy, but during a personal meeting in New York, Smith convinced her that he was "an uncommon man of lightning ability and I left his office determined to work my best for his cause." Much of her work in 1928 involved crisscrossing the state to speak to Arizona Democratic Women's Clubs to convince them to support Smith over their objections to his "wet" record. To hedge her bet, she emphasized the state ticket during the campaign, to "avoid any antagonism which might break our organization on the Smith issue." Greenway's party loyalty at this point was critical to her subsequent success in the Democratic party.[13]

Even though Al Smith failed to capture Arizona's vote and lost the national election to Herbert Hoover, Greenway's efforts attracted the attention of state Democrats, and her thoughtful evaluation and support of Smith won considerable praise. Democratic women said that "if such a woman as Mrs. Greenway can be for Al Smith he can't be so bad as he has been painted." Equally important, her political skills and hard work earned her accolades, especially from the women under her leadership. She quickly found that Democratic bosses had little use for women. The state national committeeman, Clarence Gunter, and his county chairmen were reluctant to provide Greenway with information she needed and hesitated to assign women as county vice chairs. Eleanor Roosevelt wrote stern letters to the state party leadership, and Greenway pleaded with them until a sufficient number of women were incorporated in some counties and "women were working at all times with the men." Greenway received numerous letters from women who praised her accomplishments and asked her to run for office. She decided instead to continue working as Democratic national committeewoman, bringing in hundreds of women to the newly formed county Democratic women's clubs, ready to tackle the 1932 campaign.[14]

Although Democrats enjoyed a distinct electoral advantage in the state and benefited from a dysfunctional Republican party, the old conservative and progressive factions of the Democratic party continued to battle each other and to divide themselves over candidates and issues. Greenway was uniquely qualified to unify the two factions because she was closely tied to both. Her former Progressive party membership and her close friendship with Roosevelt have led some Arizona historians to brand Greenway an "Eleanor Roosevelt liberal," an incomplete assessment. John Greenway was a former Progressive, but he was also a manager for a mining company and one of the leaders involved in the Bisbee deportation. The Greenways were also close friends with the Douglas family, the power behind the corporation wing of the Democratic party. Isabella's association with both wings of the party, her relationship with the national Democratic party, and her strong performance during the 1928 election allowed her to transcend the factionalism of the Democratic party in the 1930s and to emerge as a state party leader acceptable to both conservatives and progressives. She was a successful businesswoman who operated an airline that serviced Arizona, California, and Mexico in the early 1930s, and in 1930 she started the Arizona Inn, a luxury destination that still operates in Tucson. Few men in the state could rival her political or business accomplishments. Although reluctant to seek the help of a woman, the deeply divided state party leadership had no other choice, especially when their superiors in the national Democratic party insisted on her participation. Greenway was asked to advise national party chairman Jim Farley on political appointments and to mediate between the party's factions. She was one of only a handful of people the state party could rally around from 1928 to 1936, and she was unique, according to political scientist Martin Gruberg, because she was the only nationally known woman at the time whose power could be traced to her own achievements and personal connections, not to a husband or a father.[15]

Although Greenway was a member of Eleanor Roosevelt's close network of women, unlike other members of this circle she also was relied upon by Franklin Roosevelt. In early 1932 the Democratic National Committee was still firmly controlled by Al Smith followers, and Franklin Roosevelt chose to work at the state level to garner support for his nomination. Roosevelt wanted an instructed delegation from Arizona to the Democratic convention, but since Arizona's Democratic male leaders were unwilling to get behind him, Roosevelt asked for Greenway's support through Eleanor. Eleanor wrote Greenway that Franklin's campaign leaders were "afraid there is no man strong enough to get it through, so they have asked me to write you and urge that you do whatever you can to bring this about." Greenway worked hard to see that the first instructed delegation in Arizona history went to the convention, in full support of Franklin Roosevelt.[16]

When she arrived at the convention in Chicago, the press featured stories about "the most colorful woman in the United States," whose healthy glow came of "cow-ranching and flying over mountains in airplanes." Greenway played an important role in persuading the California delegation to swing its support to Roosevelt. John Nance Garner was putting up a good fight for the nomination, so Isabella Greenway became the "most insistent visitor" to Thomas Storke, a friend of hers and a member of the California delegation. She persuaded Storke and another delegate to meet with Roosevelt's campaign director, Jim Farley, who in turn promised Garner the vice presidency if the delegation switched to Roosevelt. On the fourth ballot the California delegation finally went for Roosevelt, and the nomination was locked up. Arizona's delegation rewarded Greenway for her work with an honorary nomination as vice president and continued to demand further recognition for her. Consequently, after his election President Roosevelt arranged to have Arizona Governor B. B. Moeur appoint Greenway as Arizona's official representative to the presidential inauguration in 1932. Roosevelt also considered her for secretary of labor before appointing Frances Perkins, who became the first female cabinet member. Increasingly, the national campaign looked to Greenway as Arizona's Democratic spokesperson, bypassing male leaders. Even outside Arizona she "was being hailed as 'a political phenomenon, if not a political genius.'"[17]

Arizona's Democratic leaders could not overlook Greenway's credentials and personal connections. She had brought women into the Democratic fold in large numbers in the late 1920s, and in 1932, when she invited Franklin Roosevelt to visit her at her ranch near Williams during his presidential campaign tour, she brought national attention to the state. During his visit, she introduced Roosevelt to Lewis Douglas, Arizona's congressman and brother of state Democratic leader Walter Douglas. It was Greenway who officially opened FDR's 1932 campaign in Arizona, announcing the visit of James Farley, chair of the national Democratic party, and it was Greenway who made the headlines, giving speech after speech, introducing candidates, and issuing press releases for the party. Arizona's national committeeman Gunter and state party chairman C. E. Addams were clearly in the background at these functions, perhaps because they were involved in destructive factional debates and were perceived as "lukewarm" toward a Roosevelt candidacy.[18]

With her political star rising, Greenway once again considered seeking office. She had briefly entertained the notion of running for governor in 1929 but decided against it because her youngest son was only four. She said, "I always believed that a woman with small children should be in a position to give them her best and if necessary her all." Franklin Roosevelt was especially supportive of the idea of her running for governor, but Arizona's male Democratic leaders had reservations. George Hunt warned her that "no Woman, no Mormon, and no Catholic could be elected governor of this State." Bill Mathews, editor of the *Arizona Daily Star* in Tucson, stated in the spring of 1932 that he felt that she had "no business running for governor, and I have been and intend to be brutally frank in telling her so. After she learns a little about the state, and about politics, she might be qualified if any woman is."[19]

Although strong local sentiment existed against a gubernatorial campaign for Greenway, Democratic bosses supported a congressional campaign because of her connections to the Roosevelts. When Lewis Douglas accepted the post of national budget director offered by President Roosevelt, his congressional seat opened up. Grace Sparkes, secretary of the Yavapai County Chamber of Commerce, briefly considered running, but in the end three Democrats threw their hats into the ring: copublisher of the *Arizona Gazette* and state senator Harlow Akers, former state legislator William Coxon, and Isabella Greenway. During the special election of 1933 Greenway easily beat Akers and Coxon, capturing 70 percent of the vote. In the general election she won with 74 percent of the vote. Voters knew she would have instant access to power in Washington, D.C., because of her friendship with the Roosevelts, and she could be trusted to help Arizona because she had done so much for the state and the Democratic party in the preceding five years. Of course she had the overwhelming support of the Democratic women in the state behind her.[20]

During her two terms as Arizona's representative in Congress, Greenway worked to help Arizona recover from its economic depression, sponsoring legislation to assure the continuation of operations of Arizona copper mines, to rescind federal cutbacks in veterans' benefits, and to increase spending for tubercular patients. She brought much-needed public works projects to the state, and her knowledge of the mining industry led her to forge a new copper code that benefited Arizona mining companies. She declined to run for a third term when family and financial obligations became too much.[21]

Perhaps Greenway's greatest political legacy was her work incorporating women into the Democratic party and breaking down the hostile relationship between men and women in state politics. She taught women to be good partisans at a time when the traditional assumption was that women were more interested in social reform than party politics. Evidence of her success can be found in the number of female appointments to vacancies in the state legislature. Before 1928 there were none. In most states it was common practice to invite a widow to take her husband's seat, but in Arizona it was not until 1931, after Greenway had completed her initial organizational work, that Mary Francis became the first woman appointed to assume her husband's position, as representative from Maricopa County. During the tenth legislature, Rose Godfrey, a member of the state Democratic Central Committee and the Maricopa County Women's Club, was rewarded for her party work and appointed to replace Renz Jennings when he resigned his seat in Maricopa County. That same session, Harriet Sprague, another party activist and a labor union member, was appointed to replace Gertrude Bryan Leeper when she left the legislature for health reasons. And in 1933 Mary Kelley took her husband's seat when he died in office. After 1930 women were viewed as reliable Democrats who could be counted on to do the party's bidding in the legislature, and therefore they were appointed by party leaders, something that would never have happened in Frances Munds's day.[22]

During the 1930s, African Americans, who had traditionally voted Republican, were increasingly drawn to the Democratic party nationwide. Many black civic leaders recognized that Roosevelt's New Deal held more promise for their community than the GOP's policies, and registration among African Americans shifted dramatically toward Democrats. In Arizona, church and civic leaders formed the Colored Jeffersonian Democratic League, and women such as Ada Walker and Estella Wright played important roles on its board of directors. African American leaders approached Greenway for assistance with their organizations, and she obliged them with donations, speakers for events, and patronage positions.[23]

The energy Greenway generated among Democratic women was profound. Six women won seats in the Arizona house in 1930, and three additional women—Rose Godfrey, Mary Francis, and Harriet Sprague—were appointed, drawing the attention of voters and giving rise to concerns that women were taking over the legislature. *Arizona Woman*, the official publication of the state women's clubs, profiled the new legislators' accomplishments and noted their collective experience in club work. These women were eager to do "women's work" in the legislature, including introducing legislation to improve schools and libraries, and according to the article they lent "a delightful bit of color to an otherwise somber body." Gertrude Bryan Leeper, a well-known writer from Phoenix and a close associate of Isabella Greenway's in the Democratic party, tried to calm any fears that women were usurping men in government, explaining that "women were not trying to take men's places. They are merely trying to find places of their own." Bridgie Porter, another Maricopa County representative, affirmed woman's traditional rationale for seeking office: "Men are not fully aware of the children's problems; it takes a woman and a mother to understand." Although the women used maternalist rhetoric to convince the press that they were in politics only to help women and children, only a handful of female legislators stuck to this traditional agenda. The more successful women quickly shouldered a wider array of issues.[24]

The tenth legislature held a tumultuous session in 1931, and one of the bills that caused the biggest ruckus was introduced by Gertrude Leeper, who tried to toughen enforcement of the state's prohibition law. Leeper had grown up in Tennessee before moving to Phoenix with her attorney husband and was the society page editor of the *Arizona Gazette* and a member of the Arizona Federation of Women's Clubs. Before her election to the legislature she had worked in Democratic politics, but she was still surprised by the tenor of the legislature. Ten minutes after her prohibition bill was read before the house, Leeper recalled, "accusations, recriminations, and challenges flew about indiscriminately. In the midst of the uproar stood our wild-eyed Speaker, his white hair flying, his always ruddy face ablaze, his arms waving. . . . 'If the damn thing passes this afternoon,' he shouted, 'I mean to see that every member of the House is in his or her seat to-morrow to vote on it. I'll show the people of Arizona what a bunch of hypocrites you are—voting dry and drinking wet!'" Prohibition lost its appeal during the depression because taxes on alcohol were important sources of state revenue, and in 1933 President Roosevelt and the Democratic Congress ushered through an amendment to undo the Eighteenth Amendment, which had outlawed the sale and manufacture of alcohol in the United States. Given the changing public attitude toward prohibition, it was not surprising that Leeper's prohibition enforcement bill failed. She had hoped to use her seat as a platform to reform the government, but she found the legislature foreign and uncomfortable and resigned after suffering a nervous breakdown.[25]

Most of the other female members of the tenth legislature were made of sterner stuff and came to the state capitol to tackle more pressing economic issues. Like Frances Munds and other early suffragist politicians, they understood that altruism did not win elections. Jessie Bevan, who represented Cochise County in 1930, said she felt sorry for "the sad faces of the men in Bisbee who have no work, and have families depending on them asking for anything to do to whereby they might make their daily bread." Her husband had been a miner, and together they had run a boarding house and hotel in Bisbee, catering to visiting politicians. Bevan knew something of suffering herself. She had lost her husband and all five of her young children to tuberculosis. She considered her work as a legislator during those turbulent years the most constructive of her life because she had a hand in developing legislation that could help others, regardless of gender. In the legislature she chaired the Child Welfare Committee, sat on the Education Committee, and became the first woman on the Mining Committee.[26]

Harriet Sprague, a member of the typographical union, was appointed to replace Gertrude Leeper, representing Maricopa County in the tenth legislature. She pledged herself to be "a friend of organized labor," determined to lower taxes, prevent wage cuts, and implement an income tax. Annie Campbell Jones, a single woman who worked as a court reporter and clerical worker for the railroads, was active in both the Prescott BPW club and Democratic party politics. In the legislature she sat on the Labor, Banking, and Military Affairs committees and introduced the bill in the house to build the Black Canyon Highway, the major road running from Phoenix to northern Arizona, which provided jobs for many unemployed men. Blanche Cavness was born in a mining camp in Pinal County and served on the Alhambra school board in Phoenix before her election to the legislature, where she served on the Agriculture and Irrigation, Child Welfare, Education, and Livestock committees. Cavness entered politics for the same reasons as most of her female colleagues, as one journalist reported: "Mrs. Cavness believes that the interest of the right type of womanhood in politics will do much to raise its standards and that women in public office have a beneficial influence upon those men with whom they are working." The women of the legislature in the 1930s were clearly at a crossroads, still bringing their unique female qualifications to government but also branching out into new areas of legislation. Perhaps the woman who did the most to push them beyond their traditional sphere of influence was a slight riverboat captain from the town of Parker named Nellie Trent Bush.[27]

When Nellie Bush first came to the legislature in 1920, she agreed with the prevailing wisdom that women had a unique role to play in state politics. "Women must live and raise families under the laws of the state, therefore they must protect that sphere in which they move. That is woman's reason

Nellie Trent Bush
represented Yuma
County for seven
sessions in the state
legislature.

for being in politics," she said. But over time she became a formidable
presence in the legislature and used her training as an attorney to put to rest
the notion that women could represent only women and children in public
office. Shrewd, aggressive, and knowledgeable, Bush, like Frances Munds,
set high standards for the women who followed her into politics and was one
of the best known early political figures, male or female, in Arizona.[28]

Born in Missouri in 1888, Bush arrived in Arizona in 1893 when her
family moved to Mesa because of her father's bronchial ailment. She spent
her early life in poverty. Her family made its home in a tent in the desert
for many years, and as a child her clothes were made of flour sacks. With
her mother she washed clothes for others, and together they provided
the sole income for the family for several years. She shelled almonds so
that she could afford to attend Tempe Normal School, where she gained

her teaching certificate. While riding the trolley to work as a teacher in Glendale, she remade the acquaintance of the inspector, Joe Bush, who had pulled her pigtails back in grade school. The pair married, and when Joe bought a ferryboat business in 1915 in Parker, he moved his bride to remote northern Yuma County. Nellie was pregnant when she made the train trip from Phoenix to Parker alone, and when she first saw the small, dusty town of thirty-five people or so, she was certain her husband had taken leave of his senses by bringing her to such a desolate spot. She resolved to leave, but after a good cry she changed her mind and began a lifetime of activity in Parker.[29]

There were no bridges in northern Yuma County in the 1910s, so the ferry business run by Joe and Nellie, which brought people and goods across the Colorado River from California to Arizona, had tremendous potential. It required long hours of strenuous labor. Nellie quickly earned her riverboat license, the first woman in the United States to do so, and worked alongside Joe guiding the boats and fixing the equipment. She supplemented the family's income by teaching school. The Bush family lived on a houseboat in those early years, and Nellie often worried that her young son might fall overboard before he had a chance to learn how to walk or swim.[30]

In 1916 Bush began her political career when she was elected to the local school board, followed by a stint as justice of the peace in 1918. Residents encouraged her to run for the legislature, and in 1920 she and Louise Boehringer were elected Yuma County's two representatives. When asked whether it was appropriate for a woman to serve at the state capitol and to be away from her family, Bush responded, "I have a husband and a big 5 year old son, yet I do not feel that they are being neglected because of my work. My folks take good care of the boy while I'm here, and my husband is right back of me in my public career."[31]

Her first session in the legislature in 1921 made Bush realize that she had insufficient legal training to achieve the effect she desired, so she attended law school at the University of Arizona in the 1920s. She brought her son, Wesley, with her to Tucson, where he was enrolled in grade school and told his friends, "Mother and I are both in the first grade." Lorna Lockwood, a future state legislator, joined Bush to become one of the only two women at the law school. Both faced discrimination because of their gender, and Nellie handled such problems with wit and intelligence. When she was told that women could not attend law classes when rape cases were discussed, she asked whether "they had ever heard of a rape case that didn't involve a woman. They let us in after that." When the state legislature met during the spring terms, Bush was forced to miss her law classes, so she attended law summer sessions at the University of California at Berkeley. Although she was never able to garner sufficient credits to graduate, she was admitted to the Arizona State Bar in 1923.[32]

With her legal education complete, Bush returned to northern Yuma County to practice law and to help Joe with his growing business interests, which included the presidency of the new local bank in Parker. Most women with legal training had trouble establishing practices because clients preferred male attorneys—but not Bush, who was the only lawyer in northern Yuma County in the 1920s. She served as the official attorney for the city of Parker, represented the Southern Pacific Railroad Company, and in 1924 was appointed the first female United States commissioner in Arizona, roughly equivalent to a federal justice of the peace. In January 1927 she returned to the state legislature with increased stature. She was given more prominent positions on committees, including the chairmanship of County Affairs, and became the first woman to chair the powerful Judiciary Committee. She also became one of six members of a joint senate and house committee convened to investigate the Highway Department, continuing her role, as the Los Angeles Times put it, as a "thorn in the side of Gov. Hunt." Her committee determined that the Highway Department "had been converted into a political machine" by the governor and recommended legislation to remedy the problem. The bill was passed by both houses but vetoed by Hunt.[33]

In 1934 Nellie Bush attracted national attention when the state of Arizona became embroiled with the federal government over the construction of the Parker diversion dam. Governor B. B. Moeur sought to halt construction of the dam because Arizona was battling other western states for its share of Colorado River water. Hoping to make a strong statement to the federal government that Arizona wanted its claim protected, Moeur proclaimed martial law on the Arizona side of the proposed Parker dam site and authorized National Guard troops to stop the construction. Nellie and Joe were enlisted as boat captains to ferry the soldiers across the river. Newspapers around the country, including the New York Times and the Los Angeles Times, carried coverage of the "Parker Dam War." Although the press treated the incident with laughter, it brought attention to the existing water problems in the West, which was what the governor wanted to do. Moeur recalled the guards when Secretary of the Interior Harold Ickes ordered construction halted, but by then Nellie had gained notoriety in national newspapers and magazines, and the governor had granted her the official title "Admiral of Arizona's Navy." A newspaper reporter wrote a poem about her exploits in the *Los Angeles Examiner*, the *New York Herald Tribune* featured her in a lengthy profile, and her photograph and life story appeared in newspapers across the nation. Even California papers warned that "if those on the California side of the line think they are playing with children, they do not know those sturdy Arizonans, particularly Senator-elect Nellie T. Bush . . . who has all the charm, the courage, the tenacity of purpose and, upon occasion, the forceful language of that 'Tugboat Annie' whom the beloved Marie Dressler made famous in films." After months of media exposure, Nellie's name was a household word in Arizona, and she became only the second woman, after Frances Munds, elected to the Arizona State Senate.[34]

The bills Bush sponsored during her seven legislative sessions in the 1920s, 1930s, and early 1940s defy categorization, as Bush did herself. She backed numerous construction bills for Yuma County, including bridges, roads, and dams. In 1931 she put herself out of business when she sponsored a bill to build a bridge at Parker, thereby eliminating the need for the Bush ferryboat service. Her willingness to support legislation that benefited her constituents at the cost of her family's income impressed her colleagues in the legislature. She also originated many economic bills, ranging from the creation of soil conservation districts and a water and power authority to bills providing for vocational rehabilitation and for the children's colony. In an interview in 1931 Bush admitted that she truly loved legislative work and politics, and "her only policy is a firm belief in as few laws as possible and adequate enforcement of those that are fundamentally necessary." Like so many of her female colleagues in politics, Nellie Bush held leadership positions with the Business and Professional Women's Clubs and the Arizona Federation of Women's Clubs. She held high-ranking positions in the Democratic party and was chosen as a delegate to the 1932 Democratic National Convention, which she attended with her friend Isabella Greenway.[35]

Nellie Bush was enormously popular among voters in Arizona and after the Parker Dam War gained a national reputation that allowed her to run for Congress in 1936 when Isabella Greenway retired. She ran as a businesswoman, an attorney, and "The best 'MAN' in the race for Congress." Bush flew her own plane around the state during her congressional campaign, giving speeches condemning political corruption and waste that resonated with Depression-weary Arizona voters. She blasted Governor Moeur for continuing Hunt's practice of using the Highway Commission to control party patronage, telling a meeting of Flagstaff Business and Professional Club Women that the Arizona Highway Commission was a "'trading machine' that participated in personal politics and ordered roads on a political basis." She was a clear favorite to win the election until a late entry candidate, Martin Phelps, drew away many of her votes. Phelps was a follower of Francis E. Townshend, a national politician who challenged the reelection of Franklin D. Roosevelt and proposed a pension plan that Bush deemed ill advised but that appealed to many destitute voters. With much of her support split by Phelps, Bush finished third in the Democratic primary. Her political career, however, continued. Her knowledge of water law and her experience on the Colorado River led to her appointment to the Colorado River Basin States Commission in the 1940s, and she continued to work in local politics as a member of the Parker City Council until her death in 1963.[36]

Like Frances Munds, Nellie Bush believed that women had a right to full participation in government, and she was adamant in her belief that women made superior legislators to men. As one California reporter put it: "More she legislators instead of he legislators are needed today in [Senator Bush's] opinion since women, she believes are more quick witted than men, more interested in the general welfare and less inclined to view an individual situation from a personal standpoint." Bush had a toughness that allowed her to command respect from political enemies and allies alike over the two decades she served in the legislature. As the national press put it in 1940, "In debate she traded blows with the best the state offered, and asked no quarter."[37]

In the 1930s women in the Arizona legislature continued to cluster on the Child Welfare, Public Health, Education, and Public Institutions committees, but led by Bush, they increasingly broke with tradition. Before 1928 only Rosa McKay was chosen to sit on the Labor Committee, a powerful assignment that acknowledged her close ties to labor unions in the state. After 1928 women were routinely assigned to Labor. They also started to appear regularly on committees traditionally dominated by men: Judiciary, Military Affairs, Ways and Means, Mining, Appropriations, Agriculture and Irrigation, and Banking and Insurance.[38]

Committee assignments not only reflected the increasing power select women held in the party but also displayed the growing range of female interests. Their names became associated with important building projects and tax bills, including the Parker bridge appropriations bill (Nellie Bush), a law prohibiting private financing by state officials for use by the state of Arizona (Jessie Bevan), and the creation of a state income tax (Annie Campbell Jones). Before 1928 just over half of all bills introduced by women were concerned with women and children, but after 1928 the proportion dropped to one-third. Much of the social housekeeping agenda promoted by suffragists had been completed, and now female legislators, backed by the Business and Professional Women's Clubs, began to demand equality for women under Arizona law. They were no longer content to see women placed in the same legal category as children and began to work to remedy laws that discriminated against them. In the 1930s the Arizona BPW lobbied the legislature extensively to pass a woman's jury bill, to block a minimum wage bill, and to pass a bill permitting the dissemination of birth control information.[39]

When Arizona women were granted the right to vote in 1912, it opened the debate over jury duty for women. In August 1914, nine women were summoned for jury duty in a Mesa courtroom, but the Maricopa County attorney, Frank H. Lyman, gave his opinion that women were ineligible for service because existing statutes stated that "a jury shall be made up of male citizens, and that as a result women are not qualified." The women were dismissed. Women were not summoned for jury duty again in Arizona until March 1945.[40]

In 1871, shortly after giving women the vote, Wyoming became the first territory to seat female jurors, but that privilege was quickly revoked. In 1879 the United States Supreme Court ruled in *Strauder v. W. Virginia* that women could be excluded from jury duty because it was not viewed as a constitutional right and therefore was not "an automatic tenet of citizenship." Only five of the first sixteen states to grant women the vote before passage of the Nineteenth Amendment (Idaho, Kansas, Michigan, Nevada, and Utah) also allowed women jurors. A few states, including Arkansas, Louisiana, Maine, North Dakota, Oregon, and Wisconsin, changed their laws immediately in 1920 and 1921, but women in other states, including Arizona, faced uphill battles to obtain the right to serve on juries because their statutes stated that jurors had to be men.[41]

Most women and men believed that women were unsuited to be jurors and that they belonged at home, not in the courtroom. At issue was the fear that jury duty would take women away from their responsibilities as wives and mothers, and they would be unable to find someone to care for their children or put dinner on the table. Earle C. Slipher, senator from Coconino County, explained that he voted against a jury bill in 1938 because he thought "women's time can be better spent than in the jury box. . . . If you put women in the jury boxes you might as well put them in the mines as muckers, make slaves of them. . . . Where is your shivalry [sic]? Where is your manhood?" A further concern was that jury duty would subject women to immoral behavior. House member William Wisener opposed it because he believed "the average woman of the state sincerely objects to leaving her home, her children, and all that a mother's heart holds dear, for the purpose of sitting as a judge in certain cases such as rape, bastardy, incest, sodomy, and murder."[42]

Some legislators thought women were quite capable of sitting on juries. Kean St. Charles, an old ally in the suffrage battle and at the time the longest-serving member of the state senate, supported women's jury service and noted that the arguments against it were "the same kind of harangue we had to listen to when men were fighting against women suffrage. . . . They have women jurors in California and no one has heard it said they cook any the worse for it." State Senator Perry McArthur, a minister, agreed, noting, "I'm a pretty good nurse . . . and if my wife wanted to answer a call for jury duty I'd certainly stay home and take care of the children. What does that have to do with the question?"[43]

Arizona women's clubs split over the issue of jury duty. Although the Arizona Federation of Women's Clubs did study and debate the issue, it never endorsed it. In 1932 the organization held a mock trial in Phoenix to demonstrate that women could perform "in any judicial capacity, from judge to juror." AFWC members were divided over the issue, and because the organization already had a firm policy of refusing to endorse political issues, it is not surprising that it refused to back a jury duty bill. In 1933 the president of the AFWC, Mrs. James Whetstine, echoed the sentiments of many male legislators, warning that women in Arizona would have to travel great distances to their county seats to serve on trials, forcing them to be away from home for long periods of time and requiring overnight stays in hotels with sequestered male jurors, which might suggest impropriety. However, Arizona Federation of Business and Professional Women's Club members were adamantly behind the issue at both the national and state levels. As working women with much at stake in the judicial system, BPW members could not afford to remain on the sidelines and believed that women would attain full citizenship only when they were granted the right to serve on juries. Women had a right to hear evidence in court cases and were just as qualified as men to return judgment. They denied that women were less capable than men of being objective and argued that women were competent to understand complex legal testimony. As taxpayers and business owners, women were subject to the same penalties under the law as men. Therefore they had an equal interest in the judicial process and demanded the right to a jury of their peers.[44]

Representatives Jessie Bevan (D-Cochise), Gertrude Bryan Leeper (D-Maricopa), Nellie Bush (D-Yuma), and Bridgie Porter (D-Maricopa), all BPW members, worked to pass a woman's jury bill during the 1930s, to no avail. Bevan introduced a bill in 1933; it passed fifty-two to eleven in the house but failed in the senate. In almost every legislative session that followed, a woman's jury bill was introduced in the house—which had a substantial number of female legislators—where it either died in committee or, if passed, was sent to the all-male, more conservative senate, where it was ignored.[45]

A 1937 national public opinion poll showed that 68 percent of all Arizonans were in favor of women's serving on juries. Just as with the suffrage issue, the public was supportive, but male legislators continued to resist women's demands. To convince male legislators of women's interest in the jury process, the Arizona BPW sponsored a jury school in 1937. Judges from around the state were invited to speak on the subject and to train women about the justice system. Superior Court Judge Martin T. Phelps supervised the schools and reported that women "compared very favorably" in their ability to "render judgments in cases." BPW legislative chairman Harriet Jean Oliver also coordinated a campaign that had every state BPW club contact or meet with its representatives on the measure, and a delegation of women from the Phoenix BPW was present at all hearings. Despite the efforts of female legislators and the BPW, jury legislation continued to meet defeat in the conservative, male-dominated senate. Senators defeated the bills because, as one gentlemen stated, "women are too emotional and sentimental for jury service, and should not be required to hear some of the degrading cases that are tried in our courts." Women would have to wait until World War II to convince Arizona's male legislators that they were capable of doing the same tasks as men, including rendering judgments in legal cases.[46]

Another issue that was important to the Arizona BPW was protective legislation. Female support for a minimum wage for women was almost universal in Arizona in 1916, when Rosa McKay negotiated her first bill through the legislature, but the United States Supreme Court ruled it, along with other state minimum wage laws, unconstitutional in 1925. The high court continued to strike down minimum wage laws until 1937, when it ruled in *West Coast Hotel Co. v. Parrish* that the protection of the health of a woman took primacy over her right to freely contract with an employer. In response, a minimum wage law for women was reintroduced in the Arizona legislature, touching off a firestorm within the Arizona BPW. President Estelle Bjerg mounted a campaign in 1937 to block the new law because it equated women with children in the workplace and because the law was based on the sex of the worker rather than on the nature of the work performed. She believed men and women should be treated the same under the law, and if a minimum wage passed, it should apply to both sexes. Nellie Bush told fellow BPW members in 1937 that whereas an earlier generation of women had asked for special protection, times had changed, and "now we are asking that you do not discriminate against them."[47]

Unlike the jury bill, which enjoyed strong popular support from voters and BPW members, the minimum wage bill was hotly debated among women. A survey of Phoenix BPW members in 1938 revealed that more than twice as many women supported a minimum wage for women than opposed it. While the BPW leadership championed equality in the workplace, many members and the general public still believed in special protection for women.[48]

The testimony at the Corporation Committee hearing in June 1937 illustrated how divisive this issue was among women. BPW president Estelle Bjerg led the protest against the bill in the legislature, accompanied by representatives from the Globe, Flagstaff, and Phoenix BPW clubs.

Bjerg testified that the bill would hurt working women because it would allow men to underbid women for positions, and the minimum wage would be used as a maximum wage for women. Nellie Bush also testified: "I won't want men to say I can't take any job for whatever wage I want to take it for. . . . If you men are afraid of your jobs, why don't you legislate for yourselves and let us alone?" Proponents of the bill, mostly female, testified as well. Teresa Schottmueller of Phoenix said she spoke for working women but believed that "any woman who fears a minimum wage law fears she cannot compete with a man at that wage." Labor unions also backed the bill, stating that it would help the lowest wage earners in the state. Despite BPW protests, the minimum wage bill for women was passed behind the vote of Representative Bridgie Porter, a BPW member. Bjerg complained in her next presidential report that "as citizens of the United States and as adults, women want to be treated as such; they want to be left free to meet the problems confronting every human being in the struggle for existence in their own way without any hobbles."[49]

During the depression, working women faced many obstacles. They often lost jobs to men, especially as teachers and librarians, because many people believed it was more important that a man, who was head of the household, to have a job than a woman. The 1932 Economy Act, passed by Congress, stipulated that when employees were released from the federal payroll to save expenses, married persons would be discharged first. Because most women working for government earned far less than their husbands, they typically were the first to lose their jobs. Many states, including Arizona, passed similar measures to reduce the government payroll. Estelle Bjerg, Arizona's BPW president, was alarmed by an almost unanimous state senate resolution stating that married women in public offices were a "detriment to the public welfare." The Arizona BPW worked diligently to combat the popular notion that married women should be forced to give up their jobs to men or single women, arguing that the salaries of married women were necessary to the average family income, and women were entitled to equality in the workforce. Nellie Bush, in her capacity as Public Affairs chairman of the Arizona BPW in 1938, worked toward "creating an enlightened public opinion" on the topic of working women, arguing that "any public opinion or legal restriction covering the economic or social activities of any group of women tends to place limitations on all women." Bjerg admonished BPW women to use their vote "while we still have it and see that a different personnel adorns the legislative halls next time."[50]

One issue on which the AFWC and the BPW agreed during the 1930s was birth control. During the depression, Arizona's rates of infant mortality were alarming, second only to New Mexico's in the nation, and many club women believed that family limitation was necessary so that parents could afford to feed their children. In 1934 Margaret Sanger, the leading birth control advocate in the world, moved to Tucson and continued her work with Arizona women to establish the Tucson Mothers' Clinic in 1935, which catered to the large population of Mexican American women in the area. Sanger also worked closely with women in Casa Grande and Phoenix, especially N. Bess Prather, who became one of the state's early birth control crusaders. As president of the AFWC, Prather was able to get two resolutions passed by her club in 1935, one to endorse the Equal Rights Amendment and the other to endorse "the proper and intelligent use of scientific contraceptive methods under the direction of reputable physicians." In 1937 the Phoenix Business and Professional Women's Club sponsored a large event to support the Phoenix Mothers' Health Clinic, hosting 300 businesswomen, the governor, the mayor, the chief justice of the Arizona Supreme Court, and other important public officials. Sponsors of the Phoenix Mothers' Health Clinic included many prominent Phoenicians, among them Margaret (Peggy) Goldwater, a public health volunteer and wife of future Senator Barry Goldwater, Republican leader Margaret Adams Rockwell, and Maie Heard, wife of publisher Dwight Heard.[51]

In 1936 the U.S. Supreme Court ruling *United States v. One Package* overturned the Comstock laws, which had prohibited the distribution of contraceptives, and birth control clinics opened all over the United States. In the same year, Esther Louise Struckmeyer, better known as Fritzi, a twenty-six-year-old single Phoenix woman, was elected to the Arizona house. She introduced a bill in 1937 that would have amended the state penal code to eliminate the ban on birth control information. Margaret Sanger praised Struckmeyer "as the first woman in any state legislature or in congress to 'have the courage to introduce legislation which would remove obstacles to the [birth control] movement which means so much to their own sex.'" Struckmeyer's birth control bill was amended in committee to stipulate that only doctors had the legal right to disseminate information on birth control, a watered-down version of her original bill.

However, it was passed in the legislature with the support of both the AFWC and the BPW, opening the way for the increased distribution of birth control information for women in Arizona.[52]

The late 1920s and 1930s were a time of transition for women in Arizona politics. Democratic women were incorporated into the party under the guidance of Isabella Greenway, and women gradually changed from altruistic reformers into partisan politicians. They entered the decade believing they were still responsible primarily for laws affecting women and children, but the Great Depression made it apparent that it was also their responsibility to care for the rest of society. Mary Alice Patterson, the daughter of Arizona's first female house member, Rachel Berry, represented Maricopa County from 1928 to 1930 and, like her mother, campaigned on improving education and the welfare of disadvantaged children. But she also promised the unions that she would pass labor legislation and bring jobs to the state. During the winter of 1909 she had hosted NAWSA field worker and labor activist Laura Gregg in St. Johns during Gregg's visits to Mormon communities to organize for suffrage. Patterson came away from the experience with an appreciation of the problems facing labor that might otherwise have escaped a Mormon woman living in rural Arizona, and she brought those concerns to the state capitol in the 1930s.[53]

Despite women's many successes, the limits to their political participation were also still apparent in the 1930s. Female legislators, the Arizona BPW, and public opinion polls were unable to persuade a majority of male legislators that women deserved the equal right of jury service, and women themselves were split over whether protective legislation did more harm than good. The world war looming on the horizon would force voters and politicians to reevaluate the role of women in society, and established female politicians began to test just how far they could go in politics.

CHAPTER 6

Professional Politicians

The 1940s

World War II brought profound changes to Arizona. Its mining, farming, and ranching industries were resuscitated as demand skyrocketed for raw materials such as copper, cotton, and beef. The military discovered that the state's wide open spaces and year-round sunshine were ideal for training pilots, and the military installations and defense industries that supported them moved to the desert Southwest, quickly transforming the economy. Although mining towns continued to thrive, the state's population became increasingly concentrated in Phoenix and Tucson, where defense contractors were located. Earlier generations, which had been attracted to Arizona by the promise of recuperation from devastating respiratory ailments or the chance to start new lives on their own land, had faced the challenges of desert heat, lack of running water and electricity, and grinding poverty. After World War II, servicemen who had trained in Arizona often moved their families to live there, attracted by the warm weather and high-paying jobs. The early pioneers were quickly displaced by midwestern immigrants who lived in planned communities, worked in air-conditioned offices, and enjoyed spectacular golf courses. Local real estate and construction businesses flourished as they scrambled to accommodate new arrivals. Postwar Arizona was no longer a hard-scrabble frontier but was becoming a modern economy dominated by the service sector. The changing demographics quickly altered the political landscape.[1]

The new postwar immigrants to Arizona were more likely to be midwestern Republicans and less likely to be strong supporters of organized labor than the prewar immigrants. A Veterans' Right to Work Committee emerged in 1945 to push a bill through the legislature that guaranteed the right to run a nonunion shop, and the law was referred to the voters in 1946. The right-to-work bill was fought with all the available resources of the state's labor unions, but more than 10,000 new voters registered in Maricopa County alone in response to the labor debate, many of them veterans looking for employment. The measure's victory signaled that the economy and politics of Arizona were shifting from the extractive, labor-intensive industries backed by Democrats to the service and financial industries favored by Republicans. Although Democrats maintained control of state government in the 1940s, Republicans, led by a new generation of men and women that included John J. Rhodes, Barry Goldwater, Eugene Pulliam, Margaret Adams Rockwell, and Margaret Hance, began to contest every race by the end of the decade.[2]

Whereas the important role men played in rebuilding the Republican party in Arizona in the 1950s is well documented, less is known about the handful of GOP female stalwarts who kept the party alive in the late 1930s and 1940s. Much of the groundwork began in 1938 when Emma Parsons worked with Freeda Marks, the first Republican woman elected to the legislature, to revive the Arizona Woman's Republican Club, which had languished. Parsons, a native of Kansas, had worked her way up in the Republican party from Pima County precinct woman to county vice chair. She then founded and chaired the Pima County Woman's Republican Club and served as state vice chairman and as national committeewoman. Parsons attended national conventions regularly and counted President Herbert Hoover and 1936 presidential candidate Alf Landon among her personal friends. In 1938 she and Marks traveled throughout the state to rally Republican women, much as Isabella Greenway had done for the Democrats ten years earlier. The two organized twenty-one clubs in fourteen counties. The state national committeewoman, Wilma Hoyal, disapproved of their attempts to affiliate their local clubs into a statewide organization, so it was not until 1941, when Hoyal had left Arizona for a national party position, that the Arizona Republican Woman's Club was affiliated with the national organization. In 1946 Parsons created a woman's division as a department of the Republican state central committee, and women finally began to receive funding for their activities from the state party budget. Much of their effort involved registering new Republican voters in every county, but the work focused on Maricopa and Pima counties, where the rapid population growth was occurring.[3]

In 1948 Margaret Adams Rockwell became Arizona's national committeewoman and joined with Parsons to strengthen the party. Rockwell was the daughter of John C. Adams, owner of the Adams Hotel, often referred to as the "third branch of the state legislature" because it was such a popular place for politicians to meet. The hotel became the primary watering hole for Arizona politicians shortly after its construction at the turn of the century because of its reputation for the best food and finest whiskey in the Southwest. Frances Munds had set up her suffrage headquarters at the Adams in 1912, knowing that it would maximize her access to affluent politicians. John Adams, a Republican lawyer, served as Phoenix mayor in the 1890s and was instrumental in the creation of the state fair and the local chamber of commerce. He catered to a clientele that was mostly Democratic before 1950, and his only resistance was a sign on the wall in the tile of the men's washroom instructing them to "Button-Up" because, according to friend Bob Creighton, "the hotel was so infested with stupid Democrats he felt that it was his public duty to help them get through the more difficult problems in life."[4]

Margaret Adams was born in 1890 and remembered when her mother, who was fortunate to own one of only two electric fans in all of Phoenix, hung wet sheets in front of the fan to cool the hotel rooms, which became infernos in the summer heat. After her father's death, Margaret ran the Adams Hotel with her husband, John Rockwell. She found no time for party activities until 1944, when her two children were grown and she was in her mid-fifties. Her affiliation with the hotel and her knowledge of politics, gleaned over the years in its "smoke-filled halls," allowed Rockwell to rise quickly in the party, serving as head of the Woman's Republican Club, as vice chair of the state party, and as candidate for Congress in 1944. Although roads had improved considerably over the years, campaign trips were still arduous affairs, and Rockwell noted that she spent weeks "living on milkshakes and hamburgers" and sleeping in "rickety hotels" to generate interest in the party.[5]

At the time, Republicans still had trouble recruiting candidates and often filled the state ticket, as one political journalist later recalled, "by twisting the arm of someone who didn't relish the dubious honor." Often women were tapped to run for "hopeless office," especially when so many men were off fighting in World War II. In 1942 Dorothy Rand, who had risen through the ranks to become president of the Arizona Woman's Republican Club, ran for state superintendent of public instruction, even though she had never held political office before. Grace Forbes Alexander ran unsuccessfully for representative from Maricopa County in 1940 and 1942 and for state senate in 1944, the same year Margaret Rockwell became a "sacrificial lamb" when she consented "to run for Congress when she knew she had no chance for election." Even though these candidates were tremendous underdogs in the prevailing anti-Republican climate, they ran against Democrats who otherwise would have run unopposed, keeping the Republican party on the ballot and visible to voters.[6]

Participants in the GOP resurgence in Arizona in the 1950s, such as Barry Goldwater's political advisor Stephen Shadegg, testify that it was Margaret Rockwell, working with other male leaders, who "had done more than breathe new life into a complacent organization. They had drafted and implemented an effective political mechanism capable of bringing Republican voters to the polls." Rockwell was well known for her organizational and speaking skills and worked with a group of activists known as the Young Republicans to draft and support candidates such as Barry Goldwater, Howard Pyle, and John Rhodes, who led the party's resurgence in the 1950s.[7]

The Republican party was also greatly aided by Eugene Pulliam, who arrived in Phoenix determined to revitalize the GOP. He took over two of the state's largest newspapers, the *Arizona Republic* and the *Phoenix Gazette*, in 1946. During World War II, as Arizona experienced an influx of conservative midwestern Republican voters, Pulliam began backing GOP candidates for office through his newspapers. Although Republicans would not outnumber registered Democrats in Arizona until 1986, the 1950s marked the beginning of the state's shift toward the two-party competition that had been largely absent during its early history.[8]

Pulliam's efforts to create a vibrant Republican party were aided by the talents of Howard Pyle's campaign manager, Barry Goldwater, who was just beginning his own political career. Goldwater came from a pioneer Arizona political family—his uncle, Morris Goldwater, had been the Democratic mayor of Prescott and served in the state senate with Frances Munds, representing Yavapai County in 1914. Morris Goldwater was a conservative, or "corporation," Democrat who consistently voted the opposite of the progressive Frances Munds on bills. Barry Goldwater claimed that he felt strongly that the state needed a two-party system, because "a one-party system put up dogs for office." But it is also clear that earlier Goldwater Democrats such as Uncle Morris had leaned heavily to the right.[9]

World War II not only changed the demographics and politics of the state but also forced Arizonans to view women in a new light as they took on men's positions in the workplace, laboring in factories, fields, offices, and even copper mines for "the duration" to release men to help with the war effort. Women's clubs rallied to support the war effort, saving scrap metal, planting victory gardens, and raising funds. In one weekend alone in 1944, members of La Asociación Hispano-Americana de Madres y Esposas, a Tucson women's group, sold more than $30,000 worth of war bonds and stamps. After years of trying to pass a woman's jury bill, the Arizona Federation of Business and Professional Women's Clubs finally found success in March 1945 when House Bill 12 was introduced by BPW member and Maricopa County representative Claire Phelps. The bill passed in both houses and was signed into law by Governor Sidney Osborn, a populist Democrat. The first six women empanelled for jury service were all members of the Phoenix League of Business and Professional Women's Clubs. Harriet Jean Oliver, the state BPW legislative chairman, believed that credit for the bill's success belonged to the BPW clubs because of their concerted effort to contact and convince their representatives to support the bill. Their jury school and legislative lobbying, which had began in the 1930s, combined with women's willingness to work outside the home to help the war effort, finally eradicated the prevailing notion that women were too sentimental to have sound judgment and too sensitive to hear criminal testimony.[10]

The National Federation of Business and Professional Women's Clubs continued to work diligently to protect women from discrimination in the workplace. Arizona BPW president Estelle Bjerg complained that eliminating the thousands of laws on the books that discriminated against women was "like bailing the oceans with a sieve." She cited legislation that denied women equal guardianship of their children, unequal inheritance laws, and minimum wage laws for women only. Although women were doing the same work as men, they were rarely paid the same wages. Bjerg also believed that "the troubled conditions existing throughout the world and evidence of reactionary forces at work in our own country to restrict economic freedom of women, make imperative the passage of the Equal Rights Amendment." In Europe, women lost many of their rights when fascist regimes came to power and declared that a woman's primary role in society was to bear children. Bjerg did not want women in Arizona to lose the ground they had won.[11]

Increasingly, women began to see the wisdom of Alice Paul and the radical suffragists who had introduced the Equal Rights Amendment in Congress in 1923. The ERA would eliminate the protective legislation and minimum wage laws that had granted women unequal treatment, and the issue was viewed favorably in the West, where Republican candidates such as Margaret Adams Rockwell supported it in the 1940s. Many BPW members had resisted eliminating the laws in Arizona in the 1930s, but during the 1940s, as even more women assumed the work of men, they began to recognize that those same laws kept women from competing with men. In 1938 BPW leaders organized a campaign aimed at Arizona Senator Henry Ashurst, chairman of the U.S. Senate Judiciary Committee. Ashurst was originally opposed to the ERA, but after receiving 3,600 telegrams about it, primarily from BPW women, he decided his constituents were in favor of it and used his influence to bring the amendment up for a hearing before his committee. That was as far as the amendment got that year.[12]

Despite pressure from women's groups, the Equal Rights Amendment did not come up for a vote in Congress until July 19, 1946. Arizona Senator Ernest McFarland pledged to support the amendment but was working in Arizona when the vote was called in Congress, and it lost thirty-eight to thirty-five. Arizona BPW leaders believed that Senator Carl Hayden had committed himself to equal rights legislation during his 1944 campaign and complained bitterly when he voted against the measure. Hayden responded that he felt that the bill would fail until a clause was attached so that "nothing in this article shall be so construed as to invalidate or prevent enactment of legislation benefiting women in their work or family status." When Hayden presented his version of the Equal Rights Amendment to Congress, he attached a provision for protective legislation, and the bill was rejected by Congress and denounced by BPW leaders. Although their efforts to pass the ERA were ultimately unsuccessful, Arizona BPW leaders worked closely with Governor Sidney Osborn to see that women were appointed to the defense council and other state boards during World War II.[13]

World War II also brought profound changes for minority populations in Arizona. The GI Bill provided loans for housing, helped pay tuition bills, and helped returning veterans find jobs. American Indians, African

Americans, and Mexican Americans had fought and defended their country with honor during the war. They returned to greater economic opportunities but still faced discrimination at home. In 1946, fifty African American women created the Women's Division of the Urban League to protest restrictive covenants that prohibited sales of homes to "those having perceptible strains of Mexican, Spanish, Asiatic, Negro or Indian blood." Their efforts were supported by two prominent white Arizona residents, Anna Roosevelt-Boettinger, who, like her mother, Eleanor Roosevelt, was a crusader for civil rights, and Kathryn R. Gammage, wife of civic leader Grady Gammage. But it was Eleanor Ragsdale, an African American real estate agent, who challenged the covenants by moving into the racially exclusive Encanto neighborhood of Phoenix in 1953. In 1944 Carl Sims and Hayzel B. Daniels became the first African American males elected to the Arizona legislature. African American women ran for office as well but faced more opposition than men. Julia McGowen ran unsuccessfully for Maricopa County recorder on the Communist party ticket, a party platform that advocated anti-lynch laws, abolition of the poll tax, and elimination of job discrimination. In 1948 a member of the executive committee of the Colored Jeffersonian Democratic League, Ada Walker, became the first female African American legislative candidate in Arizona when she ran to represent Maricopa County in the house, coming in third of four Democrats in the primary. It would be another eighteen years before an African American woman would win election to the state legislature.[14]

Anglo women, however, made substantial gains in the state legislature during the 1940s. The Arizona Federation of Business and Professional Women's Clubs resolved "to have more women in the legislature than ever before. This would be a chance to relieve the 'man power' for active combat work." Women responded, regaining their representation in the state legislature, which had waned during the late 1930s. The BPW clubs undertook an intense lobbying campaign to select Nellie Bush as house speaker in 1941, and she lost by only five votes, narrowly missing the opportunity to become the first female speaker in the United States. By 1948, 30 percent of all women running won their seats in Maricopa County, the same percentage as men.[15]

The nine female legislators who served in the 1940s were experienced politicians closely affiliated with their political parties. Unlike the early generation of suffragist candidates, who ran for office once or twice to pass legislation they felt their party was neglecting, by the 1940s women had established themselves as seasoned veterans who operated much like the men of the legislature. Although roughly one-third of legislation proposed by women still involved traditional female issues in the 1940s, the rest of the bills they introduced were concerned with the economy, taxation, defense, and public works. All female members except Louise Moore ran for multiple terms, and the only reason she did not was because she left to run for Congress in 1942.[16]

The two members of the Church of Latter-day Saints serving in the legislature in the 1940s, Laura McRae and Eva Decker, both had traditional female agendas reminiscent of those of their suffragist foremothers. Laura McRae had grown up in a pioneer family in Safford and was a Democratic representative from Maricopa County from 1938 to 1956. Besides being active in her church, she was a member of the local BPW club, served on the Democratic state executive and central committees, was a nurse's aid during World War II, and was the mother of three young children. Throughout her legislative career, McRae was a leading advocate for child welfare, sponsoring bills to protect children with physical and mental disabilities. Eva Decker, a homemaker from Snowflake, became the first female representative from Navajo County in 1946 and only the third Republican woman to serve in the legislature. She sat on traditional female committees, including Child Welfare, Education, and Public Health, and unsuccessfully tried to ban smoking on public transportation in Arizona.[17]

Clara Botzum, known as "the Mining Lady," replaced Nellie Bush as Yuma County's representative when Bush retired from the legislature in 1941. Botzum was born in Indiana but moved to the West with her family when she was seven. The family traveled down the still untamed Colorado River on a raft manned by Mohave Indians, arriving in the new town of Parker, Arizona, in 1900. After receiving a college degree and marrying in California, she returned to run mines in Parker inherited from her father. After a divorce, she went to work as secretary of the Yuma County Chamber of Commerce and became active in the Yuma Business and Professional Women's Club. Bush and Botzum were largely responsible for improving transportation in Yuma County from the 1920s to the 1960s. Bush had ushered a bill through the legislature that provided one-third of the funds for the Parker bridge, and Botzum began a campaign in 1930 to convince federal officials to raise the additional funds. She finally

Yuma County represent-
ative Clara Botzum was
largely responsible for
the construction of the
Parker bridge over the
Colorado River.

found an ally in Congresswoman Isabella Greenway. The Parker bridge
was truly a product of a female political network, and had Botzum been
a man, it surely would have been named for her when it was dedicated
in 1937. Not until 1979, however, after the modern woman's movement
forced Americans to recognize the contributions of women, was the bridge
rededicated in Clara Botzum's name at a special ceremony attended by
the eighty-six-year-old civic pioneer.[18]

Botzum's work on this and other projects in Yuma County led to her
endorsement for representative to the legislature in 1942 by civic leaders
and the Yuma BPW club. In the house she became the first woman to
chair the Mining Committee, and over the years she used her effective
lobbying skills to boost mining in the Parker area. She persuaded the
federal government to bring a government stockpile depot to the area and
to establish a conservation district, and she helped create a recreation area
on the Colorado River. Her influence brought electricity to rural northern

Yuma County and motivated local investors to start the Parker Bank. In 1978 a lengthy local article saluted Botzum for her years of dedication to the Parker area, calling her "a woman who has demonstrated the kind of backbone and business acumen which put this area on the map."[19]

Claire Phelps brought her expertise in ranching to the legislature in the 1940s. She was a college graduate with two years of law school experience, was active in the Chandler Woman's Club, served as president of the Mesa Business and Professional Women's Club, and was a housewife and a partner with her husband in running their ranch. She got involved in politics as a result of her participation in women's clubs but decided that appealing to women voters was not enough to launch a successful political career. Phelps was able to discuss farming and ranching with men, was well versed in business law, and understood water policy. She has been described as extremely assertive, energetic, and eager to combat the "good old boys" network that permeated the capitol. She ran four successful legislative elections, campaigning as an "efficient, capable, and fearless" candidate, and she beat future Arizona Congressman John J. Rhodes in 1946 to represent Maricopa County. During her years as representative from Maricopa County, from 1940 to 1947, she helped write an underground water code, sponsored a Colorado River water bill and the right-to-work bill, chaired the Mining Committee, and introduced the woman's jury bill that finally passed in 1945.[20]

Maxine Provost Brubaker grew up in a household that was devoted to improving the plight of workers in Arizona. As a young woman she served as an attaché to the legislature when her father, John Provost, was a representative, and she later noted that "the insight I had for legislation from this work at age 14 gave me the desire to be giving for the state and humanity ever since." John Provost was a well-known labor leader in Arizona who founded and presided over the Arizona Federation of Labor, ran as a Socialist candidate for governor in Colorado, and was a delegate to the Arizona constitutional convention. When Maxine entered the legislature she was married, had no children, had a master's degree, and had taught both high school and junior college. As chair of the house Labor Committee in 1941, Brubaker continued in her father's footsteps to protect the rights of working men and women. She sponsored workman's compensation legislation and was an outspoken advocate for African Americans and Mexican Americans in her district during World War II.[21]

Edwynne "Polly" Rosenbaum was born in Iowa and earned both a bachelor's and a master's degree at the University of Colorado. After teaching in Colorado and Wyoming and following a divorce, she moved to Arizona in 1929 to teach in the mining camps, but as the mines closed during the Great Depression she was forced to seek other employment. She moved to Phoenix in 1939 to work as a secretary in the state legislature, and there she met and fell in love with house speaker William "Rosey" Rosenbaum. Her legislative career began in 1949 when her husband died and she was asked to replace him as Gila County's representative. One lawmaker told her she need not bother to come down to the legislature to serve out Rosey's term, and another told her he did not want a woman on his committee. "It was tough for women back then if you let it get to you, but I didn't. They tolerated you. It was especially tough for a woman alone." Despite the negative attitudes of her fellow legislators, not only did Polly show up for work, but she remained in the legislature until 1994, out-lasting all her colleagues and becoming the longest-serving legislator in Arizona history.[22]

Lorna Lockwood brought her expertise in law to the legislature in 1938. She was the daughter of Alfred C. Lockwood, who began his political career as a pro-labor superior court judge in Cochise County and was appointed to serve on the Arizona Supreme Court in 1925. Lorna was born in Douglas, Arizona, in 1903 and earned her law degree from the University of Arizona in 1925, attending classes with Nellie Bush. The law dean discouraged Lockwood from attending, telling her "it was no place for a woman," but she found that the male students were very nice to her, and she soon became "just another student." Despite finishing near the top of her class, Lockwood faced challenges during her legal career. She originally had hoped to practice law with her father, but when he was elected to the state supreme court, she was forced to go into private practice alone. She quickly discovered that few clients were willing to hire a female attorney and reluctantly went to work as a legal secretary and clerk for her father until 1939, when she went into private practice with Loretta Savage. Even then their business struggled to find clients and failed after several years.[23]

Ironically, while she faced discrimination as a female attorney, Lorna Lockwood found success in public office, largely through the support of local women's clubs. Active in both the Democratic party and the Arizona BPW, Lockwood was recruited in 1938 to run for the legislature

Lorna Lockwood was
a representative in the
state legislature before
advancing to superior
court judge in 1950 and
state supreme court
judge in 1960.

representing Maricopa County. During her three sessions in the house she concentrated on sponsoring laws concerned with criminal procedures, including prescribing penalties for child molestation. She helped establish a commission on unemployment compensation in 1941 and introduced numerous bills concerned with transportation. She was the second woman, after Bush, chosen to chair the Judiciary Committee.[24]

Outside the state legislature, women continued to chip away and occasionally win election to nontraditional offices in the 1940s. Margaret Kober was the first woman elected to the Phoenix City Council in 1949 and served alongside political newcomer Barry Goldwater. Kober impressed colleagues with her direct style and ability to ask "pertinent questions." At the county level, with BPW assistance, women increasingly sought posts once reserved for men. Jewell Jordan, an active BPW officer and experienced accountant, was appointed sheriff of Maricopa County in 1944 when her husband, Lon, died during his third term in office. She became the first elected female sheriff in Arizona in 1946. Although Jordan remained in the office for four and a half years, she later remarked, "It was a man's job. I had some harrowing experiences and really saw all sides of life." She used her experience as sheriff to run successfully as the first female Maricopa County treasurer in 1948 and then for state auditor in 1950.[25]

Although only eleven female attorneys were listed in the 1940 census for Arizona, many of these women made remarkable progress in politics. The first female assistant county attorney, Lorna Lockwood's law partner Loretta Savage, was appointed in 1943, and Gertrude Converse was the first woman to run for county superior court judge. Converse had strong credentials for the office: former assistant attorney general, member of the county attorney's staff, and leader in the campaign for a women's jury bill. She also was endorsed by the Arizona Federation of Business and Professional Women's Clubs, but she was unable to win the nomination in the Democratic primary election in Maricopa County in 1948. However, she did set the stage for Lorna Lockwood to become the state's first female superior court judge in the following election.[26]

Despite their strong advances at the county level and in the legislature, women faced many of the same old biases when they tried to run for higher office. C. Louise Boehringer lost her third and last attempt to become superintendent of public instruction in 1940, and Dorothy Rand, the Republican write-in candidate for that office in 1942, lost in the general election. Louise Moore ran as a "woman's candidate" for Congress in 1942 after only one term in the state legislature. Despite serving briefly as a legislator, this housewife, teacher, and member of the Maricopa County Democratic Women's Club had little political experience that would have given her the stature to run for high office. She announced her candidacy at "the urgent request of women from all parts of the state who believe that women should have representation in congress on a 50–50 basis," but she lost the primary. If a woman wanted to reach Congress or other high office, she had to represent the interests of all constituents and have exceptional skills that overshadowed those of her male competitors.[27]

In 1950, however, three women, all prominent BPW members, made history running for positions traditionally reserved for men: auditor, superior court judge, and governor. Jewell Jordan was elected state auditor and served until the position was eliminated in 1969. Lorna Lockwood's work in the legislature gained her notice, and she was appointed to the Phoenix City Charter Revision Committee in 1947. She was selected as assistant attorney general in 1949 and then won election as the first female superior court judge in 1950. Lockwood later recalled that "people were surprised at her victory, but the lawyers were the ones that were a little bit against it. They didn't think a woman belonged on the bench. . . . There weren't any valid reasons given, just that a woman hadn't been there and shouldn't be."[28]

Before 1950 only two women had served as governors in the United States—Miriam A. "Ma" Ferguson of Texas and Nellie Tayloe Ross of Wyoming—and each had succeeded her husband in office. In 1950 Ana Frohmiller, a Catholic, twice-divorced female politician, attempted to make history and become Arizona's first female governor. In the primary election she ran against the incumbent governor and four other Democratic men. Politicians predicted that incumbent Dan Garvey or challenger Richard Harless would get the nomination, but observers noted that Frohmiller often outdrew these men at campaign rallies. Stephen Shadegg, who was working for Republican gubernatorial candidate Howard Pyle's campaign, was surprised when he quizzed "old-line, hard-shelled Democrats" in Bisbee who said they were supporting Garvey but expected Frohmiller to win. A voter in Graham County told him, "Ana will poll quite a few votes, especially among the women."[29]

Frohmiller's primary campaign was orchestrated to highlight her many years of experience in the state auditor's office. Her slogan was, "I offer the voters experience, not an experiment." She promised to run a fiscally responsible Arizona and pledged to "get to the bottom of the welfare fiasco and give it a good housecleaning," a slogan reminiscent of the suffragists. She was a well-known political commodity in the state after her many years of service, and it was generally acknowledged that she would receive the woman's vote in most counties.[30]

But even if many women did support Frohmiller for governor, others had reservations about a woman serving in high office. A waitress in Gila County told the press, "I wouldn't vote for a woman for governor at any time under any circumstances. I don't think it's a job for a woman." In Bisbee, Democratic civic club members expressed their opinion that Frohmiller would lose because "Arizona wasn't ready for a woman governor." Despite these misgivings, Frohmiller surprised just about everyone in the state when she beat out her five male opponents for the Democratic nomination, winning a majority in seven of the state's fourteen counties and becoming the first female gubernatorial nominee in Arizona. The *Arizona Republic* noted that "political circles were agog Wednesday as

ANA
FROHMILLER
DEMOCRAT
FOR
GOVERNOR
YOUR VOTE WILL BE
APPRECIATED

I offer you experience, not an experiment!

A campaign card from Ana Frohmiller's 1950 gubernatorial contest.

Mrs. Frohmiller forged steadily ahead in the total vote," winning by a 9,000-vote margin over her nearest competitor. But perhaps the state's politicians should not have been surprised. After all, six Democratic nominees competed in the primary, and they should have expected that the male vote would split among the five male candidates while a significant proportion of female voters would unite behind Frohmiller.[31]

Many predicted a 25,000-vote margin of victory for the Democrat Frohmiller in the general election, because Democrats were still roughly 75 percent of the registered voters, but she had two factors working against her. First, she was a woman, and Democrats historically were not inclined to put up a fight for a female candidate for major office. Indeed, the Democratic party greeted Frohmiller's primary win with "stunned surprise." Second, the Arizona political climate was changing in 1950, and Democratic candidates were no longer guaranteed a general election victory. Republican women had been busy registering new voters, and a newly defined and reinvigorated Republican party was emerging. Frohmiller would receive considerable competition from her Republican opponent, well-known radio talk show host Howard Pyle, and his campaign manager, Barry Goldwater.[32]

The Goldwater family had owned stores in Arizona since territorial days, and Barry had started his career in the family retail business. He found himself drawn to politics in the 1940s with his participation in the charter government movement in Phoenix and his subsequent election to a seat on the city council. In 1950 Goldwater teamed up with Howard Pyle and changed the nature of political campaigning in Arizona. They modernized the campaign, using the media to get out their message and spending enormous sums of money in the process.[33]

During the 1950 gubernatorial campaign, Goldwater and Pyle characterized their opponent, Ana Frohmiller, "as part of the 'political machine' which had dominated the Arizona political scene since 1912," referring to the notorious George Hunt Democratic machine. Pyle boldly proclaimed, "For years the opposition leadership has cleverly hidden behind a so-called people's program while they dished out special favors and fat tax cutbacks to special interests whose principal ownership doesn't live in Arizona and doesn't care what happens to the state." Furthermore, he challenged Frohmiller's work as state auditor, questioning her financial code and claiming that it created "tax bills that don't buy anything, that represent waste and confusion." He condemned her support of spending on state hospitals, prisons, and colleges—issues women had long championed in the state—alleging they were examples of waste and inefficiency in government. He brashly claimed that Frohmiller did not speak for herself but rather was "in the hands of others" and was "the voiceless stooge of the boys in the back room." Ironically, Frohmiller had fought for years against corrupt Democratic office holders, but the recently transplanted conservative voters were unaware of her history, and she had few resources with which to publicize her record.[34]

Pyle's campaign against the inefficiency and cronyism of traditional Democratic-controlled state government was effective. He linked Frohmiller with the Democrats, whose factional debates and patronage had dominated state politics since statehood. Throughout her campaign Frohmiller ran on her experience as state auditor, but when faced with Pyle's charges of corruption, she responded poorly. Instead of defending her distinguished record, Frohmiller stated in a radio address that if a woman was elected governor, "the state will get a tremendous amount of free publicity across the country." Frohmiller had been involved in state politics since the 1920s and still believed that women had something unique to bring to the political arena. They sponsored legislation that protected women and children and exposed corruption in the state. Eugene Pulliam, in an editorial in the *Arizona Republic*, wrote that "Ana Frohmiller's sex won't solve the problems that vex Arizona, and it won't sell the state to outsiders." Characteristically, Barry Goldwater had a blunter reaction: "What are we running in Arizona—a side-show or a state?"[35]

Frohmiller had touched the nerves of the new political establishment by striving for the highest state office, and she stimulated an avalanche of negative comments. Pulliam's *Arizona Republic* ran editorials stating that women were intended to be helpmeets and devoted mothers but not to lead government. One piece asserted that because no woman was a leader in the Bible, no woman should lead Arizona as a governor. While this argument undoubtedly appealed to some of the more conservative newcomers, long-time residents accustomed to female office holders objected. One reader responded with the observation that in the fourth chapter of Judges, "the leader of the army refused to go out to battle unless the woman leader would go with him. . . . Whether as a teacher, missionary, farmer, head of a family, business woman or Governor, given the chance and the need, she will deliver the goods." In the past, most female politicians, such as Frances Munds, Isabella Greenway, Nellie Bush, and Clara Botzum, had "delivered the goods," and therefore newspaper coverage of female campaigns was largely devoid of criticism. In this election the stakes were much higher, and there were more voters with traditional views of women, so gender became a critical issue.[36]

The biggest weakness in Frohmiller's campaign was lack of support from the Democratic party. Party officials were shocked when she was nominated and did little to raise money or find volunteers for her campaign. Frohmiller had no choice but to run her gubernatorial campaign as she had conducted her career: simply and efficiently. She refused to place billboards and posters along Arizona's roads, arguing that they cluttered the countryside. She refused to raise money from special interest groups and instead collected only from individual private donors. She chose to manage her own campaign when Dick Smith, her campaign manager, died of a heart attack midway through the contest. Without a campaign headquarters, without a fund-raising organization, and equipped only with an unpaid staff of mostly female volunteers, Frohmiller could not keep pace with the Republicans. When the votes were counted, she had

spent only $875, whereas most gubernatorial candidates in the 1940s aver-
aged $5,000 on campaigns. Her Republican opponent, Howard Pyle, had
spent $11,428.[37]

Frohmiller's loss to Pyle was as bitter as it was close. Democrats still
greatly outnumbered Republicans in the state and had predicted a huge
victory, yet Pyle narrowly won the election by 3,000 votes. Frohmiller was
urged by supporters to contest the election because of alleged voter fraud,
but characteristically, she was unwilling to pay for the recount and left
politics disenchanted, telling her brother, "I never wanted to ride a horse
in a damn parade anyway." She went on to become the founding treasurer
of Southwest Savings and Loan Association.[38]

Democratic leaders blamed Frohmiller's failure on the fact that she
was a woman. Party workers were reluctant to support her and did not work
"to get the vote out in heavy Democratic precincts of Maricopa County,
where Pyle amassed his greatest lead." But female candidates had always
enjoyed strong support in the past in Maricopa County, especially where
women's clubs were active, and Frohmiller was a member of the BPW.
Its political pull was no match for Pulliam's virulent campaign against
Frohmiller in the *Republic* and *Gazette*. By attacking her record, her
honesty, and her ability to lead, Pulliam and Goldwater openly suggested
that women were unqualified for the highest state office. A *Gazette* editorial the day after the election asked, "Did thousands turn against Mrs.
Frohmiller because she was a woman and because they wanted the strong
hand of a man at the helm in these perilous times? Or was the vote for Pyle
simply a protest against Democratic misgovernment for many years at the
Capitol?" In the end, the column concluded that it was the "Democratic
record of misrule" that was Frohmiller's main handicap, but clearly her
gender was an obstacle as well.[39]

Another factor in Frohmiller's defeat was undoubtedly the hard work
conducted by GOP women to register new voters and make sure they
turned out at the polls. Emma Parsons, Margaret Adams Rockwell, and
other Republican women had played crucial roles in keeping the party
alive in the 1930s and 1940s and paved the way for the success of men
like Howard Pyle and Barry Goldwater in the 1950s. However, Republican women were disappointed with their treatment by the new male
leadership. In return for their hard work on the campaign, female party
leaders expected appointments to government boards and commissions or

to vacancies in the legislature. In 1951 Rockwell wrote to state chairman Randolph Evjen that she was disappointed that Governor Pyle was not appointing women to those positions and that he was even threatening to eliminate many state and county boards that women traditionally served on in order to cut state expenditures. The boards that governed education, the state hospital, the children's colony, and public welfare all faced elimination under the new welfare plan proposed by Pyle. Silencing women's voices in government, she stressed, "will make a very serious impression on the thinking women voters in the state. I am sure that there will be political pressure to keep women out of the picture and it will probably come as always from those who are more concerned with politics and patronage than welfare." Women had played an important role in the Republican party in its early years, when it existed in the shadow of the Democrats, but as the fortunes of the party rose in the 1950s, it relegated women to a lesser role, much as the Democrats had done when they firmly controlled state politics.[40]

During the 1940s women made great strides and experienced notable defeats in Arizona politics. They ran for the legislature primarily on their business and legal expertise, were elected to multiple sessions, and earned seniority. As the chairs of important committees, they ushered through legislation relevant to all segments of the state's population. They continued to serve on political party committees but also worked with the BPW to pass laws giving equal rights to women. One woman, Ana Frohmiller, garnered enough respect from voters to become a legitimate contender for the state's highest office. Party officials continued to hold female candidates at arm's length, but it was clear in 1950 that women had chipped away at many of the arguments against them and stood poised to take the final step toward political equality.

Conclusion

In 1948, Frances Willard Munds died in her Victorian home on Mount Vernon Street in Prescott at the age of 82. She had arrived in Arizona when it was still a frontier and spearheaded the suffrage campaign. During that long battle Munds discovered that although most male voters were receptive to opening the franchise to women, the political parties had little interest in her cause. She could win the right to vote only if she used political leverage to force the hands of party leaders. From 1903 to 1912 she built a strong coalition of supporters drawn from labor, Socialists, and Mormons. Much of the early success of Arizona women in politics was a result of her extraordinary leadership. She publicly confronted party leaders, legislators, congressional candidates, and even the governor, demanding rights and respect for women. Munds's style stood in direct contrast to what society perceived a woman to be: submissive and restrained. She had fed ranch hands, lived and taught under primitive conditions, and dealt with drunken brawls in her classroom. Like most of the women who followed her into the state legislature, Munds was unfazed by the cursing, drinking, and tobacco spitting that were inevitable aspects of the all-male environment, and she enjoyed sparring with her male adversaries.

Early on, former suffragists such as Frances Munds recognized that the state legislature was the most effective place to advance their political agenda. During the campaigns of the 1910s and 1920s, most female candidates were teachers and mothers, so they positioned themselves as alternatives to males, highlighting their expertise in education, public health, and social welfare and their work with civic clubs. But two other attributes were also important: most women candidates had business experience, and most were born or raised in the West. They had contributed to the early economic and civic growth of the territory and state and could boast of deep roots in their communities at a time when most people were newcomers. The skills and expertise they brought to their campaigns allowed them to compete on an equal basis with male candidates. Local newspapers supported women in politics as long as they did not seek to direct the votes of other women or run for high office.

Democratic leaders, who controlled state politics, were suspicious of women voters. They believed women would vote more conservatively than men, and to a certain extent they were proved correct. But by excluding female leaders and leaving registration work primarily to women's clubs, Democrats created an adversarial relationship that lasted until the late 1920s. Women remained united long after the suffrage battle was won and ran for office to challenge male domination of state politics. Although the Republicans were able to find a few women willing to help them, most Democratic women refused to work for their own party. Starting in 1920, the Arizona Federation of Business and Professional Women's Clubs, whose members included many of the educated, professional working women of the state, became the dominant voice for politically active Anglo women. This organization demanded the inclusion of women on the rolls for jury service, sought the elimination of protective legislation that discriminated against women, worked for access to birth control information, and petitioned Congress for the Equal Rights Amendment. Its leaders were deeply committed to equality in the workplace, and they recruited and provided the funding and moral support for female candidates for county, legislative, and state offices. These women often had educational and business credentials equal or superior to those of their male competitors, making them credible alternatives to male office holders.

At the county level before 1950, few women sought office to affect policy or to advance their political careers. Rather, women ran for economic reasons. Many candidates were single women, sometimes widows with young families, who sought steady employment. Experienced teachers, bookkeepers, and clerical workers campaigned on their experience, integrity, and reliability for the positions of county school superintendent, recorder, treasurer, and court clerk, and they won in large numbers. Once they established themselves as qualified candidates, women often dominated these positions with little competition from male candidates. They challenged men only occasionally for positions in law enforcement and those requiring legal experience.

When Isabella Greenway arrived in Arizona, she discovered many talented female politicians running for office, but few were involved in party politics. In contrast to Munds, with her confrontational style, Greenway worked tirelessly in 1928 to organize women in the state's Democratic party, managing to soothe many of the hard feelings that divided men and women and encouraging women to run for party committee positions and for office. Her personal political connections were supplemented with astute business and political skills that allowed her to achieve unprecedented power for a woman. Ultimately, her work incorporating women into the Democratic party is her most important political legacy, and her achievement allowed women to transition from outsiders to insiders in state government.[1]

After 1928 a second generation of women politicians entered the legislature with even greater legal and business experience. They continued to serve on legislative committees that oversaw education and public welfare issues, but many also had the expertise to serve with confidence on committees concerned with labor, agriculture, law, and mining. They were becoming legislators first and women second. In the 1930s, Arizona's female legislators redefined the existing parameters for women politicians and sponsored bills concerned with taxation, water codes, and mining laws on an equal basis with the men of the legislature. The lives of most female candidates were intimately connected to the politics of the state because they worked as teachers, business owners, lawyers, ferryboat pilots, government clerks, ranchers, and mine owners and therefore understood the problems of all their constituents, both male and female. When Jessie Bevan campaigned for reelection from Cochise County in 1932, she pointed to her work on three committees—Education, Mines and Mining, and Public Institutions—noting that she was the only candidate in the race who truly understood the needs of all the county's residents, including its children, widows, and miners.[2]

Women's early successes in the legislature established a permanent role for them in state politics, allowing easier access for the female candidates who followed. As Arizona journalist Dorothy Challis Mott accurately predicted in 1930: "No doubt as the years go on a larger and yet larger number will be elected to the state law making bodys [sic] until their strength cannot be denied and their ultimate goal will have been accomplished." By the time of Munds's death in 1948, women were no longer anomalies but veteran politicians, able to win multiple elections and hold prominent positions on committees.[3]

The importance of the work completed by female politicians before 1950 in Arizona becomes more apparent when viewed in comparison with the accomplishments of women in California, a state that saw few early victories. After gaining the right to vote in 1911, women in California faced fierce opposition in running for the legislature. Women's clubs and political parties were unsupportive of their campaigns. Only 14 of the 366 female candidates for the California Assembly won seats between 1912 and 1968. After the modern woman's movement, female representation escalated rapidly to between 10 and 15 percent in the 1980s, and it finally reached 20 percent in the 1990s. Political scientist Beth Reingold conducted a study comparing female legislators in California and Arizona in the 1990s and discovered startling differences between the two groups. In California, women were relative newcomers to politics in the 1990s and felt they were very much in the minority in the state assembly. In interviews they revealed that they believed they were working as outsiders in a hostile environment, and they tended to place priorities on issues concerning women and children over other legislation. The study also revealed that women held twice as many seats in the Arizona legislature in 1998 as their California counterparts, were less likely to represent women's interests, did not view their gender as a disadvantage, and enjoyed higher status in the legislature. The difference was that Arizona women had started in politics much earlier. In the 1910s and 1920s they were the outsiders, campaigning on women's issues. By 1950 they had established themselves as legitimate politicians, drawing powerful committee assignments, introducing important legislation, and beginning the transition from minority status to that of equal partners in government. Once they established themselves in the state legislature, they were ready to advance to statewide office.[4]

At the state level, competition was intense, campaign expenses were high, and public attitudes were biased against female candidates. An individual legislator or a lone county official wields little influence, but state executive officers control budgets, hire and fire personnel, and establish policy in their departments. Although many women believed they were entitled to representation in state office, especially as superintendent of public instruction and secretary of state, the voting public did not agree. Only Ana Frohmiller, as state auditor, was successful in holding state office for more than one term before 1950.

Throughout the years from 1883 to 1950, women tested the limits of female participation in Arizona politics. As a group, they would not emerge as a political force until after the modern woman's movement, but as individuals, some women did achieve and wield political power. Sometimes they achieved this power in geographic clusters, such as the women who represented Yuma County and Maricopa County for so many years. Some women, including Frances Munds, Nellie Bush, and Isabella Greenway, challenged male political bosses. Their personal experiences growing up under harsh conditions, living in tents or log cabins, hauling water, and navigating rivers prepared them for the rough world of male politics. Their lives were not defined by domestic responsibilities, church, women's clubs, and civic activities. They also worked outside the home, raised families without husbands, and paid the bills. Most women in the United States would not have similar experiences until the 1960s and 1970s, when women entered the workforce in large numbers and discovered that they were not given equal protection under the law. Arizona women were forced to face this reality early in state history, and it jarred them into demanding equal rights and representation in government. By the time of the modern woman's movement, when women in most other states were just receiving their political baptism, Arizona's female politicians had already paid their dues and were poised to advance to the next level.

Epilogue

A comprehensive history of women in Arizona politics after 1950 remains unwritten. What follows is a brief overview of some of their accomplishments.

In the 1950s women made rapid progress and captured 11 percent of the total legislature and almost 14 percent of the house. Other states would not experience similar gains by women until the 1970s, after the modern women's movement. By 1960, every county except Graham had sent a woman to the state legislature. These female representatives resembled the women who had preceded them in many ways. Most were married, college educated, born or raised in western states, active in women's clubs and political parties, and worked outside the home. Eleven of the seventeen women elected in the 1950s represented Maricopa County, all served in the house, and all were Anglos. Whereas earlier female legislators were drawn from business, ranching, the law, or education, the female representatives of the 1950s were more likely to come from the emerging service sector and were real estate brokers, nurses, or insurance agents. Their political affiliation changed abruptly as well: of the seventeen women serving in the 1950s, nine were Republicans and eight Democrats. Only three Republican women had been elected to the house before 1950, but now, because of the work done by Emma Parsons and Margaret Adams Rockwell in organizing the Woman's Republican Club and a party women's division in the 1940s, GOP women were energized to take advantage of the shift in state politics more quickly than men. During the 1950s only 30 percent of the total legislature was Republican, but more than half of all female representatives came from the GOP.[1]

Another significant change in the 1950s was the increase in the number of women appointed to the legislature. Appointments are used to reward service to a political party, and no woman was appointed until Isabella Greenway's organizational work in 1928 resulted in a flurry of female Democratic appointments in the 1930s. During the 1940s, women did not receive appointments because returning veterans were given priority over women for their war service. But starting in 1949, when Polly Rosenbaum assumed her husband's seat, appointments were once again used to reward female party workers, and 30 percent of all women in the legislature (five Democrats and one Republican) were appointed from 1950 to 1960. Democrat Thelma Bollinger replaced her husband in the senate, but the other five filled open seats created by the death or resignation of an unrelated legislator or by reapportionment. Once in the legislature, these women usually ran numerous times and represented their districts for years.[2]

In the wake of the civil rights movement, African American women began to make advancements in Arizona politics. Ethel Maynard, a Democrat from Tucson, became the first African American woman elected to the legislature, in 1966. Maynard, a nurse and community activist, had moved to Arizona in 1946 and was married to a doctor. She served as an officer of the Tucson Council for Civic Unity, an organization that worked to desegregate public facilities and housing, and on the executive board of the National Association for the Advancement of Colored People.[3]

Although American Indians were granted full rights of citizenship in 1924 when Congress passed the Indian Citizenship Act, the Arizona State Supreme Court decided in 1928, in *Porter v. Hall*, that a person living on a reservation was like a person under guardianship and therefore, according to the Arizona Constitution, ineligible to vote. It was not until 1948 that the Arizona State Supreme Court overruled *Porter* in *Harrison v. Laveen*, and American Indians were allowed to vote in the state. Eighteen years later, in 1966, the first American Indian, Lloyd House, an Apache from Window Rock, was elected to the Arizona State Legislature. Residents of reservations, however, did not win the right to run for elected office until 1973, when a member of the Navajo reservation, Tom Shirley, contested the issue in the Arizona Supreme Court. Shirley won a seat on the Apache County Board of Supervisors in 1973, but Anglo board members refused to certify his election because he did not own property. The state supreme court decided in Shirley's favor, and he was allowed to hold elective office. By the mid-1970s American Indians were exercising more power and voting in large numbers, but not until 1996 was the first woman, Debora Norris, a member of the Navajo nation, elected to the legislature.[4]

In 1941, LULAC, the League of United Latin American Citizens, was established in Phoenix to foster ethnic pride and fight discrimination.

Mexican American women became active in LULAC, labor unions, and Parent Teacher Associations after World War II. But only Mexican American men ran for public office in Arizona until 1973, when Carmen Cajero of Tucson was appointed to fill her husband's seat in the state legislature. She served until 1996.[5]

Many white female college students working for black voting rights in the South in the 1960s began to realize that women were marginalized in business, politics, and education. Ever since the success of the national suffrage movement in 1920, women's issues had been in retreat. In the 1960s and 1970s, many of the arguments raised by Alice Paul and the Business and Professional Women's Clubs in the 1920s concerning equal rights in the workplace again took center stage as moderate groups such as the League of Women Voters joined liberal feminists in the National Organization for Women and radical feminists on college campuses to demand the Equal Rights Amendment.[6]

As public opinion toward women changed in the 1960s, many of the old obstacles women had faced in politics began to disappear. In the Arizona legislature in the 1960s, veteran house members such as Isabel Burgess and Edna Thode were elected to the senate in the 1960s, and female representation surged to 14 percent in the house. Lorna Lockwood continued to pioneer women's roles in the judiciary. In 1965 she became the nation's first female chief justice of a state supreme court. Her pioneering work as a female jurist attracted national attention as well, and she was recommended by Senator Carl Hayden for appointment to vacancies on the U.S. Supreme Court in 1965 and 1967. Lockwood was passed over and did not become the first woman on the highest court, but she said, "I don't think a woman should be denied a seat on the court just because she is a woman and I don't think she should be given one just on the basis of being a woman either. The job is too important to be judged on this basis alone." In 1968 Polly Rosenbaum and the other seven women in the house—Etta Mae Hutcheson, Elizabeth Rockwell, Ethel Maynard, Bess Stinson, Gladys Gardner, Polly Getzwiller, and Ruth Peck—sat down together and eliminated all language that discriminated against women in state laws. They tried to pass a concurrent resolution to amend the state constitution to eliminate the requirement that only "male citizens" could hold statewide office. The bill never made it out of committee.[7]

In the 1970s, women made inroads in municipal and state government that had eluded their predecessors. They increasingly sought seats on city councils, capturing almost 12 percent of those positions by 1978, and began to use their experience on municipal boards and committees to run for mayor. Margaret Hance was an early member of the Young Republicans and had worked with the Phoenix Parks and Recreation Advisory Board and with the Charter Government Committee in the early 1970s. Despite her strong qualifications and name recognition with voters, Hance was bypassed as a candidate for Phoenix mayor by the Charter Government Committee because she was a woman. With the help of mostly female volunteers, she launched an independent campaign and won a decisive victory in 1975 to become one of the first female mayors of a major city. Her leadership provided a powerful catalyst for other women, and by the time she stepped down in 1983, women were 11 percent of the state's mayors.[8]

Progress in the legislature escalated in the 1970s. Ten percent of the senate and almost 17 percent of the house was female in 1970, and by the end of the decade women had captured 20 percent of all legislative seats, a level not achieved in most other states for another twenty years. The fifty-seven women who sat in the legislature in the 1970s and 1980s created a strong pool of candidates capable of moving to higher office, such as Karan English, who served in the legislature from 1987 to 1992 before becoming Arizona's second female representative to Congress.

Over the years, women in Arizona always had to fight for acceptance by male political leaders. The parties rarely supported females for high office unless they were put up to run as "hopeless candidates," and Democrats had all but sabotaged Ana Frohmiller's campaign for governor. The attitudes of some leading politicians finally changed in the 1970s, and women found their strongest allies in two Democratic governors. In 1977, when Governor Raul Castro was appointed an ambassador, Secretary of State Wesley Bolin became governor and appointed Rose Mofford to his old position to reward her for years of service in the state treasurer's office. When Bolin died in office after only four months of service, Bruce Babbitt, the attorney general, was next in line because Mofford was appointed, not elected, as secretary of state. Babbitt continued the process begun by Bolin of appointing women to high-ranking boards and offices in the state, regardless of their political affiliation. Because so many women in the state had excellent business and political experience, Babbitt found numerous qualified candidates and during his nine years in office appointed women to 30 percent of the 2,100 positions in government. By 1985 the state ranked fifth in the nation for women holding cabinet-level offices. Not only were women finally rewarded for the many years they had served in government, but many were able to take advantage of their appointments to move even farther up the political ladder. In 1985 Governor Babbitt appointed Republican Betsey Bayless to run the Arizona Department of Administration. Subsequently, Bayless served on the Maricopa County Board of Supervisors before her election as secretary of state in 1998.[9]

Another Republican woman who benefited from a Babbitt appointment was Sandra Day O'Connor. She had grown up on her family's ranch in the remote southeastern corner of Arizona, not far from Isabella Greenway's ranch, where she was the only female participant in the annual cattle roundups and performed chores alongside the cowboys. The family had no indoor plumbing, running water, or electricity during the 1930s, and if something needed to be fixed, she had to do it herself. O'Connor commented in her autobiography that it "was no country for sissies, then or now." Like so many Arizona female politicians who came before her, she grew into a confident and independent woman. Her intelligence and work ethic allowed her to graduate third in her class from Stanford law school in 1952, but when she went looking for a job, potential employers wanted to know how well she typed. She was told by one California interviewer, "If you type well enough, I might be able to get you a job as a legal secretary. But we have never hired a woman as a lawyer here. And we don't anticipate doing it." The story would have sounded familiar to Lorna Lockwood, Loretta Savage, Alice Birdsall, Olive Failor, and the other female lawyers who came before O'Connor. Like them, O'Connor turned to public office as an alternative.[10]

After exemplary work in the Arizona attorney general's office, O'Connor was rewarded with an appointment by the Republican party to fill a seat in the Arizona State Senate vacated by Isabel Burgess when Burgess was appointed to serve on the National Transportation Safety Board in Washington, D.C., in 1970. O'Connor, with no prior elective office experience, initially had doubts about her qualifications. "I lacked any legislative experience, and I didn't know how that body operated. But because of my legal training and state experience, I was immediately made chairman of the State, County, and Municipal Affairs Committee."

O'Connor quickly went to work revising aspects of Arizona law that discriminated against women, and she supported the Equal Rights Amendment. Her fellow senators selected her senate majority leader, the first female in a majority leadership position in U.S. history. In 1974 she was elected to Lorna Lockwood's old seat on the Maricopa County Superior Court, and her work on the court led Governor Babbitt to appoint her to the state appellate court in 1979. There she drew the attention of the Reagan administration, which in 1981 appointed her the first female justice on the U.S. Supreme Court. In 1995, the Frances Lillian Willard Munds Award was created to honor the accomplishments of modern women who had fulfilled Munds's vision of equal participation in Arizona politics. The first recipient was Supreme Court Justice Sandra Day O'Connor.[11]

Although many prejudices against female office holders in Arizona had been laid to rest by the 1980s, women still faced stiff resistance when it came to the office of governor. In 1986, after twelve years serving as the state's superintendent of public instruction, Carolyn Warner won the Democratic primary nomination for governor. Isabella Greenway had been encouraged by President Franklin Roosevelt, and Senator Barry Goldwater had pressed Sandra Day O'Connor to run for governor, but both women had declined. Warner was only the second woman, after Ana Frohmiller, to be nominated for governor in Arizona. Business and political leaders were unhappy with Warner's selection and encouraged Democratic businessman William Schulz to enter as an independent, which split the Democratic vote. Like Frohmiller, Warner had difficulty raising funds for her campaign and narrowly lost to Republican Mormon car dealer Evan Mecham. Ironically, Warner's loss would set the stage for the first woman to become Arizona's governor just two years later.[12]

Ever since Frances Munds had run for secretary of state in 1916, voters and politicians had worried that a woman might become governor through the back door of the office of secretary of state, and that was just what happened. Rose Mofford was appointed secretary of state in 1977 and served in that position until 1988, when Evan Mecham was removed from office and she became governor. In 1988, with Mofford as governor, a ballot proposition was overwhelmingly approved by voters that finally eliminated the clause in Article V, Section 2, of the state constitution stating that only men were qualified to hold statewide executive office. Jane Hull replaced Mofford as secretary of state and became governor

From left to right: Superintendent of Public Instruction Lisa Graham-Keegan; Attorney General Janet Napolitano, Governor Jane Hull, former state legislator Edwynne "Polly" Rosenbaum, Supreme Court Justice Sandra Day O'Connor, Treasurer Carol Springer, and Secretary of State Betsey Bayless at the 1999 Arizona inauguration.

in 1997 when Governor Fife Symington was forced to resign after being convicted of bank fraud charges.[13]

In 1998, women captured the top five positions in Arizona state government and occupied 37 percent of the seats in the state legislature. None of the women elected to state executive office was a newcomer to politics. Jane Hull was elected to the Arizona house in 1978 and served first as majority whip and then as speaker of the house. Lisa Graham-Keegan used her experience in the legislature from 1991 to 1994 to run successfully for superintendent of public instruction, and Carol Springer served in the legislature from 1991 to 1998 before her election as state treasurer. Betsey Bayless campaigned for secretary of state on her experience as director of the Department of Administration and Maricopa County Supervisor, and Janet Napolitano started her political career as U.S. attorney for the District of Arizona before her election as state attorney general. When Napolitano was elected governor in 2002, Arizona became the first state to have two elected female governors in succession. Female representation in the legislature dipped from a high of 37 percent in 1998 to 34 percent in 2006 as many women moved up the political ladder to head government agencies or run for higher office. In 2006 Gabrielle Giffords became the state's third congresswoman, and Arizona led the nation with the most women in legislative, executive, and judicial positions. Almost 39 percent of state positions were held by women. In a state traditionally known for its political conservatism, Arizona's female politicians continue to challenge conventional notions about a woman's role in politics.[14]

Appendix

Women Elected and Appointed to the Arizona Legislature, 1914–1950

Women Elected and Appointed to the Arizona Legislature, 1914–1950

Name	County	Office and years	Party[a]	Religion	Highest level of education	Occupation	Place of birth	Marital status[b]
Rachel Berry	Apache	House, 1914–15	D	LDS	Secondary	Teacher	Utah	M
Frances Munds	Yavapai	Senate, 1914–15	D	Baptist, Christian Science	Secondary	Teacher, businesswoman	California	M
Theodora Marsh	Santa Cruz	House, 1916–17	D	None noted	Normal school	Teacher, business owner	Illinois	W
Rosa McKay	Cochise, Gila	House, 1916–19, 1922–23	D	Presbyterian	Elementary	Homemaker	Colorado	M
Pauline O'Neill	Maricopa	House, 1916–19	D	Catholic	Normal school	Teacher	California	WM
Nellie Hayward	Cochise	House, 1918–19	D	Unspecified Christian	Business college	Clerical	Illinois	WM
Anna Westover	Yuma	House, 1918–19	D	Baptist	Secondary	Newspaper owner	Kentucky	M
C. Louise Boehringer	Yuma	House, 1920–21	D	Lutheran	Postgraduate	Teacher, school administrator	Illinois	S
Nellie Bush	Yuma	House, 1920–23, 1926–27, 1930–33; Senate, 1934–35; House, 1940–41	D	Methodist	Postgraduate	Lawyer, business owner	Missouri	M
Vernettie Ivy	Maricopa	House, 1922–23, 1926–29	D	Unspecified Christian	Normal school	Teacher, homemaker	Missouri	M
Freeda Marks	Maricopa	House, 1922–23	R	Jewish	Secondary	Homemaker	Russia	M

Name	County	Office and years	Party[a]	Religion	Highest level of education	Occupation	Place of birth	Marital status[b]
Gladys Walker	Santa Cruz	House, 1926–27	D	Episcopalian	Postgraduate	Teacher	Nogales, AZ	S
Ione Breinholt	Maricopa	House, 1928–29	R	LDS	Secondary	Homemaker	Mesa, AZ	M
Virginia Harris	Yuma	House, 1928–29	D	Nonsectarian	College	Mine owner	Georgia	M
Annie C. Jones	Yavapai	House, 1928–33	D	Episcopalian	Some college	Clerical, library	Virginia[c]	S
Mary Alice Patterson	Maricopa	House, 1928–29	D	LDS	Some college	Teacher, stenographer	Utah	M
Jessie Bevan	Cochise	House, 1930–33	D	Episcopalian	Some postgraduate	Teacher	Utah	W
Blanche Cavness	Maricopa	House, 1930–31	D	Catholic	Unknown	Homemaker	Pinal, AZ	M
Mary Francis[d]	Maricopa	House, 1930–33	D	Unknown	Secondary	Homemaker	New Jersey	W
Rose Godfrey[d]	Maricopa	House, 1930–31	D	Presbyterian	Secondary	Homemaker, landlord	Iowa[c]	M
Gertrude Leeper	Maricopa	House, 1930–31	D	Methodist	College	Newspaper editor	Tennessee	M
Bridgie Porter	Maricopa	House, 1930–37	D	Catholic	Secondary	Clerical	Illinois[c]	WM
Harriet Sprague[d]	Maricopa	House, 1930–31	D	Methodist	Secondary	Printer, nurse	Missouri[c]	M
Mary Kelley[d]	Gila	House, 1932–33	D	Catholic	Secondary	Homemaker	Iowa	W
Fritzi Struckmeyer	Maricopa	House, 1936–37	D	Episcopalian	College	Journalist, teacher	Phoenix, AZ	S
Lorna Lockwood	Maricopa	House, 1938–41, 1946–47	D	Congregationalist	Postgraduate	Attorney	Douglas, AZ	S

Women Elected and Appointed to the Arizona Legislature, 1914–1950 (continued)

Name	County	Office and years	Party[a]	Religion	Highest level of education	Occupation	Place of birth	Marital status[b]
Laura McRae	Maricopa	House, 1938–55	D	LDS	College	Homemaker	Safford, AZ	M
Maxine Brubaker	Maricopa	House, 1940–41	D	Unspecified Christian	Postgraduate	Business owner, teacher	Phoenix, AZ	M
Louise Moore	Maricopa	House, 1940–41	D	Catholic	College	Teacher	Texas	M
Claire Phelps	Maricopa	House, 1940–47	D	Episcopalian	Postgraduate	Rancher, homemaker	Mississippi	M
Clara Botzum	Yuma	House, 1942–49, 1958–61	D	Christian Science	College	Mine owner, secretary	Indiana[c]	D
Eva Decker	Navajo	House, 1946–49	R	LDS	College	Homemaker, missionary	Arizona	M
Edwynne Rosenbaum[d]	Gila	House, 1948–94	D	Episcopalian	Postgraduate	Teacher, clerical	Iowa	DW
Mary Dwyer	Maricopa	House, 1950–53	D	Catholic	College	Business owner	Arkansas	D
Julliette Willis	Pima	House, 1950–57	R	Protestant	College	Homemaker	Iowa	M

Sources: Legislative Files, obituary files, ASLAPR.

[a]D = Democrat, R = Republican.

[b]M = Married, S = Single, D = Divorced, W = Widowed.

[c]Moved to the West before age twelve.

[d]Appointed.

Notes

Abbreviations Used in the Notes

AHF	Arizona Historical Foundation, Hayden Library, Arizona State University, Tempe
AHS, Tempe	Arizona Historical Society, Central Archives Collections, Tempe
AHS, Tucson	Arizona Historical Society, Southern Archives Division, Tucson
ASLAPR	Arizona State Library, Archives, and Public Records, Phoenix
ASU	Arizona Collection, Hayden Library, Arizona State University, Tempe
BMHM	Bisbee Mining and Historical Museum, Bisbee
HL	Huntington Library, San Marino, California
KL	King Library, University of Kentucky, Lexington, Kentucky
NAWSA	National American Woman Suffrage Association Records, Stanford University, Stanford, California
PAHS	Parker Area Historical Society, Parker
PPL	Phoenix Public Library, Arizona Room, Burton Barr Central Library, Phoenix
SHM	Sharlot Hall Museum, Prescott

Introduction

1. The only men elected to statewide office in 1998 were the three members of the corporation commission and the state mining inspector. *Chicago Sun-Times*, 31 October 1999; *New York Times*, 6 January 1999.

2. Cox, *Women State and Territorial Legislators*, 29–30; Werner, "Women in Congress, 1917–1964," 40; Center for American Women and Politics, *Facts on Women Candidates and Elected Officials*. Marshall Trimble is quoted in the *Arizona Republic*, 24 March 2006.

3. Hietter, "Lawyers, Guns, and Money."

4. Mead, "How the Vote Was Won," 3.

5. Mead, *How the Vote Was Won*, 2.

6. For a discussion of the relationship between African American and white women during the suffrage campaigns, see Giddings, *When and Where I Enter*, and Terborg-Penn, *African American Women in the Struggle for the Vote, 1850–1920*. Suffragists and English language newspapers at this time often used the term "Americans" to denote people with non-Hispanic, European ancestry, and "Spanish" to represent people originally from Mexico. "White" was often used to describe anyone who was not African American. I have

used the term "Anglo" to identify people of European ancestry and "Mexican American" to define people who traced their ancestry to Mexico.

7. Matthew Whitaker, *Race Work*, 14; Mead, "How the Vote Was Won," 283. Kotlanger, in "Phoenix, Arizona," 396, makes the argument that Phoenix was established to be "run by Anglos for Anglos," but after statehood this assessment applies to the whole state. Although the Voting Rights Act of 1965 abolished literacy requirements for voting, Arizona's state law was not overturned until 1972. Chinese Americans were only a small fraction of Arizona residents, and few of them were American citizens. The female Chinese American population was too small to engage in significant political activity during this period. Luckingham, *Minorities in Phoenix*, 80–83, 84.

8. Cott, *The Grounding of Modern Feminism*, 85; Baker, "The Domestication of Politics"; Young, *Understanding Politics*, 12; Freeman, *A Room at a Time*, 5; Cox, *Women State and Territorial Legislators*, 12–13.

9. Early studies of female politicians in the United States include Breckenridge, *Women in the Twentieth Century*; Gruber, *Women in American Politics*; Young, *Understanding Politics*; Sanders, *The Lady and the Vote*; Werner, "Women in Congress, 1917–1964"; and Cott, *Grounding of Modern Feminism*, 85. Mead, in *How the Vote Was Won*, 172, calls for "a substantive reanalysis of the long-standing historical question of what women did with the vote after it was won" by refocusing on state rather than national studies of female political activity.

10. McCormick and McCormick, *Equality Deferred*, 12–14; Kelly, "Where Conservatism and Feminism Meet," 2; Petrik, *No Step Backward*, xiii. Studies of women in state politics include Andersen, *After Suffrage*; Cox, "The Three Who Came First"; Diamond, *Sex Roles in the State House*; Gordon, *After Winning*; Jensen, "'Disfranchisement Is a Disgrace'"; McCormick and McCormick, *Equality Deferred*; MacKay, "Women in Politics: Power in the Public Sphere"; Muncy, "Women Demand Recognition"; Salas, "Soledad Chávez Chacón, Adelina Otero-Warren, and Concha Ortiz y Pino"; Thompson, "After Suffrage"; and Van Ingen, "Campaigns for Equality."

11. Cox, *Women State and Territorial Legislators*, 29–30. Lotchin, in "Hispanics, Women, and Western Cities," also discusses the states where women were successful.

12. Riley, *Building and Breaking Families*, 5; Guy, "The Economics of Widowhood in Arizona, 1880–1940," 196–97, 211.

Chapter 1. The Battle Begins

1. *Arizona Daily Star*, 21 February 1883; Snapp, "Defeat the Democrats," 28; Gienapp, "'Politics Seem to Enter into Everything,'" 30.

2. Goldberg, *Barry Goldwater*, 2.

3. U.S. Bureau of the Census, *Population of the United States*, 1870, 1880, 1890; Sheridan, *Arizona*, 3, 50–52, 70. Susan L. Johnson provides an excellent discussion of Anglo and Mexican women in early territorial Arizona in "Sharing Bed and Board: Cohabitation and Cultural Difference in Central Arizona Mining Towns."

4. Fischer, "A Profile of Women in Arizona in Frontier Days," 48; Guy, "Economics of Widowhood," 196, 211. The contributions of married women were actually far greater

than these numbers suggest, because census workers did not report women who either took part-time jobs or were not the primary wage earner for the family. Glenda Riley, *Building and Breaking Families in the American West*, 134–36. Melcher, in "Tending Children, Chickens, and Cattle," 2, 46, notes that 33 percent of farms and ranches were without electricity in 1940, and only 15 percent had telephones.

5. Sheridan, *Arizona*, 232–33; Benton, "What about Women in the White Man's Camp?" 143, 276; Guy, "Economics of Widowhood," 196, 201; Sheridan, *Los Tucsonenses*, 142–43; Reynolds, "'We Made Our Life as Best We Could,'" 44. Tuberculosis was estimated to affect 10 percent of the U.S. population at the turn of the century. Scientists identified the tuberculosis bacillus in 1900, but doctors had no cure and continued to prescribe a dry climate for those suffering from all forms of bronchial diseases. Thousands of these "health seekers" came to Arizona and lived in tents, regardless of social class, to achieve the perceived benefits of the southwestern air.

6. Barbara Welter, "The Cult of True Womanhood, 1820–1860," 151–74.

7. *The Revolution*, 19 May 1870. See Cott, *The Grounding of Modern Feminism*, for a detailed account of the national suffrage movement.

8. Rothman, *Woman's Proper Place*, 63. On the role of the WCTU, see also Epstein, *The Politics of Domesticity*, and Bordin, *Frances Willard*.

9. West, *The Saloon on the Rocky Mountain Mining Frontier*, 132–38; Berman, *Arizona Politics and Government*, 11; Beeton, *Women Vote in the West*, 7.

10. MacKay, "Women in Politics," 369; Iversen, "The Mormon-Suffrage Relationship," 9–12; Beeton, *Women Vote in the West*, 23–25; Beeton, "How the West Was Won for Woman Suffrage," 107. Polygamy is defined in *Webster's Ninth New Collegiate Dictionary* as "marriage in which a spouse of either sex may have more than one mate at the same time." Mormons practiced polygyny, which is the "practice of having more than one wife or female mate at one time," but most people referred to it as polygamy.

11. Lyman, "Elimination of the Mormon Issue from Arizona Politics, 1889–1894," 206. Arizona legislators passed a law in 1885 requiring a test oath aimed at disfranchising Mormon voters who refused to disavow polygamous marriage.

12. McClintock, *Arizona*, vol. 2, 385–86; Connors, *Who's Who in Arizona*, 602–4.

13. Lykes, "Phoenix Women in the Development of Public Policy," 45; Work Projects Administration (WPA) Pioneer Interviews, Josephine Brawley Hughes, ASLAPR.

14. Boehringer, "Josephine Brawley Hughes," 102; McClintock, *Arizona*, vol. 3, 384; *Phoenix Gazette*, 1 July 1964; Ware, "Alcohol, Temperance and Prohibition in Arizona," 129.

15. Ware, "Alcohol, Temperance and Prohibition," 95, 112; Wagoner, *Arizona Territory, 1863–1912*, 320.

16. "Annual Report of the Arizona Woman's Christian Temperance Union for 1885 and 1887," AHS, Tucson; Tisdale, "The Prohibition Crusade in Arizona," 6; Ware, "Alcohol, Temperance and Prohibition," 129; Lykes, "Phoenix Women in the Development of Public Policy," 34.

17. Connors, *Who's Who in Arizona*, 103, 602–8; McClintock, *Arizona*, vol. 2, 385; Wagoner, *Arizona Territory*, 320.

18. Kasper, "Arizona's First Woman Lawyer," 1, 4, 6, 8.

19. Pry, "Statehood Politics and Territorial Development," 408–9; *Arizona Gazette*, 19 September 1891.

20. Boehringer, "Josephine Brawley Hughes," 103.

21. *Arizona Daily Gazette*, 4 February 1899; "Proceedings of the 30th Annual Convention," NAWSA Records, 13–19 February 1899; Graham, *Woman Suffrage and the New Democracy*, 8.

22. Louis Hughes was forced to resign as territorial governor in 1896 for exercising "undue influence" on the legislature, but his unpopularity probably stemmed more from his liberal views than any actual wrongdoing. Wagoner, *Arizona Territory*, 321; Anthony and Harper, *The History of Woman Suffrage*, vol. 4, 472–73.

23. Berman, *Reformers, Corporations*, 33–34.

24. Ibid., 22; Larson, *Populism in the Mountain West*.

25. Pry, "Statehood Politics and Territorial Development," 422; Sheridan, *Arizona*, 173; Berman, *Reformers, Corporations*, 18–26.

26. Buckey O'Neill to N. O. Murphy and John Hendron, 12 October 1894, William O'Neill Collection, SHM; Berman, *Reformers, Corporations*, 37; Tessman, "Buckey O'Neill, Rough Rider and Fiction Writer," 21–22.

27. Foster, "The Right Kind of Girl," 33–35, 42.

28. Buckey O'Neill to James McClintock, 14 July 1897, McClintock Collection, PPL; Lauerman, "Desexing the Ballot Box," 12; Frances Munds, "Report for the National Suffrage Convention, 1910," Women's Suffrage Collection, ASLAPR.

29. Mead, *How the Vote Was Won*, 68–69, 92–95; Marilley, *Woman Suffrage and the Origins of Liberal Feminism in the United States, 1820 to 1920*, 155; Beeton, "How the West Was Won," 113.

30. *Arizona Gazette*, 9 February 1899.

31. Foster, "Right Kind of Girl," 39–40, 42. The Prescott Women's Club changed its name to the Monday Club to end criticism that it was a suffrage club. Laura Gregg described it as the most conservative club she had met with in some time. Laura Gregg to Anna Howard Shaw, 9 October 1909, Women's Suffrage Collection, ASLAPR.

32. *Arizona Daily Gazette*, 8 February 1899; Catt and Shuler, *Woman Suffrage and Politics*, 129; Anthony and Harper, *The History of Woman Suffrage*, vol. 4, 472–73. Thomas Lauerman asserts that Goldwater was not even present for the initial vote to bring the bill out of committee and that he voted with the minority the second time the motion was defeated. Lauerman, "Desexing the Ballot Box," 13. Morris Goldwater was Senator Barry Goldwater's uncle. During the territorial period, the upper house of the legislature was called the council. After statehood it was renamed the senate.

33. *Arizona Daily Gazette*, 15 February 1899; Berman, *Arizona Politics and Government*, 9–11; Lamar, *The Far Southwest, 1846–1912*, 17.

34. Berman, *Reformers, Corporations*, 71–75.

35. Ibid., 69–72.

36. *Woman's Journal*, 14 February 1903; Frances Munds to James McClintock, 4 April 1915, McClintock Collection, PPL.

37. *Arizona Republican*, 17 March 1903.

38. Fowler, *Carrie Catt*, 82; Frances Munds to Alice Park, 27 January 1913, Alice L. Park Papers, HL.

39. Harper, *History of Woman Suffrage*, vol. 6, 10; Frances Munds to James McClintock, 4 April 1915, McClintock Collection, PPL; *Arizona Republican*, 17 and 19 March 1903. Ironically, the suffrage movement's male champion, Kean St. Charles, was a well-known alcoholic. Over the years, his sobriety was a concern to Munds. In 1909, when she made the last big legislative push for suffrage, she told Laura Clay that she was counting on St. Charles to convince another legislator to change his vote. "I told him to do it, and he will, if he stays sober long enough." Frances Munds to Laura Clay, 11 February 1909, Clay Collection, KL.

40. Frances Munds to James McClintock, 4 and 15 April 1915, McClintock Collection, PPL; McClintock, *Arizona*, vol. 3, 386; Laura Gregg to Anna Howard Shaw, 1 January 1910, Women's Suffrage Collection, ASLAPR; *Arizona Republican*, 20 March 1903.

41. *Woman's Journal*, 9 May 1903, 146; *Arizona Republican*, 21 March 1903.

42. Frances Munds to James McClintock, 15 April 1915, McClintock Collection, PPL; McClintock, *Arizona*, vol. 3, 386; Frances Munds report to NAWSA, 1910, Women's Suffrage Collection, ASLAPR.

43. Frances Munds to Mary Colista Willard Scott, 27 March 1903, held privately by L. Spencer Leister, courtesy of Karen Willard, both descendents of Alexander Hamilton Willard Sr.; Anthony and Harper, *History of Woman Suffrage*, vol. 4, 472–73; Pauline O'Neill to Laura Clay, 3 April 1909, Clay Collection, KL.

44. Harper, *History of Woman Suffrage*, vol. 6, 11; Lykes, "Phoenix Women," 47; Williams, *History of Valuable Pioneers of the State of Arizona*, 75.

Chapter 2. The Battle Is Won

1. Mead, *How the Vote Was Won*, 3, 67, and 94, discusses the nonpartisan bent of NAWSA.

2. Fuller, *Laura Clay and the Woman's Rights Movement*, 106–8.

3. Maxwell, *A Passion for Freedom*, 106–8. Hall's appointment brought up the question of the legality of female office holding, "but the Governor [Sloan], a lawyer of long acquaintance with the territorial statutes, has concluded that his action will stand review." *Los Angeles Times*, 2 October 1909.

4. Frances Munds to Laura Clay, 7, 8, 9, and 11 February 1909, Laura Clay Collection, KL; *Journal of the Arizona House of Representatives*, 1909; *Journal of the Arizona Senate*, 1909; Fuller, *Laura Clay*, 105–6; Goodman, *Bitter Harvest*, 49.

5. Laura Clay to Pauline O'Neill, 31 March 1909, Clay Collection, KL.

6. Frances Willard Munds biography file, ASLAPR; Williams, *Valuable Pioneers*, 9–10.

7. Willard, *An Old-timer's Scrapbook*, 27–28; Williams, *Valuable Pioneers*, 41.

8. John Munds (grandson of Frances Munds) to Heidi Osselaer, 24 October 1994. Frances was the fifth cousin, once removed, of Frances Elizabeth Lillian Willard of the WCTU. Karen Willard, Willard family genealogist, e-mail to author, 31 August 2007.

9. Williams, *Valuable Pioneers*, 17–18; Karen Willard, Willard family genealogist, e-mail to author, 31 August 2007.

10. Williams, *Valuable Pioneers*, 20–23; Dolph Willard Memoirs, SHM, 3–5.

11. Willard, *Old-timer's Scrapbook*, 27, 57; Williams, *Valuable Pioneers*, 28–29, 36–41; Berman, *Reformers, Corporations*, 16.

12. Williams, *Valuable Pioneers*, 39.

13. Ibid., 38, 41; *Arizona Republic*, 19 April, 1931.

14. John Munds biography file, SHM.

15. Telephone interview with John Munds, grandson of Frances Munds, 15 October, 1994; Laura Gregg to Anna Howard Shaw, 22 December 1909, Women's Suffrage Collection, ASLAPR.

16. Frances Munds to Mary Colista Willard Scott, 27 March 1903, held privately by L. Spencer Leister, courtesy of Karen Willard, both descendents of Alexander Hamilton Willard Sr.

17. The percentage of Mormon leaders could have been higher. Religious and organizational affiliations could not be identified for all members. Berman, *Reformers, Corporations*, 10; Snapp, "Defeat the Democrats," 33–34.

18. Laura Gregg to Frances Munds, 24 November 1909, Laura Gregg to Anna Howard Shaw, 9 October 1909 and 1 January 1910, Women's Suffrage Collection, ASLAPR.

19. Anna Howard Shaw to Laura Gregg, 23 March 1910, Women's Suffrage Collection, ASLAPR.

20. Frances Munds to Laura Clay, 8 February 1909, Clay Collection, KL; Berman, "Gender and Issue Voting after Suffrage Expansion in Arizona," 844–47; Laura Gregg to Frances Munds, 24 November 1909, Laura Gregg to Anna Howard Shaw, 9 October and 22 December 1909 and 1 January 1910, Inez Lee to Mary Sumner Boyd, 10 February 1917, Women's Suffrage Collection, ASLAPR.

21. Laura Gregg to Anna Howard Shaw, 1 January 1910.

22. Goodman, *Bitter Harvest*, 49.

23. Connors, *Who's Who in Arizona*, 612–15; *Portrait and Biographical Record*, 225; Eppinga, "Dr. Rosa Goodrich Boido, M.D.," 1–4, 10.

24. Howard, "Creating an Enchanted Land," 53; *Messenger*, 3 February 1917; Sheridan, *Los Tucsonenses*, 108–9, 114–18, 140–42; Eppinga, "Dr. Rosa Goodrich Boido," 1–4.

25. Jensen, "'Disfranchisement Is a Disgrace,'" 599.

26. Fuller, *Laura Clay and the Woman's Rights Movement*, 105; Laura Gregg to Anna Howard Shaw, 1 January 1910, Women's Suffrage Collection, ASLAPR; Laura Clay to Harriet Taylor Upton, 4 March 1909, Clay Collection, KL; Harper, *History of Woman Suffrage*, vol. 6, 14; Luckingham, *Minorities in Phoenix*, 49; Benton, "What about Women?" 296; U.S. Bureau of the Census, *Population of the United States*, 1910, 585; Sheridan, *Los Tucsonenses*, 178. The African American community was less affected by the literacy test, with an 8.4 percent illiteracy rate. The illiteracy rate for native-born whites was 3.3 percent.

27. *Progressive Weekly*, 15 February 1913; Berman, *Reformers, Corporations*, 75.

28. Laura Gregg to Caroline I. Reilly, 26 December 1910, Women's Suffrage Collection, ASLAPR; Laura Clay's report to the NAWSA board, 29 March 1909, Clay Collection, KL.

29. Will H. Robinson, *The Story of Arizona*, 358–59.

30. Kearney, "Arizona Legislature 1912–1914," 237; Berman, "Male Support for Woman Suffrage," 291; *Arizona Republican*, 19 October 1912.

31. Sheridan, *Arizona*, 175–76; *Progressive Weekly*, 15 February 1913. Byrkit, in *Forging the Copper Collar*, 47, notes that all of Pima County's delegation to the convention was conservative and voted against ratification.

32. Frances Munds to Anna Howard Shaw, 23 February 1910, Women's Suffrage Collection, ASLAPR.

33. Laura Gregg to Anna Howard Shaw, 16 March and 31 May 1910, Women's Suffrage Collection, ASLAPR; Laura Clay to Mrs. John L. Munds, 26 March 1909, Clay Collection, KL.

34. Hunt Biography, George W. P. Hunt Collection, Arizona Collection, Hayden Library, ASU.

35. "The Right of Franchise to Women," Women's Suffrage Collection, ASLAPR; Frances Munds to George Hunt, 20 and 24 August 1910, Hunt Collection, Arizona Collection, ASU; Berman, "Male Support for Woman Suffrage," 282–83.

36. Frances Munds to George Hunt, 24 August 1910, Hunt Collection, Arizona Collection, ASU.

37. *Arizona Republican*, 3 November 1910; *Progressive Weekly*, 15 February 1913; Laura Gregg to Caroline I. Reilly, 26 December 1910, Women's Suffrage Collection, ASLAPR.

38. Frances Munds to George Hunt, 27 January 1911, Hunt Collection, Arizona Collection, ASU.

39. *Progressive Weekly*, 15 February 1913; Frances Munds's report to *Woman's Journal*, 1913, Women's Suffrage Collection, ASLAPR; Byrkit, *Copper Collar*, 44; Berman, *Reformers, Corporations*, 32–33; Pry, "Arizona and the Politics of Statehood," 263.

40. Berman, *Reformers, Corporations*, 92; *Woman's Journal*, 13 April 1912; Frances Munds to George Hunt, 10 November 1910, Hunt Collection, Arizona Collection, ASU. Frances Munds to J. H. McClintock, 4 April 1915, McClintock Collection, PPL, summarizes the suffrage battle.

41. *Miners Magazine*, 2 May 1912.

42. Frances Munds to James McClintock, 4 April 1915, McClintock Collection, PPL; *Graham County Guardian*, 16 February and 14 June 1912; *Woman's Journal*, 13 April and 10 July 1912; Fowler, *Carrie Catt*, 82; Shaw, *The Story of a Pioneer*, 302; *Arizona Gazette*, 3, 5, and 12 October 1912; 1912 Women's Suffrage Initiative Petitions, ASLAPR.

43. *Woman's Journal*, 13 October 1912; *Arizona Gazette*, 7 September 1912; Frances Munds's report to *Woman's Journal*, 1913, Women's Suffrage Collection, ASLAPR; Williams, *Valuable Pioneers*, 77; Frances Munds to Mac Willard, 5 September 1916, Hunt Collection, Arizona Collection, ASU. There is no evidence that Madge Udall was related to the politically prominent Udall family of Arizona.

44. *Woman's Journal*, 7 and 14 September, 2 November 1912.

45. *Arizona Gazette*, 4 November 1912; *Parker Post*, 2 November, 1912.

46. *Graham County Guardian*, 1 November 1912; Munds, "Do Arizona Women Want the Ballot?" Munds biography file, Arizona Collection, ASU.

47. Munds, "Do Arizona Women Want the Ballot?" Munds biography file, Arizona Collection, ASU; Angela H. Hammer to Frances Munds, 17 February 1910, Women's Suffrage Collection, ASLAPR.

48. *Arizona Gazette*, 12 and 25 October, 7 September 1912.

49. Berman, *Reformers, Corporations*, 69, 71; *Progressive Weekly*, 15 February 1913. Berman, in "Male Support for Woman Suffrage," 286, and "Voters, Candidates, and Issues in the Progressive Era," 257, confirms that support for suffrage was significantly higher among Socialist voters than among members of any other political party.

50. *Arizona Gazette*, 7 September 1912; *Woman's Journal*, 5 October 1912; *Progressive Weekly*, 15 February 1913; "Report to the National, 1911–1912," Women's Suffrage Collection, ASLAPR; Berman, "Male Support for Woman Suffrage," 283.

51. *Arizona Gazette*, 30 September, 3 and 5 October 1912; "Minutes of the Suffrage Convention, Arizona report by Frances Willard Munds, 1912," Women's Suffrage Collection, ASLAPR; *Progressive Weekly*, 15 February 1913.

52. *Progressive Weekly*, 15 February 1913; *Arizona Gazette*, 30 September 1912.

53. Frances Munds to Alice Park, 21 November 1912, Alice L. Park Collection, HL.

54. Ibid. Davis did not win a U.S. Senate seat.

55. Shaw, *The Story of A Pioneer*, 301–2; Robinson, *The Story of Arizona*, 354, 356; Berman, "Male Support for Woman Suffrage," 286. Berman, in "Voters, Candidates, and Issues," 257, states that turnout was just 29 percent of eligible male voters.

56. Laura Clay to NAWSA Official Board, 29 March 1909, Clay Collection, KL; Frances Munds to Alice Parks, 21 November 1912, Park Collection, HL; *Progressive Weekly*, 15 February 1913; *Arizona Gazette*, 30 September 1912.

57. *Prescott Journal-Miner*, 1 September 1914.

58. *Woman's Journal*, 2 January 1915.

59. Ibid.

Chapter 3. The War Is Not Over

1. *New York Times*, 4 May 1913; *Woman's Journal*, 2 January 1915; Robinson, *The Story of Arizona*, 356.

2. Freeman, *A Room at a Time*, 85; Harvey, *Votes without Leverage*, 112–17, 155.

3. Freeman, *A Room at a Time*, 4–7; Cox, *Women State and Territorial Legislators*, 12–13; Edwards, *Angels in the Machinery*, 8–11.

4. Catt and Shuler, *Woman Suffrage and Politics*, 491; Blair, "Why I Am Discouraged about Women in Politics"; "Many Roads Lead Women into Politics," *New York Times Magazine*, 28 October 1928, 7; Roosevelt and Hickok, *Ladies of Courage*, 38; Ware, *Partner and I*, 150. Similar observations about women in political parties have been made in Low, "Women in the Election," 313; Brown, *Setting a Course*, 68; and Harvey, "Culture or Strategy?" 87–89.

5. Frances Munds to George Hunt, 23 September 1916, Hunt Collection, Arizona Collection, ASU; "Arizona Women Urge Reform," March 19, 1913, Arizona Women in Government file, Arizona Collection, ASLAPR.

6. *Graham County Guardian*, 28 March 1922; James A. Farley to William P. Stuart, 28 February 1936, Stuart Family Papers, Arizona Collection, ASU; Frances Munds to Alice Park, 7 March 1913, Park Collection, HL; Freeman, *A Room at a Time*, 115, 117, 276. Andersen, in *After Suffrage*, 90–91, notes that the other seven states without equal representation were Georgia, Maryland, Mississippi, Nevada, North Dakota, Virginia, and Wisconsin.

7. *Nogales Daily Herald*, 23 September 1920; *Arizona Capitol Times*, 4 January 1984; "History of the Arizona Woman's Republican Club," Joseph and Grace Alexander Papers, Arizona Collection, ASU; Secretary of State, *Arizona Blue Book*, 1925–26. Percentages for third party registration are not included.

8. Reference files, McClintock Collection, PPL; *Arizona Gazette*, 1 January 1920; *Arizona Republic*, 22 August 1999.

9. Susan Seavy, "The Life Story of Nellie Bush," Nellie Bush Collection, PAHS, 317; Frances Munds to George Hunt, 18 November 1914, Women in Government file, Arizona Collection, ASLAPR; *Bisbee Daily Review*, 17 March 1985. Byrkit, in *Copper Collar*, 72, claims that mining companies controlled all aspects of Arizona's economic, political, social, and religious life.

10. Frances Munds to Alice Park, 4 January 1913, Park Collection, HL; *Dunbar's Weekly*, 19 September and 10 October 1914.

11. *Arizona Republican*, 16 August, 4 September, and 3 November 1914; *Parker Post*, 1 June 1912; Goff, *George W. P. Hunt and His Arizona*, 57.

12. *Arizona Republican*, 4 October 1914; *Dunbar's Weekly*, 29 August, 5 September, and 17 October 1914.

13. Berman, *Reformers, Corporations*, 125, 139–40; *Arizona Woman*, August 1930, BPW Collection, AHS, Tempe; *Woman's Journal*, 2 January 1915; *Arizona Republican*, 7 September 1920. J. Morris Richards, in *The History of the Arizona State Legislature*, vol. 4, part 1, 60, comments that "there were some predictions from time to time that certain members would succeed in defeating themselves for reelection by the way they had cast their votes on women's suffrage" as well as other issues. For examples of male politicians proclaiming their pro-suffrage stance, see *The Oasis*, 5 September 1914; *Graham County Guardian*, 31 October 1924; *Prescott Journal-Miner*, 1 November 1914; and *Dunbar's Weekly*, 10 October 1914.

14. Lunardini, *From Equal Suffrage to Equal Rights*, xiii–xiv.

15. Telegram from Mrs. E. B. O'Neill to Dr. Anna Howard Shaw, 8 October 1914, Library of Congress microfiche, O'Neill Collection, NAWSA Records; *Prescott Journal-Miner*, 1 November 1914.

16. "Resolutions of the Women's Woodrow Wilson League of Arizona," Arizona Collection, ASU; "Testimony of the Western States on the Anti-Democratic Policy of the Congressional Union," NAWSA Records; Snapp, "Defeat the Democrats," 137; Pincus, quoted in Lunardini, *From Equal Suffrage to Equal Rights*, 95.

17. *Prescott Journal-Miner*, 18 September 1914; *Woman's Journal*, 16 August 1913.

18. *Woman's Journal*, 1 February 1913; *Bisbee Daily Review*, 2 November 1914; "Governor Campbell Pays High Tribute to Women Voters of State and Political Activities," 1917, Arizona Women in Government file, Arizona Collection, ASLAPR.

19. *Bisbee Daily Review*, 3 November 1914; *Arizona Republican*, 22 August 1914.

20. Ware, "Alcohol, Temperance and Prohibition," 224; *The Oasis*, 12 September 1914; Berman, *Reformers, Corporations*, 121; Berman, "Gender and Issue Voting," 849; *Christian Science Monitor*, 28 April 1915; press release by Grady Gammage, "Arizona," Women's Suffrage Collection, ASLAPR; *Woman's Journal*, 2 January 1915.

21. U.S. Bureau of the Census, *Population of the United States*, 1910; *Arizona Republican*, 4 and 6 September, 3 November 1924; Frances Munds to Alice Park, 27 January 1913, Park Papers, HL.

22. Rothman, *Woman's Proper Place*, 4; Epstein, *The Politics of Domesticity*, 148.

23. Whitaker, *Race Work*, 38; Kotlanger, "Phoenix, Arizona," 463–64.

24. Crudup, "African Americans in Arizona," 322–24; White, quoted in Whitaker, "In Search of Black Phoenicians," 89.

25. Kotlanger, "Phoenix, Arizona," 459, 464; Luckingham, *Minorities in Phoenix*, 34, 53–54, 142; Benton, "What about Women?" 129–30. The state legislature passed a bill in 1923 banning the use of masks for purposes of intimidation, and the KKK's influence waned by 1925.

26. McFarland, "A Power for Good," 84–85; Reynolds, "'We Made Our Life,'" 23.

27. Raquel Rubio-Goldsmith, in "Shipwrecked in the Desert," 40, provides an example of how women in the Mexican religious order known as the Company of Mary "created their own marginal world as an enclave of comfort and solace from the male-dominated existence they experienced." Because Mexican American women before World War II operated within the confines of organizations run by men, rather than in separate female organizations, the work they performed remains almost invisible to historians. Until more research is conducted on these organizations, it is impossible to present an accurate assessment of the extent of Mexican American women's contributions to political life in Arizona. See www.asu.edu/lib/archives/website/intro.htm for more information on the Chicano-Chicana experience in Arizona.

28. *Arizona Federation of Women's Clubs Yearbook*, 1917, AHS, Tempe.

29. Secretary of State, *Arizona Blue Book*, 1915–16, 1923–24, 1927–28; Freeman, *A Room at a Time*, 115, 117, 276; *Arizona Republic*, 21 May 1950.

30. Frances Munds to Alice Park, 27 January 1913, Park Collection, HL.

31. *Arizona Republican*, 4 January 1913.

32. *Woman's Journal*, 16 August 1913; *Arizona Gazette*, 20 January 1915.

33. "Arizona Federation of Women's Clubs Minutes, 1911 to 1924," Alexander Papers, Arizona Collection, ASU; McFarland, "Power for Good," 99.

34. Frances Munds to Grace Alexander, 18 January 1916, Alexander Papers, ASU.

35. "My Memories of Grace Alexander, 1874–1957," by Eleanor Alexander Wiebeck, Alexander Papers, ASU.

36. Grace Alexander to Frances Munds and Mrs. C. M. Roberts, 6 January 1916, Grace Alexander to Pauline O'Neill, 19 February 1917, Alexander Papers, ASU.

37. Grace Alexander to Mary Wood, 15 May 1919, Alexander Papers, ASU; Darnall, "Women and Politics," 19; Gullett, *Becoming Citizen*, 2–5; Van Ingen, "Campaigns for Equality," 265.

38. *Arizona Republican*, 22 March 1919.

39. Sturgeon, "Arizona Women and the Sheppard-Towner Act"; Guy, "Economics of Widowhood," 201–2; Ross, "The Tale Is Told," Ross Papers, Arizona Collection, ASU, 28. The Secretary of State's *Arizona Blue Books* for 1920–30 list members of the child welfare boards.

40. Ross, "The Tale Is Told," Ross Papers, Arizona Collection, ASU, 21. Most women who belonged to neither the AFWC nor the BPW were Mormons, who were active instead in the LDS Relief Society.

41. Arizona Federation of Business and Professional Women, *Women Who Made a Difference*, vol. 1, 3.

42. Cott, *Grounding of Modern Feminism*, 128–29, 141–42. In Arizona in 1910, only thirty-eight women worked in manufacturing. U.S. Bureau of the Census, *Population of the United States*, 1910.

43. Freeman, *A Room at a Time*, 138; *Arizona Republican*, 6 August 1928. Dye, *As Equals and Sisters*, is one example of studies of the WTUL.

44. Arizona Federation of Business and Professional Women, *Women Who Made a Difference*, vol. 1, 21; "Greetings from First State President, Arizona State Federation of B & P W Clubs," B. & P.W.C. of Phoenix, Inc., newsletter, 1944, BPW Collection, ASLAPR.

45. Guy, "Economics of Widowhood," 211; "The Lookout," May 1938, BPW Collection, ASLAPR.

46. Joy, *Angela Hutchinson Hammer*, 138, 148, 177; Angela Hammer to Frances Munds, 17 February 1910, Women's Suffrage Collection, ASLAPR; Arizona Federation of Business and Professional Women, *Women Who Made a Difference*, vol. 1, 55.

47. "Western Women," June–July 1929, "The Rodeo," February 1939, BPW Collection, ASLAPR; *Arizona Woman*, April 1932, BPW Collection, AHS, Tempe. Voter registration figures for the 1920s are from Secretary of State, *Arizona Blue Book*.

48. "Minutes of the Fourth Annual Convention, April 24, 1924," "Minutes of the Eighth Annual State Convention of Arizona Federation of Business and Professional Women's Clubs, 4–5 March 1928," "National Business Women's Week, 10–16 March 1930," BPW Collection, AHS, Tempe; *Phoenix Gazette*, 7 June 1961; Arizona Federation of Business and Professional Women, *Women Who Made a Difference*, vol. 1, 43, vol. 2, 13. The National Federation of Business and Professional Women's Clubs claimed 56,000 members in 1930.

49. "The Rodeo," February 1938, April 1939, BPW Collection, ASLAPR. Evidence of the national BPW's continued support of women's candidacies can be found in Doris Herrick Cochrane's letters to all state legislative chairmen, 30 October 1944, Arizona Women in Government file, Arizona Collection, ASLAPR.

50. Van Ingen, "Campaigns for Equality," 2, 33, 151, 173, 193; Gullett, *Becoming Citizen*, 2–5.

51. *Woman's Journal*, 24 April 1915.

Chapter 4. "A Woman for a Woman's Job"

1. *Arizona Gazette*, 12 January 1915.

2. Schramm, "Women and Representation," 53; Witt, Paget, and Matthews, *Running as a Woman*, 31; Breckenridge, *Women in the Twentieth Century*, 295; Andersen, *After Suffrage*, 33; Young, *Understanding Politics*, 180; Sanders, *The Lady and the Vote*, 19.

3. Cox, *Women State and Territorial Legislators*, 12–13; Center for Women in Government and Civil Society, "Women in State Policy Leadership, 1998–2005."

4. Rothschild and Hronek, "A History of Arizona Women's Politics," 11; Petrik, *No Step Backward*, xiii; Rothschild and Hronek, *Doing What the Day Brought*, xx; Miller, *Isabella Greenway*, 151; Cox, *Women State and Territorial Legislators*, 13. Female office holding in Oregon and Washington remains unexamined.

5. Cox, "Three Who Came First," 18; Muncy, "Women Demand Recognition," 45.

6. Sheridan, *Los Tucsonenses*, 141–43; Melcher, "Tending Children," 12; Salas, "Soledad Chávez Chacón," 163–64. In New Mexico, "Hispano" and "Hispanic" are customary usage rather than "Mexican American."

7. MacKay, in "Women in Politics," 360, asserts that Utah women were "consistently ranked lowest in the West for percentage of women in elective office," according to the Center for American Women and Politics, but that organization did not begin to collect data until 1971. Elizabeth Cox's data show that Utah had above average success sending women to the legislature before the 1950s. Cox, *Women State and Territorial Legislators*, 276–77.

8. Berman, "Male Support for Woman Suffrage," 286; U.S. Bureau of the Census, *Population of the United States*, 1910. Place of birth was identified for 73 female candidates in Arizona: 14 had been born in Arizona, 4 in California, 2 in Colorado, 1 in Idaho, 4 in Montana, 1 in New Mexico, 2 in Oregon, and 4 in Utah. For statistics on male legislators, I collected a random sample of men elected between 1914 and 1950 and identified their places of birth from obituary files and legislative files. Guy notes in "Economics of Widowhood," 201, that the term *pioneer* was a code word for Anglo.

9. *Woman's Journal*, 1 May 1915; *New York Times*, 17 November, 1915; *The Oasis*, 14 November 1914; Lucretia Roberts vertical file, ASLAPR.

10. Colorado women were nominated for state legislature by party officials. Cox, "Three Who Came First," 16. California women were nominated in a primary election. Van Ingen, "Campaigns for Equality," 31. Until more state studies are conducted, it is difficult to determine the relevance of the nomination process on female candidates.

11. Karning and Walter, "Election of Women to City Councils," 610–11; Kotlanger, "Phoenix, Arizona," 397, 482; *Nogales Daily Herald*, 20 May 1916; Osselaer, "'A Woman for a Woman's Job,'" 305; Frances Munds to Alice Park, 27 January 1913, Park Collection, HL. A list of candidates for municipal elections in Arizona is not available, and local newspapers gave cursory and uneven coverage to these campaigns. Therefore it is difficult to fully assess the role women played in municipal government. Voters wishing to participate in municipal elections were required to register separately from their county and state registration and were forced to travel to the city clerk in person every year until 1934. After 1934 they

had to register only every two years. In 1948, recognizing the injustice of this process, the League of Women's Voters led a drive to eliminate the system of double registration, and women's participation in local elections jumped significantly. Rockstroh, "An Analysis of Phoenix Municipal Administration," 58, 104.

12. *Arizona Capitol Times*, 29 October 1986; *Arizona Labor Journal*, 15 and 22 February 1923; Arizona First Event Card File, Arizona Collection, ASLAPR.

13. "Grace Marian Sparkes, Territorial Women's Memorial Rose Garden," SHM; Grace Sparkes Collection, AHF.

14. Secretary of State, *Arizona Blue Book*, 1914–32; *Arizona Daily Star*, 22 April 1927, 26 January 1949.

15. *Arizona Republican*, 2 November 1914. I identified candidates for county office through election coverage and campaign advertisements in the major newspapers for five counties: Cochise, Maricopa, Graham, Santa Cruz, and Yavapai. Together these counties accounted for more than half the population of the state and included a mix of urban and rural populations, Mormons, Mexican Americans, farmers, ranchers, and miners that mirrored the state's overall population. In addition, I assembled the names of women elected to all county offices from 1914 to 1950 from newspaper articles. Unsuccessful women candidates for office in the five counties totaled 109 out of the 200 women in this database; those who won office constituted the remaining 91. I collected biographical information on these women from obituary files, WPA Pioneer Interviews, legislative files at the Arizona State Archives, newspaper articles, and biographical guides including Connors, *Who's Who in Arizona*, *Portrait and Biographical Record*, Goff, *Arizona Biographical Dictionary*, Peplow, *History of Arizona*, and McClintock, *Arizona*. The newspapers I used to collect information on candidates included the *Bisbee Daily Review*, the *Arizona Republic/Republican*, the *Arizona/Phoenix Gazette*, the *Nogales Daily Herald*, *The Oasis*, the *Graham County Guardian*, the *Prescott Journal-Miner*, and the *Prescott Evening Courier*. See Osselaer, ""A Woman for a Woman's Job'" for more details on county office holding in Arizona.

16. Arizona Women in Government file, Arizona Collection, ASLAPR; *Arizona Republic*, 19 May 1940; Andersen, *After Suffrage*, 120; MacKay, "Women in Politics," 377; Secretary of State, *Arizona Blue Book*, 1915–32. Female justices of the peace included Nellie Bush in Yuma County and Beva Ferguson, Diantha Bratcher, and Fay Boswell in Graham County. The first female county supervisor in Maricopa County was Ruth O'Neill, who was appointed to the position to replace her deceased husband. *Arizona Gazette*, 25 May 1959.

17. Cothran, "Local Government in Arizona," 54–55; *Nogales Daily Herald*, 11 September 1916; Rockstroh, "Analysis of Phoenix Municipal Administration," 58, 104.

18. *Prescott Journal-Miner*, 10 September 1916. Not all men were as chivalrous as Eli Perkins. E. A. McSwiggins challenged Ruffner in the primary, and William Ebel challenged her in the general election.

19. *Prescott Evening Courier*, 3 November 1930; *Arizona Woman*, January 1933, BPW Collection, AHS, Tempe.

20. According to Kyte, in "A Tough Job for a Gentle Lady," 386, the state attorney general determined that the practice of prohibiting married women from teaching was illegal.

The actual number of widows running for office might have been much higher, because the exact marital status of many women could not be determined. The marital status of 82 female candidates was as follows: single, 16; married, 18; widowed, 17; divorced, 2; women who used "Mrs." but whose exact status could not be determined, 29. See Osselaer, "'A Woman for a Woman's Job,'" 317, for more information on marital status.

21. "1918 Election for Cochise County School Superintendent," Elsie Toles Scrapbook, AHS, Tucson; Brown, *More than Petticoats*, 72.

22. Kyte, "Tough Job," 397; "1918 Election for Cochise County School Superintendent," Elsie Toles Scrapbook, AHS, Tucson.

23. Elsie Toles Scrapbook, AHS, Tucson; Kyte, "Tough Job," 397.

24. Kyte, "Tough Job," 390–93; Benton, "What about Women?" 521.

25. Miller, *Isabella Greenway*, 160; Robinson, "Arizona's Mothers of Law," 5. Byrkit, in *Copper Collar*, 47, states that all five of Pima County's delegates to the 1910 constitutional convention represented the interests of the Southern Pacific Railroad, and all voted against the progressive state constitution. This suggests that it was difficult for women in Pima County to win election on a reform ticket.

26. *Yuma Morning Sun*, 31 October 1920. In 1924 legislative districts were reapportioned, and many incumbents, both male and female, were not reelected. Rosa McKay left the house to run for county supervisor, Freeda Marks and Vernettie Ivy narrowly lost reelection, and Nellie Bush took a leave to attend law school.

27. *Arizona Republican*, 16 September 1914.

28. Leeper, "Lady in the Legislature," 55; *Arizona Labor Journal*, 1 March 1923; Susan Seavy, "The Life Story of Nellie Bush," Nellie Bush Collection, PAHS, 264.

29. Etulain, "Contours of Culture in Arizona and the Modern West," 29–30.

30. Mason and Hink, *Constitutional Government in Arizona*, 78; *Arizona Republic*, 1 September 1940. Brown and Jones, in "The Arizona Legislature," 27, assert that in comparison with the legislatures of other states, the Arizona legislature "has relatively moderate powers, operating under rather strict constitutional limitations." A random survey of thirty-five legislators serving from 1914 to 1950 shows that 46.3 percent ran once, 22 percent ran twice, 7.3 percent ran three or four times, and 2.4 percent ran five times or more. The 1910 Arizona Constitution established that the state senate would be composed of nineteen senators, two each from the five most populous counties (Maricopa, Cochise, Gila, Pima, and Yavapai), and one each from the remaining counties, a formula that remained unchanged before 1950. After statehood, representation in the lower house was based on the population of the whole county, and initially members were chosen at large from each county. In 1918 representation was refined to reflect voters, not population. Legislative districts were based on one representative for each 1,500 votes cast in the prior gubernatorial race in the county, granting greater representation to districts with the highest turnouts. Over the years, as population and voters increased, the number of representatives increased from thirty-five in 1914 to sixty-four in 1932. Under pressure to reduce government expenses during the Great Depression, representation was reduced to one member for each 2,500 votes, reducing the number of representatives from sixty-four to fifty-one.

31. Leeper, "Lady in the Legislature," 55.

32. Telephone interview with John Munds, grandson of Frances Munds, 15 October 1994; *Arizona Gazette*, 1 January 1920.

33. Diamond, *Sex Roles in the State House*, 36; *Arizona Republic*, 15 May 1975.

34. Percentages were calculated on the basis of the 1948 Maricopa County race results. This was the first year enough women ran to allow a statistical analysis of their performance.

35. Freeda Marks legislative file, ASLAPR.

36. *Arizona Republican*, 16 September 1914; "Tenth Legislature Has a Lucky Seven," Arizona Women in Government file, Arizona Collection, ASLAPR. Campaign ads were surveyed in the *Bisbee Daily Review*, the *Arizona Republican/Republic*, the *Arizona/Phoenix Gazette*, the *Prescott Journal-Miner*, the *Prescott Evening-Courier*, the *Arizona Daily Star*, the *Graham County Guardian*, the *Nogales Daily Herald*, and *The Oasis* for the years 1914–1950.

37. *Prescott Journal-Miner*, 1 September 1914; *Arizona Gazette*, 17 September 1914; *Woman's Journal*, 14 November 1914; *Christian Science Monitor*, 28 April 1915.

38. *Arizona Republican*, 25 August and 17 September 1914; *Prescott Journal-Miner*, 1 September 1914.

39. *Arizona Gazette*, 12 January and 8 February 1915.

40. *Arizona Magazine*, February 1915, Arizona Women in Government file, Arizona Collection, ASLAPR; *Arizona Gazette*, 19 January 1915; Williams, *Valuable Pioneers*, 79; *Dunbar's Weekly*, 16 January 1915. Smoking bans apparently hit a raw nerve with Arizona reporters. In 1895, when women in Colorado's legislature demanded the enforcement of a smoking ban, the *Arizona Republican* complained vehemently about the action, according to Cox, in "Three Who Came First," 19.

41. *Arizona Gazette*, 12 January 1915; 1 January 1920 article, Nellie Bush biography file, ASU; Jessie Bevan to C. A. Campbell, 16 February 1931, Jessie Bevan Collection, BMHM.

42. *Woman's Journal*, 26 December 1914; *Arizona Gazette*, 29 January 1915.

43. Guy, "Economics of Widowhood," 201; *Journal of the Arizona Senate*, 1915; *Journal of the Arizona House of Representatives*, 1915.

44. *Arizona Gazette*, 25 February, 1915; *Arizona Labor Journal*, 1 April 1915.

45. Brown and Jones, "Arizona Legislature," 29; Frances Munds to George Hunt, 18 November 1914, Hunt Collection, ASU; Arizona Women in Government file, Arizona Collection, ASLAPR.

46. *Journal of the Arizona House of Representatives*, 1915–1927. I categorized and counted bills introduced by men and women in the house to determine the effect of gender on legislation.

47. Buckey O'Neill file, McClintock Collection, PPL. Women legislators introduced more bills on average than men: in 1917 the three women in the legislature introduced 24 bills, in comparison with the 161 bills introduced by the thirty-two men. In 1923, women averaged 5.75 bills each, and men averaged 4.2. *Journal of the Arizona House of Representatives* and *Journal of the Arizona Senate*, 1917, 1923; *Arizona Republic*, 15 November 1939; Guy, "Economics of Widowhood," 201.

48. C. Louise Boehringer biography file, AHS, Tucson; Brown, *More than Petticoats*, 79.

49. "Arizona Women Demonstrate They Can Exert Same Power in Legislature as Home," 12 January 1923, McClintock Collection, PPL; "Arizona's Minimum Wage Victory," Arizona Women in Government file, Arizona Collection, ASLAPR; *Messenger*, 3 February 1917; *Arizona Labor Journal*, 15 February 1923; Benton, "What about Women?" 467–68; *Arizona Republic*, 23 March 1934.

50. "Trying to Recall Mrs. Rosa M'Kay in Cochise County," May 1917, Arizona Women in Government file, Arizona Collection, ASLAPR; O'Neill "A Community Divided," 105.

51. Byrkit, *Copper Collar*, 209, 255; *Prescott Courier*, 29 November 1919; *Dunbar's Weekly*, 18 August 1917; O'Neill, "Community Divided," 106. Ludlow, Colorado, was a mining town where guards hostile to striking mine workers burned the tents housing families and killed fourteen innocent people, including eleven children, in 1914. *Prescott Courier*, 29 November 1919; *Messenger*, 15 November 1924.

52. *Arizona Gazette*, 15 August 1918; Frances Munds to George Hunt, 14 November 1918, Hunt Collection, ASU; *Journal of the Arizona House of Representatives*, 1917, 1919; Byrkit, *Copper Collar*, 317; Goff, *George W. P. Hunt*, 112.

53. *Journal of the Arizona House of Representatives*, 1920, special session; *Journal of the Arizona Senate*, 1920, special session; Cox, *Women State and Territorial Legislators*, 23.

54. *Woman's Journal*, 24 April, 1915; "Men of Arizona Remain Gallant," Arizona Women in Government file, Arizona Collection, ASLAPR; *Arizona Capitol Times*, 15 November 1996; Cox, *Women State and Territorial Legislators*, 327; Peirce, *The Mountain States of America*, 221. U.S. Census statistics show the rural gender ratio in 1910 at 61 percent male to 39 percent female, and the urban ratio at 57 percent male to 43 percent female. The 1920 rural ratio was 58 percent male to 42 percent female, and the urban ratio was 53 percent male to 47 percent female. U.S. Bureau of the Census, *Population of the United States*, 1910, 1920.

55. "Mrs. Nellie A. Hayward," Arizona Women in Government file, Arizona Collection, ASLAPR; *Dunbar's Weekly*, 12 September 1914; *Arizona Republican*, 9 October 1916.

56. Frances Munds to George Hunt, 12 September 1918, Hunt Collection, ASU; *Dunbar's Weekly*, 12 September 1914; Article V, Section 2, Arizona Constitution; Kelly, "Women, Politics, and Public Policy," 104; *Arizona Republic*, 22 August 1999.

57. Secretary of State of Arizona, Official Canvass, General Election Results, 1914–50.

58. *Phoenix Tribune*, 28 October 1922; press release by the Republican State Committee from the *Glendale News*, Elsie Toles Scrapbook, AHS, Tucson.

59. "Anti-Mormon Pamphlet," 18 August 1920, "A Statement by Miss Toles," Elsie Toles Scrapbook, AHS, Tucson; *Arizona Capitol Times*, 4 January 1984. Benton, in "What about Women?" 522, notes that Elsie Toles naïvely believed that her choice of political party was irrelevant.

60. Elsie Toles Scrapbook, AHS, Tucson; *True West Magazine*, April 1965.

61. C. Louise Boehringer biography file, AHS, Tucson; press release by the Republican State Committee from the *Glendale News*, Elsie Toles Scrapbook, AHS, Tucson; "Elsie

Toles," in Tod and Crowe, *Arizona Women's Hall of Fame*; *Graham County Guardian*, 5 November 1912, 6 September 1940.

62. Salas, "Soledad Chávez Chacón," 161; *Tucson Daily Citizen*, 16 September 1918; George Hunt to Frances Munds, 18 September 1918, Hunt Collection, ASU.

63. Jones, "Ana Frohmiller," 360; *Arizona Republic*, 9 and 10 September 1950.

64. Secretary of State of Arizona, Official Canvass, Primary Election Returns, 1926–30; *Arizona Republican*, 5 September 1926; Shadegg, *Arizona Politics*, 36; Arizona Federation of Business and Professional Women's Clubs, *Women Who Made a Difference*, vol. 2, 57.

65. *Arizona Republic*, 17 July 1946; Mason and Hink, *Constitutional Government in Arizona*, 137; Jones, "Ana Frohmiller," 351.

66. Jones, "Ana Frohmiller," 355–59. Although Frohmiller was the daughter of Irish parents, the name Anastasia led many to assume she was Russian.

67. "Arizona Women Demonstrate," 12 January 1923, McClintock Collection, PPL.

Chapter 5. "Mis"-Representatives

1. "Tenth Legislature," Arizona Women in Government file, Arizona Collection, ASLAPR; Sheridan, *Arizona*, 253–54, 262.

2. "The Rodeo," December 1937, BPW Collection, ASLAPR; "Minutes of the Sixteenth Annual Convention of the State Federation of Business and Professional Women's Clubs, 8–10 May 1936," BPW Collection, AHS, Tempe. McFarland, in "Power for Good," 113, notes that membership in the Women's Club of Phoenix, an AFWC affiliate, declined from a high of 400 in the 1920s to 191 in 1944.

3. Shadegg, *Arizona Politics*, 12; Berman, *Parties and Elections in Arizona 1863–1984*, 18–27, 48, 58; *Arizona Republic*, 2 October 1940; Goff, *Arizona*, 98.

4. Wilma Hoyal biography file, AHS, Tucson.

5. Emma Parsons to Mrs. Albert G. Sims, 23 October 1939, Emma Parsons Collection, AHS, Tucson.

6. Morrison, "Isabella Greenway," 5; Cook, *Eleanor Roosevelt*, vol. 1, 174.

7. Miller, *Isabella Greenway*, 36; Miller, "A Volume of Friendship," 124.

8. Miller, *Isabella Greenway*, 63–64.

9. Ibid., 111–24; Morrison, "Isabella Greenway," 5.

10. Miller, *Isabella Greenway*, 144, 148, 149; Morrison, "Isabella Greenway," 11; Arizona Federation of Business and Professional Women, *Women Who Made a Difference*, vol. 1, 75; Connor, *Who's Who in Arizona*, 465; *Phoenix Gazette*, 6 September 1974; Miller, "A Volume of Friendship," 141.

11. Morrison, "Isabella Greenway," 11; Arizona Federation of Business and Professional Women, *Women Who Made a Difference*, vol. 1, 75; Connor, *Who's Who in Arizona*, 465; *Phoenix Gazette*, 6 September 1974; Miller, "A Volume of Friendship," 142.

12. Isabella Greenway to Mrs. Franklin D. Roosevelt, 10 and 24 October 1928, John Campbell and Isabella Selmes Greenway Collection, AHS, Tucson.

13. *Arizona Republican*, 1 August 1928; Isabella Greenway to Mrs. W. V. Whitmore, 16 August 1928, Mattilee Duncan to Isabella Greenway, 26 November 1928, Greenway

Collection, AHS, Tucson; *Nogales Daily Herald*, 3 November, 1928.

14. Opal Le Baron Whitmore to Isabella Greenway, 17 October 1928, Greenway Collection, AHS, Tucson; Miller, *Isabella Greenway*, 160.

15. Sheridan, *Arizona*, 263; C. E. Addams to Bill Stuart, 26 July 1932, Bill Matthews to Bill Stuart, 12 March 1932, Stuart Family Papers, Arizona Collection, Hayden Library, ASU; Miller, *Isabella Greenway*, 164; Gruberg, *Women in American Politics*, 156.

16. Miller, *Isabella Greenway*, 168–71.

17. Ibid., 171–80; Mary Dewson to Isabella Greenway, 5 January 1931, Greenway Collection, AHS, Tucson; Bill Matthews to William Stuart, 12 March 1932, Stuart Family Papers, ASU; Morrison, "Isabella Greenway," 13–14; *Arizona Labor Journal*, 19 November 1932; *New York Times*, 28 and 30 June 1932.

18. *Arizona Republic*, 21 and 26 September 1932, 10 November 1932; Miller, *Isabella Greenway*, 180–82; *Prescott Evening Courier*, 12 September 1932; *Nogales Daily Herald*, 2 July 1932.

19. Isabella Greenway, quoted in Miller, *Isabella Greenway*, 157, 162; Bill Matthews to William Stuart, 17 March 1932, Stuart Family Papers, ASU. Roosevelt wrote to Greenway that "apparently people are getting rather tired of the factional disturbances caused by the perennial candidacy of Governor Hunt and feel that you would satisfy all factions. More than that, they say that you would make a splendid Governor." Franklin Delano Roosevelt to Isabella Greenway, 21 October 1929, Greenway Collection, AHS, Tucson.

20. Isabella Greenway to Grace Sparkes, 20 April 1933, Sparkes Collection, AHF; Secretary of State of Arizona, Official Canvass, Primary and General Election Results, 1933, ASLAPR; Berman, *Arizona Politics and Government*, 49; Miller, *Isabella Greenway*, 187; Morrison, "Isabella Greenway," 13–14. Governor George Hunt originally backed Greenway's run for Congress but changed his mind, opening the door to speculation that Grace Sparkes would run. "Political Potpourri," undated *Gazette* article in Stuart Family Papers, ASU.

21. Arizona Federation of Business and Professional Women, *Women Who Made a Difference*, vol. 1, 75.

22. Miller, *Isabella Greenway*, 153, 160; legislative files of women who served from 1914 to 1950, ASLAPR.

23. African American file, Greenway Collection, AHS, Tucson. There are no records of Mexican American organizations in Isabella Greenway's extensive catalog of correspondence with official Democratic organizations in the 1930s.

24. "Tenth Legislature," Arizona Women in Government file, Arizona Collection, ASLAPR. In 1930, six women were elected, two more (Godfrey and Francis) were appointed to replace men, and Sprague was appointed to replace an elected woman, Leeper. Nine women served in the legislature that session, but only eight women, or 12.7 percent of the house, served at any give time. There were sixty-three house members altogether that year.

25. Leeper, "Lady in the Legislature," 58.

26. Jessie Bevan to Edward J. Moran, 15 January 1931, Bevan Collection, BMHM.

27. *Arizona Labor Journal*, 3 September 1932; *Prescott Evening Courier*, 3 November; "Tenth Legislature," Arizona Women in Government file, Arizona Collection, ASLAPR.

28. "Tenth Legislature," Arizona Women in Government file, Arizona Collection, ASLAPR; Nellie Trent Bush Collection, Arizona Collection, ASU.

29. *Parker Pioneer*, 1 November 1963.

30. *Arizona Republic*, 17 January 1963.

31. Tod and Crowe, *Arizona Women's Hall of Fame*, 83–84; *Arizona Gazette*, 1 January 1920.

32. *Arizona Republic*, 17 January 1963.

33. Ibid.; Nellie T. Bush legislative file, ASLAPR; *Journal of the Arizona House of Representatives*, 1927; *Los Angeles Times*, 16 November 1927; *Dunbar's Weekly*, 19 February 1927; *Arizona Republican*, 19 March 1927.

34. *Los Angeles Examiner*, 18 July 1935; *New York Herald Tribune*, 14 November 1934; *Santa Barbara Daily News*, 13 November 1934; Susan Seavy, "The Life Story of Nellie Bush," Nellie Bush Collection, PAHS, 313.

35. *Arizona Labor Journal*, 1 March 1923; *Arizona Republic*, 11 February 1931, 16 and 17 January 1963; *Arizona Gazette*, 19 and 26 November 1934; "Tenth Legislature," Arizona Women in Government file, Arizona Collection, ASLAPR.

36. *Arizona Republic*, 6 and 10 September, 9 October 1936; *Arizona Gazette*, 4 March 1936.

37. *Imperial Valley Press*, 11 April 1935; *Arizona Gazette*, 1 January 1920; *Arizona Republic*, 19 May 1940.

38. *Journal of the Arizona House of Representatives*, 1928–1940.

39. Ibid.

40. *Arizona Republican*, 19 and 20 August 1914.

41. Hebard, "The First Woman Jury," 1301; Thompson, "After Suffrage," 157; Weisbrod, "Images of the Woman Juror," 65; Lemons, *The Woman Citizen*, 69.

42. "Rights for Women," March 1938, McClintock Collection, PPL; *Journal of the Arizona House*, 1933, 138.

43. Newspaper article, 23 February 1933, Alexander Papers, ASU; "C.S.N. 31," January 1933, McClintock Collection, PPL; *Journal of the Arizona House of Representatives*, 1931.

44. *Arizona Woman*, January 1930, January 1932, April–May 1933, BPW Collection, AHS, Tempe; *Arizona Republic*, 28 October 1930; Thompson, "After Suffrage," 151.

45. *Journal of the Arizona House of Representatives* and *Journal of the Arizona Senate*, 1930–40.

46. Cantril, *Public Opinion*, 1052; "The Rodeo," December 1937, "Harriet Jean Oliver's Legislative Report, 1938–1939," BPW Collection, ASLAPR; newspaper article, 23 February 1933, Alexander Papers, ASU.

47. *Journal of the Arizona House of Representatives*, second special session, 1937, 122; personal BPW files of Jan LoVecchio, BPW historian.

48. "The Lookout," 10 May 1938, BPW Collection, ASPLAR.

49. "Testimony at Hearing," June 1937, personal BPW files of Jan LoVecchio; *Journal of the Arizona House of Representatives*, 1937, second special session, 134.

50. *Arizona Republic*, 19 May 1940; "The Rodeo," October 1938, BPW Collection, ASLAPR.

51. Moore, "The United States Birth Control Movement and Arizona Women," 23, 47–48, 55, 58, 75, 81.

52. Ibid., 75–79; Fritzi Struckmeyer Ryley biography file, AHF.

53. *Arizona Labor Journal*, 8 November 1928; Laura Gregg to Anna Howard Shaw, 22 December 1909, Women's Suffrage Collection, ASLAPR.

Chapter 6. Professional Politicians

1. Sheridan, *Arizona*, 270–73.

2. *Arizona Republic*, 2 November 1946; Sheridan, *Arizona*, 276–77.

3. Marion Martin to Emma Parsons, 6 March 1939, Emma Parsons to Margaret Adams Rockwell, 7 September 1946, Parsons Collection, AHS, Tucson.

4. "First Federal Savings Reporter," January 1952, Bob Creighton to Miss Biddle, Rockwell Family Papers, AHS, Tempe; *Mesa Tribune*, 4 January 1983. Byrkit, in *Copper Collar*, 86, calls the Adams Hotel "the real capitol of Arizona."

5. *Arizona Republic*, 27 April 1962; "First Federal Savings and Loan Reporter," January 1951, Rockwell Family Papers, AHS, Tempe.

6. *Mesa Tribune*, 4 January 1983; *Arizona Republic*, 17 October 1942.

7. Shadegg, *Arizona Politics*, 44, 59; Sheridan, *Arizona*, 175; "First Federal Savings Reporter," January 1952, Rockwell Family Papers, AHS, Tempe.

8. Berman, *Parties and Elections*, 29.

9. *Phoenix Gazette*, 4 February 1915; Goldwater, quoted in Peirce, *The Mountain States of America*, 221.

10. Marin, "La Asociación Hispano-Americana," 7; "Harriet Jean Oliver's Legislative Report, 1944–45," BPW Collection, ASLAPR. The jury bill allowed women to exempt themselves from jury service if they wished. Opponents of the bill asserted that most women would exempt themselves from jury duty rosters, but estimates in local newspapers and by the BPW suggest that only about 10 percent of all women asked for exemptions. In 1951 the state supreme court declared the exemption unconstitutional.

11. *Phoenix Gazette*, 6 April 1938; *Prescott Evening Courier*, 12 September 1942; "The Rodeo," April 1938, BPW Collection, ASLAPR.

12. "Resume of Women's Activities Shows Increasing Co-operation," *Arizona Republican* editorial, no date, Marie Good Scrapbooks, 1937–38, League/BPW, personal files of Jan LoVecchio; campaign material, Rockwell Family Papers, AHS, Tempe.

13. "Senator Hayden Votes Against Equal Pay Bill," August 1946, "Merry Mental Tinkle," November 1946, BPW Collection, AHS, Tempe.

14. Whitaker, *Race Work*, 86, 105; Crudup, "African Americans in Arizona," 330–32; *Arizona Republic*, 12 September 1948. Walker lost to incumbent Wing Ong, the first Chinese American elected to a state legislature in the United States.

15. "Twenty-Second Annual Convention of the Arizona State Federation of Business and Professional Women's Clubs, 24–26 April 1942," BPW Collection, ASLAPR; Sheridan, *Arizona*, 271; State Legislature First Event Card File, Arizona Collection, ASLAPR; Secretary of State, *Arizona Blue Book*, 1995–96, 11, 14; "Harriet Jean Oliver's Legislative

Report, 1940–1941," BPW Collection, ASLAPR. There were 52 members, all Democrats, in the Arizona house in 1941.

16. *Journal of the Arizona House of Representatives*, 1940–1950.

17. Arizona legislative files, ASLAPR.

18. *Lakeside Arizona Desert Sun*, May 1967; Nellie T. Bush biography file, Arizona Collection, ASU; Clara Botzum Collection, ASLAPR; *Parker Pioneer*, 9 November 1978.

19. *Parker Pioneer*, 9 November 1978.

20. Interview with Barbara Nielsen, grandniece of Claire Phelps, 15 March 2001; *Arizona Republic*, 4 August 1950. Most biographies of John J. Rhodes state that his first campaign was a losing battle for attorney general of Arizona in 1950, but Rhodes ran in the District 9 race and lost to Phelps in 1946. *Arizona Republic*, 2 November 1946.

21. Maxine Provost Brubaker biography file, AHS, Tucson.

22. *Arizona Republic*, 22 August, 1999.

23. Johnson, *Arizona Politicians*, 142–43. This was the second female law partnership formed in the state; the first was Alice Birdsall and Sarah Sorin.

24. Philip VanderMeer, "Lorna C. Lockwood," 190–93; Byrkit, *Copper Collar*, 312; Arizona Federation of Business and Professional Women, *Women Who Made a Difference*, vol. 1, 97; *Phoenix Gazette*, 18 September 1975, 24 September 1977.

25. Laurens L. Henderson, "Fifty Years of Arizona Political and Judicial Recollections," Arizona Collection, ASU; "Harriet Jean Oliver's Legislative Report, 1944–45," BPW Collection, ASLAPR; *Woman's Journal*, 1 May 1915; *Arizona Republic*, 8 June 1975. The first female deputy sheriff was appointed in 1914, and in 1936 Belle Talley was appointed to replace her husband as sheriff. First Event File Card, ASLAPR; Secretary of State, *Arizona Blue Book*, 1925–26, 17–19.

26. U.S. Bureau of the Census, *Population of the United States*, 1940; *Arizona Republic*, 6 September 1938; *Arizona Woman*, October 1948, BPW Collection, ASLAPR.

27. *Arizona Republic*, 6 March and 23 July 1942. Hattrude Hughes was another female congressional candidate in the Democratic primary of 1942, but she came in thirteenth out of eighteen candidates.

28. Johnson, *Arizona Politicians*, 144.

29. Shadegg, *Arizona Politics*, 38.

30. *Arizona Republic*, 29 August, 3, 9, and 10 September 1950.

31. Shadegg, *Arizona Politics*, 38; *Arizona Republic*, 3 and 14 September 1950; *Nogales Daily Herald*, 14 September 1950; *Phoenix Gazette*, 17 September, 1950.

32. *Phoenix Gazette*, 17 September, 1950

33. Peirce, *The Mountain States of America*, 221. Goldwater and Pyle are often credited with pioneering the use of airplanes in campaigns in Arizona, but Nellie Bush and Isabella Greenway had flown planes in their campaigns across the state years before those men appeared on the political radar.

34. Jones, "Ana Frohmiller," 362; *Arizona Republic*, 30 October 1950, 6 November 1950; *Nogales Daily Herald*, 2 November 1950; Arizona Federation of Business and Professional Women's Clubs, *Women Who Made a Difference*, vol. 2, 57.

35. *Arizona Republic*, 2 November 1950; *Nogales Daily Herald*, 2 November 1950.

36. *Arizona Republic*, 38 October and 4 November 1950.

37. Jones, "Ana Frohmiller," 361, 363; Arizona Federation of Business and Professional Women's Clubs, *Women Who Made a Difference*, vol. 2, 56.

38. *Prescott Evening Courier*, 8 November 1950; Arizona Federation of Business and Professional Women's Clubs, *Women Who Made a Difference*, vol. 2, 57.

39. *Arizona Republic*, 9 November 1950; *Phoenix Gazette*, 8 November 1950.

40. Margaret Adams Rockwell to Colonel Randolph Evjen, 14 February 1951, Rockwell Family Papers, AHS, Tempe; *Arizona Republic*, 10 November 1966.

Conclusion

1. Miller, *Isabella Greenway*, 160.

2. Bevan Collection, BMHM.

3. "Tenth Legislature," Arizona Women in Government file, Arizona Collection, ASLAPR.

4. Reingold, *Representing Women*, 90–92; Van Ingen, "Campaigns for Equality," 363.

Epilogue

1. *Arizona Capitol Times*, 4 January 1984.

2. Legislative files for female members, 1950–60, ASLAPR.

3. Whitaker, *Race Work*, 83–87; Arizona Women's Hall of Fame, ASLAPR, http://dev .lib.az.us/awhof/women/mayard.cfm.

4. McCool, Olson, and Robinson, *Native Vote*, 7, 11, 15–18, 20; Steiner, *The New Indians*, 233; Debora Norris legislative file, ASLAPR.

5. Luckingham, *Minorities in Phoenix*, 48–49, 71.

6. See Evans, *Personal Politics*, for an excellent overview of the origins of the modern woman's movement.

7. Johnson, *Arizona Politicians*, 148; *Journal of the Arizona House of Representatives*, 1968.

8. Burt-Way, "Women in the Electoral Process," 28.

9. *Arizona Capitol Times*, 4 January 1984; Center for Women in Government and Civil Society, "Women in State Policy Leadership," 4.

10. O'Connor and Day, *Lazy B*, 43; *U.S. News and World Report*, 30 October 2006, 18.

11. Tod and Crowe, *Arizona Women's Hall of Fame*, 6–7; *Arizona Republic*, 24 September 1995. "Speculation was rampant that Babbitt made the bold bipartisan move at least in part to remove O'Connor as a potential rival in the next gubernatorial race, a motive that he denied," according to McFeatters, *Sandra Day O'Connor*, 45, 48–50.

12. Kelly, *Women and the Arizona Political Process*, 146–47.

13. *Journal of the Arizona House of Representatives*, 1988, 1302.

14. Center for Women in Government and Civil Society, "Women in State Policy Leadership," 4.

Bibliography

Manuscript Collections

Arizona Collection, Hayden Library, Arizona State University, Tempe
    Alexander, Joseph and Grace, Papers
    Bush, Nellie Trent, Collection
    Hayden, Carl T., Family Papers
    Hughes, Josephine Brawley, Collection
    Hunt, George W. P., Papers
    Ross, Margaret Wheeler, Papers
    Stuart Family Papers
Arizona Federation of Business and Professional Women's Clubs
    Files held by club historian, Jan LoVecchio, Tucson
Arizona Historical Foundation, Hayden Library, Arizona State University, Tempe
    Sparkes, Grace, Collection
Arizona Historical Society, Central Archives Collections, Tempe
    Arizona Federation of Business and Professional Women's Clubs Collection
    Rockwell Family Papers
Arizona Historical Society, Southern Archives Division, Tucson
    Greenway, John Campbell and Isabella Selmes, Collection
    Parsons, Emma, Collection
    Toles, Elsie, Scrapbook
Arizona State Library, Archives, and Public Records, Phoenix
    Arizona Federation of Business and Professional Women's Clubs Collection
    Botzum, Clara, Collection
    Women's Suffrage Collection
    Women's Suffrage Initiative Petitions
    Work Projects Administration (WPA) Pioneer Interviews
Bisbee Mining and Historical Museum, Bisbee
    Bevan, Jessie, Collection
Hoover Institution Archives, Stanford University, Stanford, California
    Park, Alice L., Collection
Huntington Library, San Marino, California
    Park, Alice L., Papers
King Library, University of Kentucky, Lexington, Kentucky
    Clay, Laura, Collection

National American Woman Suffrage Association Records, Stanford University, Stanford, California
Parker Area Historical Society, Parker
    Bush, Nellie, Collection
Phoenix Public Library, Arizona Room, Burton Barr Central Library, Phoenix
    McClintock, James H., Collection
Sharlot Hall Museum, Prescott
    O'Neill, William, Collection
    Willard, Dolph, Memoirs

Periodicals

Arizona Capitol Times
Arizona Daily Star
Arizona Daily Gazette/Arizona Gazette
Arizona Labor Journal
Arizona Magazine
Arizona Republican/Republic
Arizona Silver Belt
Bisbee Daily Review
Chicago Sun-Times
Christian Science Monitor
Dunbar's Weekly
Graham County Guardian
Imperial Valley Press
Los Angeles Times
Mesa Tribune
The Messenger
Miners Magazine
New York Herald Tribune

New York Times
New York Times Magazine
Nogales Daily Herald
Nogales Daily Review
The Oasis
Parker Post
Parker Pioneer
Phoenix Gazette
Prescott Courier/Evening Courier
Prescott Journal-Miner
Progressive Weekly
The Revolution
True West Magazine
Tucson Daily Citizen
U.S. News and World Report
Woman's Journal
Yavapai Magazine
Yuma Morning Sun

Government Documents

Journal of the Arizona House of Representatives. Arizona State Legislature, various years.
Journal of the Arizona Senate. Arizona State Legislature, various years.
Secretary of State of Arizona. Arizona Blue Book, 1912–13, 1915–16, 1917–18, 1919–20, 1921–22, 1923–24, 1925–26, 1927–28, 1929–30, 1931–32, 1995–96.
Secretary of State of Arizona. Official Canvass, General Election Results, 1914–50.
U.S. Bureau of the Census. Historical Statistics of the United States: Colonial Times to 1970. Washington, DC: U.S. Government Printing Office, 1975.
U.S. Bureau of the Census. Population of the United States, 1870, 1880, 1890, 1900, 1910, 1920, 1930. Washington, DC: U.S. Government Printing Office.

Secondary Sources

Andersen, Kristi. *After Suffrage: Women in Partisan and Electoral Politics before the New Deal*. Chicago: University of Chicago Press, 1996.

Anthony, Susan B., and Ida Husted Harper, eds. *The History of Woman Suffrage*, vol. 4. Salem, NH: Ayer Company, 1900.

Arizona Federation of Business and Professional Women. *Women Who Made a Difference*. 3 vols. Tucson: Arizona Business and Professional Women's Foundation, 1994.

Baker, Paula. "The Domestication of Politics: Women and American Political Society, 1780–1920." *American Historical Review* 89 (1984): 620–47.

Beeton, Beverly. "How the West Was Won for Woman Suffrage." In *One Woman, One Vote: Rediscovering the Woman Suffrage Movement*, edited by Marjorie Spruill Wheeler, 99–116. Troutdale, OR: New Sage Press, 1995.

———. *Women Vote in the West: The Woman Suffrage Movement, 1869–1896*. New York: Garland, 1986.

Benton, Katherine Alexa. "What about Women in the White Man's Camp? Gender, Nation, and the Redefinition of Race in Cochise County, Arizona, 1853–1941." Ph.D. diss., University of Wisconsin, Madison, 2002.

Berman, David R. *Arizona Politics and Government: The Quest for Autonomy, Democracy, and Development*. Lincoln: University of Nebraska Press, 1998.

———. "Gender and Issue Voting after Suffrage Expansion in Arizona." *Social Science Quarterly* 74 (1993): 838–50.

———. "Male Support for Woman Suffrage: An Analysis of Voting Patterns in the Mountain West." *Social Science History* 11 (1987): 281–94.

———. *Parties and Elections in Arizona, 1863–1984*. Tempe, AZ: Morrison Institute for Public Policy, School of Public Affairs, College of Public Programs, Arizona State University, 1985.

———. *Reformers, Corporations, and the Electorate: An Analysis of Arizona's Age of Reform*. Niwot: University Press of Colorado, 1992.

———. "Voters, Candidates, and Issues in the Progressive Era: An Analysis of the 1912 Presidential Election in Arizona." *Social Science Quarterly* 67 (1986): 256–66.

Blair, Emily Newell. "Why I Am Discouraged about Women in Politics." In *Major Problems in American Women's History*, 2nd edition, edited by Mary Beth Norton and Ruth M. Alexander, 331–33. Lexington, MA: D. C. Heath, 1996.

Boehringer, C. Louise. "Josephine Brawley Hughes—Crusader—Statebuilder." *Arizona Historical Review* 2 (1930): 98–107.

Bordin, Ruth. *Frances Willard: A Biography*. Chapel Hill: University of North Carolina Press, 1986.

Breckenridge, Sophonisba P. *Women in the Twentieth Century: A Study of Their Political, Social and Economic Activities*. New York: McGraw-Hill, 1933.

Brown, Dorothy M. *Setting a Course: American Women in the 1920s*. Boston: Twayne Publishers, 1987.

Brown, Douglas A., and Robert L. Jones. "The Arizona Legislature." In *Politics and Public Policy in Arizona*, edited by Zachary A. Smith, 26–49. Westport, CT: Praeger, 1993.

Brown, Wynne. *More than Petticoats: Remarkable Arizona Women.* Guilford, CT: Globe Pequot Press, 2003.

Burt-Way, Barbara J. "Women in the Electoral Process: As Voters, Candidates, and Municipal Officeholders." In *Women and the Arizona Political Process: Second Arizona Women's Town Hall,* edited by Rita Mae Kelly, 21–40. Lanham, MD: University Press of America, 1988.

Byrkit, James. *Forging the Copper Collar: Arizona's Labor-Management War of 1901–1921.* Tucson: University of Arizona Press, 1982.

Cantril, Hadley, ed. *Public Opinion, 1935–1946.* Princeton, N.J.: Princeton University Press, 1951.

Catt, Carrie Chapman, and Nettie Rogers Shuler. *Woman Suffrage and Politics: The Inner Story of the Suffrage Movement.* Seattle: University of Washington Press, 1923.

Center for American Women and Politics. *Facts on Women Candidates and Elected Officials, 1969–2006* (http://cawp.rutgers.edu/Facts/Officeholders/cawpfs.html, viewed July 2007).

Center for Women in Government and Civil Society. "Women in State Policy Leadership, 1998–2005: An Analysis of Slow and Uneven Progress." Albany, NY: State University of New York, 2006 (http://cwig.albany.edu).

Connors, Jo, compiler. *Who's Who in Arizona.* Tucson: Press of the *Arizona Daily Star,* 1913.

Cook, Blanche Wiesen. *Eleanor Roosevelt,* vol. 1. New York: Viking, 1992.

Cothran, Dan A. "Local Government in Arizona." In *Politics and Public Policy in Arizona,* edited by Zachary A. Smith, 53–66. Westport, CT: Praeger, 1993.

Cott, Nancy. *The Grounding of Modern Feminism.* New Haven, CT: Yale University Press, 1987.

Cox, Elizabeth M. "The Three Who Came First." *State Legislatures* (Nov. 1994): 12–19.

———. *Women State and Territorial Legislators, 1895–1995.* Jefferson, NC: MacFarland, 1996.

Crudup, Keith Jerome. "African Americans in Arizona: A Twentieth-Century History." Ph.D. diss., Arizona State University, 1998.

Darnall, Kris. "Women and Politics: The Arizona Federation of Women's Clubs, 1912–1920." Unpublished paper, Arizona State University, in possession of the author.

Diamond, Irene. *Sex Roles in the State House.* New Haven, CT: Yale University Press, 1977.

Dye, Nancy Shrom. *As Equals and Sisters: The Labor Movement and the Women's Trade Union League of New York.* Columbia: University of Missouri Press, 1980.

Edwards, Rebecca. *Angels in the Machinery: Gender in American Party Politics from the Civil War to the Progressive Era.* New York: Oxford University Press, 1997.

Eppinga, Jane. "Dr. Rosa Goodrich Boido, M.D." Tucson: Arizona Historical Society, Southern Arizona Division.

Epstein, Barbara Leslie. *The Politics of Domesticity: Women, Evangelism, and Temperance in Nineteenth Century America.* Middleton, CT: Wesleyan University Press, 1981.

Etulain, Richard W. "Contours of Culture in Arizona and the Modern West." In *Arizona at Seventy-Five: The Next Twenty-Five Years,* edited by Beth Luey and Noel Stowe, 11–53. Tucson: University of Arizona Press, 1987.

Evans, Sara. *Personal Politics: The Roots of Women's Liberation in the Civil Rights Movement and the New Left*. New York: Random House, 1979.

Fischer, Christiane. "A Profile of Women in Arizona in Frontier Days." *Journal of the West* (1977): 42–53.

Foster, Anne L. "The Right Kind of Girl: Pauline M. O'Neill." In *Rough Writings: Perspectives on Buckey O'Neill, Pauline M. O'Neill, and Roosevelt's Rough Riders*, compiled by Janet Lovelady, 33–46. Prescott, AZ: Sharlot Hall Museum Press, 1998.

Fowler, Robert Booth. *Carrie Catt: Feminist Politician*. Boston: Northeastern University Press, 1986.

Freeman, Jo. *A Room at a Time: How Women Entered Party Politics*. Lanham, MA: Rowman and Littlefield, 2000.

Fuller, Paul E. *Laura Clay and the Woman's Rights Movement*. Lexington: University of Kentucky Press, 1975.

Giddings, Paula. *When and Where I Enter: The Impact of Black Women on Race and Sex in America*. New York: W. Morrow, 1984.

Gienapp, William E. "'Politics Seem to Enter into Everything': Political Culture in the North, 1840–1860." In *Essays on Antebellum Politics, 1840–1860*, edited by S. E. Maizlish and J. J. Kushma, 15–69. College Station: Texas A & M Press, 1982.

Goff, John S. *Arizona: An Illustrated History of the Grand Canyon State*. Northridge, CA: Windsor Publications, 1988.

———. *Arizona Biographical Dictionary*. Cave Creek, AZ: Black Mountain Press, 1983.

———. *George W. P. Hunt and His Arizona*. Pasadena, CA: Socio Technical Publications, 1973.

Goldberg, Robert Alan. *Barry Goldwater*. New Haven, CT: Yale University Press, 1995.

Goodman, Clavia. *Bitter Harvest: Laura Clay's Suffrage Work*. Lexington: University of Kentucky Press, 1946.

Gordon, Felice D. *After Winning: The Legacy of the New Jersey Suffragists, 1920–1947*. New Brunswick, NJ: Rutgers University Press, 1986.

Graham, Sara Hunter. *Woman Suffrage and the New Democracy*. New Haven, CT: Yale University Press, 1996.

Gruberg, Martin. *Women in American Politics: An Assessment and Sourcebook*. Oshkosh, WI: Academia Press, 1968.

Gullett, Gayle Ann. *Becoming Citizen: The Emergence and Development of the California Women's Movement, 1880–1911*. Urbana: University of Illinois Press, 2000.

Guy, Donna. "The Economics of Widowhood in Arizona, 1880–1940." In *On Their Own: Widows and Widowhood in the American Southwest, 1848–1939*, edited by Arlene Scadron, 195–223. Urbana: University of Illinois Press, 1988.

Harper, Ida Husted, ed. *History of Woman Suffrage*, vol. 6. Salem, NH: Ayer Company, 1906.

Harvey, Anna L. "Culture or Strategy? Women in New York State Parties, 1917–1930." In *We Have Come to Stay: American Women and Political Parties, 1880–1960*, edited by Melanie Gustafson, Kristie Miller, and Elisabeth Israels Perry, 87–96. Albuquerque: University of New Mexico Press, 1996.

——. *Votes without Leverage: Women in American Electoral Politics*. Lanham, MA: Rowman and Littlefield, 2000.

Hebard, Grace. "The First Woman Jury." *Journal of American History* 7 (1913): 1293–303.

Hietter, Paul T. "Lawyers, Guns, and Money: The Evolution of Crime and Criminal Justice in Arizona Territory." Ph.D. diss., Arizona State University, 1999.

Howard, Kathleen L. "Creating an Enchanted Land: Curio Entrepreneurs Promote and Sell the Indian Southwest, 1880–1940." Ph.D. diss., Arizona State University, 2002.

Iversen, Joan. "The Mormon-Suffrage Relationship: Personal and Political Quandaries." *Frontiers* 11 (1990): 8–16.

Jensen, Joan. "'Disfranchisement Is a Disgrace': Women and Politics in New Mexico, 1900–1940." In *History of Women in the United States: Historical Articles on Women's Lives and Activities*, vol. 18, part 2, edited by Nancy F. Cott, 301–31. Munich: K. G. Saur, 1992.

Johnson, James W. *Arizona Politicians: The Noble and the Notorious*. Tucson: University of Arizona Press, 2002.

Johnson, Susan L. "Sharing Bed and Board: Cohabitation and Cultural Difference in Central Arizona Mining Towns." *Frontiers* 7 (1984): 36–42.

Jones, Kay F. "Ana Frohmiller: Watchdog of the Arizona Treasury." *Journal of Arizona History* 25 (1984): 349–68.

Joy, Betty E. Hammer. *Angela Hutchinson Hammer: Arizona's Pioneer Newspaper Woman*. Tucson: University of Arizona Press, 2005.

Karning, Albert K., and B. Oliver Walter. "Election of Women to City Councils." *Social Science Quarterly* 56 (1976): 605–43.

Kasper, Jacquelyn. "Arizona's First Woman Lawyer: Sarah Herring Sorin." Tucson: Arizona Historical Society, Southern Arizona Division.

Kearney, Sharon Faye. "Arizona Legislature 1912–1914: A Study of State Progressivism." M.A. thesis, California State University, Fullerton, 1977.

Kelly, Rita Mae. "Where Conservatism and Feminism Meet: Gender and Politics in Arizona." In *Women and the Arizona Political Process: Second Arizona Women's Town Hall*, edited by Rita Mae Kelly, 1–4. Lanham, MD: University Press of America, 1988.

——. "Women, Politics, and Public Policy." In *Politics and Public Policy in Arizona*, edited by Zachary A. Smith, 103–14. Westport, CT: Praeger, 1993.

Kotlanger, Michael J. "Phoenix, Arizona: 1920–1940." Ph.D. diss., Arizona State University, 1989.

Kyte, Elinor C. "A Tough Job for a Gentle Lady." *Journal of Arizona History* 25 (1984): 385–98.

Lamar, Howard Roberts. *The Far Southwest, 1846–1912: A Territorial History*. New York: Norton, 1970.

Larson, Robert. *Populism in the Mountain West*. Albuquerque: University of New Mexico Press, 1986.

Lauerman, Thomas. "Desexing the Ballot Box: The History of Woman Suffrage in Arizona, 1883–1922." M.A. thesis, Arizona State University, 1973.

Leeper, Gertrude Bryan. "Lady in the Legislature." *Forum* (July 1932): 54–59.

Lemons, Stanley. *The Woman Citizen: Social Feminism in the 1920s.* Urbana: University of Illinois Press, 1973.

Lotchin, Roger W. "Hispanics, Women, and Western Cities: 'Setting the Pace' — Political Emergence and the Renaissance of Western Exceptionalism." *Western Historical Quarterly* 29 (1998): 293–315.

Low, A. Maurice. "Women in the Election." *Yale Review* (1921): 311–22.

Luckingham, Bradford. *Minorities in Phoenix: A Profile of Mexican American, Chinese American, and African American Communities, 1860–1992.* Tucson: University of Arizona Press, 1994.

Lunardini, Christine A. *From Equal Suffrage to Equal Rights: Alice Paul and the National Woman's Party, 1910–1928.* New York: New York University Press, 1986.

Lykes, Aimee De Potter. "Phoenix Women in the Development of Public Policy: Territorial Beginnings." In *Phoenix in the Twentieth Century: Essays in Community History*, edited by G. Wesley Johnson Jr., 33–50. Norman: University of Oklahoma Press, 1993.

Lyman, Edward Leo. "Elimination of the Mormon Issue from Arizona Politics, 1889–1894." *Arizona and the West* 24 (1982): 205–28.

MacKay, Kathryn L. "Women in Politics: Power in the Public Sphere." In *Women in Utah History: Paradigm or Paradox?* edited by Patricia Lyn Scott and Linda Thatcher, 360–93. Logan: Utah State University Press, 2005.

Marilley, Suzanne M. *Woman Suffrage and the Origins of Liberal Feminism in the United States, 1820 to 1920.* Cambridge, MA: Harvard University Press, 1996.

Marin, Christine, "La Asociación Hispano-Americana de Madres y Esposas: Tucson's Mexican American Women in World War II." In *La Mexicana/Chicana*, edited by Ignacio M. Garcia, 5–18. Tucson: Mexican American Research Center, University of Arizona, 1985.

Mason, Bruce B., and Heinz R. Hink. *Constitutional Government in Arizona: Arizona Town Hall,* 2nd edition. Tempe: Arizona State University Bureau of Government Research, 1965.

Maxwell, Margaret F. *A Passion for Freedom: The Life of Sharlot Hall.* Tucson: University of Arizona Press, 1982.

McClintock, James H. *Arizona: Prehistoric, Aboriginal, Pioneer, Modern.* 3 vols. Chicago: S. J. Clarke, 1916.

McCool, Daniel, Susan M. Olson, and Jennifer L. Robinson. *Native Vote: American Indians, the Voting Rights Act, and the Right to Vote.* Cambridge: Cambridge University Press, 2007.

McCormick, Richard P., and Katheryne C. McCormick. *Equality Deferred: Women Candidates for the New Jersey Assembly, 1920–1993.* New Brunswick, NJ: Center for the American Woman and Politics, Rutgers University, 1994.

McFarland, Janet Suzanne. "A Power for Good in the Community: The Phoenix Woman's Club, 1900–1930." M.A. thesis, Arizona State University, 1994.

McFeatters, Ann Carey. *Sandra Day O'Connor: Justice in the Balance.* Albuquerque: University of New Mexico Press, 2005.

Mead, Rebecca J. "How the Vote was Won: Woman Suffrage in the Western United States,

1868–1914." Ph.D. diss., University of California, Los Angeles, 1999.

———. *How the Vote Was Won: Woman Suffrage in the Western United States, 1868–1914*. New York: New York University Press, 2004.

Melcher, Mary S. "Tending Children, Chickens, and Cattle: Southern Arizona Ranch and Farm Women, 1910–1940." Ph.D. diss., Arizona State University, 1994.

Miller, Kristie. "A Volume of Friendship: The Correspondence of Isabella Greenway and Eleanor Roosevelt, 1904–1953." *Journal of Arizona History* 40 (1999): 121–56.

———. *Isabella Greenway: An Enterprising Woman*. Tucson: University of Arizona Press, 2004.

Moore, Darby Jane. "The United States Birth Control Movement and Arizona Women: Biography, Social Action, and Community." M.A. thesis, Arizona State University, 1999.

Morrison, Betty. "Isabella Greenway: Arizona's First Congresswoman." M.A. thesis, Arizona State University, 1977.

Muncy, Robyn. "'Women Demand Recognition': Women Candidates in Colorado's Election of 1912." In *We Have Come to Stay: American Women and Political Parties, 1880–1960*, edited by Melanie Gustafson, Kristie Miller, and Elisabeth Israels Perry, 45–54. Albuquerque: University of New Mexico Press, 1996.

O'Connor, Sandra Day, and H. Alan Day. *Lazy B: Growing Up on a Cattle Ranch in the American Southwest*. New York: Random House, 2002.

O'Neill, Colleen. "A Community Divided: A Social History of Bisbee." M.A. thesis, New Mexico State University, 1989.

Osselaer, Heidi J. "'A Woman for a Woman's Job': Arizona Women in Politics, 1900–1950." Ph.D. diss., Arizona State University, 2001.

Peirce, Neil R. *The Mountain States of America: People, Politics, and Power in the Eight Rocky Mountain States*. New York: W. W. Norton, 1972.

Peplow, Edward H. *History of Arizona*. 3 vols. New York: Lewis Historical Publishing Co., 1958.

Petrik, Paula. *No Step Backward: Women and Family on the Rocky Mountain Mining Frontier, Helena, Montana, 1865–1900*. Helena: University of Montana Press, 1987.

Portrait and Biographical Record of Arizona. Chicago: Chapman Publishing Co., 1901.

Pry, Mark E. "Arizona and the Politics of Statehood, 1889–1912. Ph.D. diss., Arizona State University, 1995.

———. "Statehood Politics and Territorial Development: The Arizona Constitution of 1891." *Journal of Arizona History* 35 (1994): 397–426.

Reingold, Beth. *Representing Women: Sex, Gender and Legislative Behavior in Arizona and California*. Chapel Hill: University of North Carolina Press, 2000.

Reynolds, Jean A. "'We Made Our Life as Best We Could with What We Had': Mexican American Women in Phoenix, 1930–1949." M.A. thesis, Arizona State Univ., 1998.

Richards, J. Morris. *The History of the Arizona State Legislature, 1912–1967*. Phoenix: Arizona Legislative Council, 1979.

Riley, Glenda. *Building and Breaking Families in the American West*. Albuquerque: University of New Mexico Press, 1996.

Robinson, Geroid. "Arizona's Mothers of Law." *Overland Monthly* (1916): 3–6.

Robinson, Will H. *The Story of Arizona.* Phoenix: Berryhill Publishing, 1919.

Rockstroh, Stephen D. "An Analysis of Phoenix Municipal Administration, 1881–1952." M.A. thesis, Arizona State University, 1952.

Roosevelt, Eleanor, and Lorena Hickok. *Ladies of Courage.* New York: G. P. Putnam's Sons, 1954.

Rothman, Sheila M. *Woman's Proper Place: A History of Changing Ideals and Practices, 1870 to the Present.* New York: Basic Books, 1978.

Rothschild, Mary Logan, and Pamela Claire Hronek. *Doing What the Day Brought: An Oral History of Arizona Women.* Tucson: University of Arizona Press, 1992.

———. "A History of Arizona Women's Politics." In *Women and the Arizona Political Process: Second Arizona Women's Town Hall,* edited by Rita Mae Kelly, 5–20. Lanham, MD: University Press of America, 1988.

Rubio-Goldsmith, Raquel. "Shipwrecked in the Desert: A Short History of the Adventures and Struggles for Survival of the Mexican Sisters of the House of the Providence in Douglas, Arizona, during Their First Twenty-Two Years in Existence, 1927–1949." In *La Mexicana/Chicana,* edited by Ignacio M. Garcia, 39–66. Tucson: Mexican American Research Center, University of Arizona, 1985.

Salas, Elizabeth. "Soledad Chávez Chacón, Adelina Otero-Warren, and Concha Ortiz y Pino: Three Hispana Politicians in New Mexico Politics, 1920–1940." In *We Have Come to Stay: American Women and Political Parties, 1880–1960,* edited by Melanie Gustafson, Kristie Miller, and Elisabeth Israels Perry, 161–73. Albuquerque: University of New Mexico Press, 1996.

Sanders, Marion K. *The Lady and the Vote.* Boston: Houghton Mifflin, 1956.

Schramm, Sarah Slavin. "Women and Representation: Self-Government and Role Change." *Western Political Quarterly* 34 (1981): 46–59.

Shadegg, Stephen C. *Arizona Politics: The Struggle to End One-Party Rule.* Tempe: Arizona State University, 1986.

Shaw, Anna Howard. *The Story of a Pioneer.* New York: Harper and Brothers, reprinted 1970.

Sheridan, Thomas E. *Arizona: A History.* Tucson: University of Arizona Press, 1995.

———. *Los Tucsonenses: The Mexican Community in Tucson, 1854–1941.* Tucson: University of Arizona Press, 1986.

Smith, Zachary A., ed. *Politics and Public Policy in Arizona.* Westport, CT: Praeger, 1993.

Snapp, Meredith A. "Defeat the Democrats: The Congressional Union for Woman Suffrage in Arizona, 1914 and 1916." *Journal of the West* 14 (1975): 131–39.

———. "Defeat the Democrats: The Arizona Campaigns for the Congressional Union for Woman Suffrage." M.A. thesis, Arizona State University, 1976.

Steiner, Stan. *The New Indians.* New York: Harper and Row, 1968.

Sturgeon, Melanie I. "Arizona Women and the Sheppard-Towner Act: 'For Every Baby a Square Deal.'" Arizona Historical Foundation, Arizona State University, 1994.

Terborg-Penn, Rosalyn. *African American Women in the Struggle for the Vote, 1850–1920.* Bloomington: Indiana University Press, 1998.

Tessman, Norm. "Buckey O'Neill, Rough Rider and Fiction Writer." In *Rough Writings: Perspectives on Buckey O'Neill, Pauline M. O'Neill, and Roosevelt's Rough Riders*, compiled by Janet Lovelady, 22–32. Prescott, AZ: Sharlot Hall Museum Press, 1998.

Thompson, Ruth Anne. "After Suffrage: Women, Law, and Policy in Tennessee, 1920–1980." Ph.D. diss., Vanderbilt University, 1944.

Tisdale, Nancy K. "The Prohibition Crusade in Arizona." M.A. thesis, University of Arizona, 1965.

Tod, Diane, and Rosalie Crowe. *Arizona Women's Hall of Fame*. Tempe: Arizona Historical Society, Central Arizona Division, 1985.

VanderMeer, Philip. "Lorna C. Lockwood." In *Encyclopedia of Women in the American West*, edited by Gordon M. Bakken and Brenda Farrington, 190–93. Thousand Oaks, CA: Sage Publications, 2003.

Van Ingen, Linda. "Campaigns for Equality: Women Candidates for California State Office, 1912–1970." Ph.D. diss., University of California, Riverside, 2000.

Wagoner, Jay J. *Arizona Territory, 1863–1912: A Political History*. Tucson: University of Arizona Press, 1970.

Ware, Harry David. "Alcohol, Temperance, and Prohibition in Arizona." Ph.D. diss., Arizona State University, 1995.

Ware, Susan. *Partner and I: Molly Dewson, Feminism, and New Deal Politics*. New Haven, CT: Yale University Press, 1987.

Weisbrod, Carol. "Images of the Woman Juror." *Harvard Women's Law Journal* 9 (1986): 59–82.

Welter, Barbara. "The Cult of True Womanhood, 1820–1860." *American Quarterly* 18 (1966): 151–74.

Werner, Emmy. "Women in Congress, 1917–1964." *Western Political Quarterly* 19 (1966): 16–30.

West, Elliot. *The Saloon on the Rocky Mountain Mining Frontier*. Lincoln: University of Nebraska Press, 1979.

Whitaker, Matthew C. *Race Work: The Rise of Civil Rights in the Urban West*. Lincoln: University of Nebraska Press, 2005.

———. "In Search of Black Phoenicians: African American Culture and Community in Phoenix, Arizona, 1868–1940." M.A. thesis, Arizona State University, 1997.

Willard, Don. *An Old-timer's Scrapbook*. Private printing, Arizona Collection, Hayden Library, Arizona State University, 1984.

Williams, Sally. *History of Valuable Pioneers of the State of Arizona*. Private printing, Arizona Collection, Hayden Library, Arizona State University, 1979.

Witt, Linda, Karen M. Paget, and Glenna Matthews. *Running as a Woman: Gender and Power in American Politics*. New York: Free Press, 1994.

Young, Louise M. *Understanding Politics: A Practical Guide for Women*. New York: Pellingrini and Cudahy, 1950.

Illustration Credits

Arizona Historical Foundation
Helen Duett Ellison Hunt (Roscoe G. Willson Collection, MS FM MSS 46)

Arizona Historical Society, Tucson
Isabella Greenway, Eleanor Roosevelt, and Elliot Roosevelt (Buehman Collection, BN 3472)

Arizona Labor Journal, 7 September 1922
Hattie Mosher's campaign advertisement

Arizona State Library, Archives and Public Records, Archives Division, Phoenix
Josephine Brawley Hughes (97-6546)
Pauline O'Neill (97-7790)
Frances Willard Munds (97-7430)
Laura Gregg Cannon (97-6269)
C. Louise Boehringer (97-6236)
Elsie Toles (98-8995)
Rachel Berry (93-9972)
Governor Hunt signing minimum wage bill (02-0200)
Nellie Trent Bush (98-9900)
Clara Botzum (98-1577)
Lorna Lockwood (97-7013)
Ana Frohmiller campaign card (97-8530)
Arizona state officials' inauguration, 1999 (99-9049)

Mike McDearmon
Arizona counties, county seats, and major cities, 1910–1982

Library of Congress
Madge Udall (George Grantham Bain Collection, Prints and Photographs Division, LC-DIG-ggbain-12599)
National Woman's Party banner (Women of Protest: Photographs from the Records of the National Woman's Party, MNWP 276018)

Index

About the Author

Heidi J. Osselaer received her undergraduate degree in history at the University of California, Berkeley, and earned both her master's degree and doctorate in U.S. history at Arizona State University. She teaches at Arizona State University and lives in Phoenix with her husband, Tom, and two college-age children, Ryan and Shannon.

CPSIA information can be obtained at www.ICGtesting.com
Printed in the USA
LVOW100749080412

276619LV00001B/5/P